ISBN 978-1-331-68859-4
PIBN 10221673

For support please visit www.forgottenbooks.com

1 MONTH OF
FREE
READING

at

www.ForgottenBooks.com

By purchasing this book you are
eligible for one month membership to
ForgottenBooks.com, giving you
unlimited access to our entire
collection of over 700,000 titles via
our web site and mobile apps.

To claim your free month visit:

www.forgottenbooks.com/free221673

English
Français
Deutsche
Italiano
Español
Português

www.forgottenbooks.com

Mythology Photography **Fiction**
Fishing Christianity **Art** Cooking
Essays Buddhism Freemasonry
Medicine **Biology** Music **Ancient
Egypt** Evolution Carpentry Physics
Dance Geology **Mathematics** Fitness
Shakespeare **Folklore** Yoga Marketing
Confidence Immortality Biographies
Poetry **Psychology** Witchcraft
Electronics Chemistry History **Law**
Accounting **Philosophy** Anthropology
Alchemy Drama Quantum Mechanics
Atheism Sexual Health **Ancient History**
Entrepreneurship Languages Sport
Paleontology Needlework Islam
Metaphysics Investment Archaeology
Parenting Statistics Criminology
Motivational

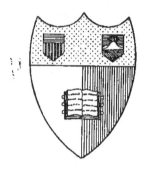

Date Due

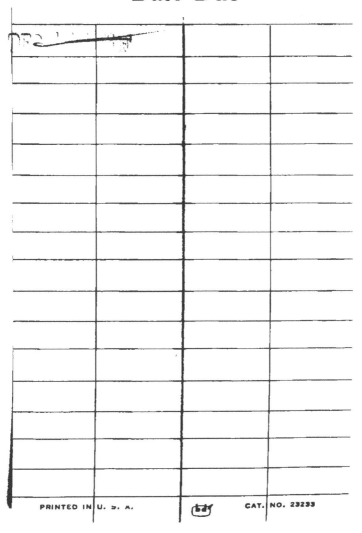

PRINTED IN U. S. A.   CAT. NO. 23233

LUKE THE HISTORIAN
IN THE LIGHT OF RESEARCH

LUKE THE HISTORIAN
N THE LIGHT OF RESEARCH

BY

A. T. ROBERTSON, M.A., D.D., LL.D., Litt.D.

PROFESSOR OF NEW TESTAMENT INTERPRETATION, SOUTHERN BAPTIST
THEOLOGICAL SEMINARY, LOUISVILLE, KY.

"Having traced the course of all things
accurately from the first."

NEW YORK

CHARLES SCRIBNER'S SONS

1920

TO

THE MEMORY OF

DR. AND MRS. J. B. MARVIN

DISTINGUISHED LIKE LUKE

IN SERVICE FOR THE BODIES AND

SOULS OF MEN

PREFACE

The work of the last fifteen years has created new interest in the writings of Luke. The relation of Luke's Gospel to Mark's Gospel and the Logia of Jesus has sharply defined his own critical methods and processes. The researches of Harnack, Hobart, and Ramsay have restored the credit of Luke with many critics who had been carried away by the criticism of Baur, and who looked askance upon the value of Luke as the historian of early Christianity. It has been like mining—digging now here, now there. The items in Luke's books that were attacked have been taken up one by one. The work has been slow and piecemeal, of necessity. But it is now possible to gather together into a fairly complete picture the results. It is a positively amazing vindication of Luke. The force of the argument is cumulative and tremendous. One needs to have the patience to work through the details with candor and a willingness to see all the facts with no prejudice against Luke or against the supernatural origin of Christianity. It is not claimed that every difficulty in Luke's books has been solved, but so many have been triumphantly removed that Luke is entitled to the benefit of the doubt in the rest or at any rate to patience on our part till further research can make a report. Luke should at least be treated as fairly as Thucydides or Polybius when he makes a statement that as yet has no other support or seems in conflict with other writers. Modern scholars are no longer on the defensive about Luke. His books can be used with confidence. The work of research has thrown light in every direction and the story is fascinating to every lover of truth.

These lectures, delivered to the Northfield Christian Workers' Conference, August 2–16, 1919, at the invitation of Mr. W.

R. Moody, have been greatly enlarged for publication. But the toil has been brightened by the memory of the crowds in Sage Chapel who first heard them.

"The long series of discoveries by Sir W. M. Ramsay and his coadjutors in Asia Minor has established the Acts narrative in a position from which later research is unlikely to dethrone it." (*London Times Literary Supplement*, March 13, 1920.) But the work of research goes on with vigor. New books continue to come out concerning Luke's writings, like Carpenter's *Christianity According to S. Luke* and McLachlan's *St. Luke: The Man and His Work*. Both of them I found useful and stimulating. Vol. I of *The Beginnings of Christianity*, by Foakes-Jackson and Kirsopp Lake, came too late to use. It is an ambitious attempt to set forth the historical atmosphere of the Acts, and assumes the thesis that Jesus preached only repentance with no world programme such as later Christianity provided. Lieutenant MacKinlay also has in press a new book on *Luke*.

I have to thank Rev. J. McKee Adams, Louisville, Kentucky, who put the manuscript in typewritten form and for other tokens of interest in the work. The splendid Indices were prepared by Rev. J. Allan Easley, Jr., Manning, South Carolina, whose careful work will make the volume more useful to students. A few of the chapters have appeared as articles in journals, whose publishers have graciously agreed to their use in this volume.

A. T. ROBERTSON.

LOUISVILLE, KY.,
August, 1920.

TABLE OF CONTENTS

LUKE THE HISTORIAN IN THE LIGHT OF RESEARCH

CHAPTER I

THE AUTHORSHIP OF THE GOSPEL AND THE ACTS

"The former treatise I made, O Theophilus" (Acts 1:1)

1. *The Importance of the Lukan Writings.*—Modern research has revived interest in the Gospel according to Luke and the Acts of the Apostles. In part this fact is due to the natural reaction against the extreme view of Baur, who bluntly said that the statements in Acts "can only be looked upon as intentional deviations from historic truth in the interest of the special tendency which they possess."[1] It is true that Luke in Acts is not a blind Paulinist, as Moffatt[2] shows. Both Peter and Paul are heroes with Luke, but the weaknesses and short-comings of both apostles appear. Undoubtedly Luke reveals his sympathies with Paul, but he is not hostile to Peter and is quite capable[3] of doing justice to both Peter and Paul. The work of Baur has not discredited Luke in the final result as a writer who sought to cover up the friction between Peter and Paul and between Barnabas and Paul. The struggles in early Christianity stand out with sufficient clearness in the Acts, and it is now seen to be quite possible that Luke has drawn the narrative with a true perspective. Schweitzer[4] argues that the account in Acts is more intelligible than that in the Pauline Epistles: "When the Tübingen school set up the axiom that Acts is less trustworthy than the Epistles, they made things easy for themselves"—easy, one may add, by slurring over plain facts in the Acts.

[1] Baur, *Paul*, vol. I, p. 108.
[2] *Intr. to the Literature of the N. T.*, p. 302.
[3] *Ibid.*, p. 302.   [4] *Paul and His Interpreters*, p. 126.

But Baur compelled diligent study of the Acts. The critics, like the Berœans after Paul preached, went to "examining the scriptures daily, whether these things were so" (Acts 17 : 11). As a result of a half-century of such research Maurice Jones[1] can say: "There is no book in the whole of the New Testament whose position in the critical world has been so enhanced by recent research as the Acts of the Apostles." It cannot, however, be claimed that modern critics are at one either in crediting the Gospel and the Acts to Luke or in attaching a higher value to the so-called Lukan writings. The long prejudice against these books has not entirely disappeared. Pfleiderer[2] can still claim that "the Gospel of Luke was probably written at the beginning of the second century by an unknown heathen Christian," though he admits that Luke, "the pupil of Paul," wrote the memoirs of his journey with Paul (the "we" sections of Acts). Jülicher[3] considers it "a romantic ideal" to attribute these books to Luke. And Weizsäcker[4] as late as 1902 says: "The historical value of the narrative in Acts shrinks until it reaches a vanishing-point." But these are modern protests against the new evidence that were to be expected. The judgment of Maurice Jones about the new estimate placed upon the Acts and upon Luke's Gospel remains true.

Much of the credit for this outcome is due to Sir W. M. Ramsay, who was himself at first a disciple of Baur. It was patient research that proved that Baur was wrong and that enabled Ramsay to reconstruct the world of Luke and Paul in the light of their own writings and the archæological discoveries made by Ramsay and others in Asia Minor. The results of this revolution in Ramsay's literary outlook appear in his various volumes, like *The Historical Geography of Asia Minor, The Church in the Roman Empire, St. Paul the Traveller and Roman Citizen, Luke the Physician, Pauline and Other Studies, The Cities of St. Paul, Was Christ Born at Bethlehem? The Bearing of Recent Discovery on the Trustworthiness of the New Testament.*

It is not too much to say that these volumes mark an epoch

---

[1] *The New Testament in the Twentieth Century*, p. 227.
[2] *Christian Origins*, p. 238.
[3] *Introduction to the N. T.*, pp. 447 f.
[4] *Apostolic Age*, pp. 106 f. With this Von Soden agrees, *History of Early Christian Lit.*, p. 243.

in the study of the writings of Luke and Paul. Ramsay is conscious that he began with a strong current of adverse criticism against him. He boldly asks[1] the critics: "Shall we hear evidence or not?" Ramsay[2] sharply says: "Criticism for a time examined the work attributed to Luke like a corpse, and the laborious autopsy was fruitless. Nothing in the whole history of literary criticism has been so waste and dreary as great part of the modern critical study of Luke." This charge is true, but Ramsay[3] is able to say: "It has for some time been evident to all New Testament scholars who were not hidebound in old prejudice that there must be a new departure in Lukan criticism. The method of dissection had failed." Ramsay took the new path that has led out of the wilderness.

Others were at work along different lines. Hawkins[4] had done real service on the synoptic problem and had brought into sharp relief the place of Luke's Gospel in relation to Mark and Matthew. Hobart[5] had shown that the author of both Gospel and Acts employed medical terms to a surprising degree. The evidence pointed to Luke and reinforced the work of Ramsay.

In time Adolph Harnack was led to notice the work of these men. He was convinced that they were right and he reversed his position and took up the cudgels for the Lukan authorship of both Gospel and Acts. He says:[6] "All the mistakes which have been made in New Testament criticism have been focussed into the criticism of the Acts of the Apostles." That is a daring statement from the new convert who ridicules "the intolerable pedantry" of the critics who cannot see the facts for their theories. Harnack is aware of the supercilious scorn of many who have refused to notice the arguments in favor of Luke. He sees also the great importance[7] of Luke's writings: "The genuine epistles of St. Paul, the writings of St. Luke, and the history of Eusebius are the pillars of primitive Christian history. This fact has not yet been sufficiently recognized in the case of the Lukan writings; partly because critics are convinced that these writings are not to be assigned to St.

---

[1] *Pauline and Other Studies*, chap. I.
[2] *Luke the Physician*, p. 3.
[3] *Ibid.*
[4] *Horæ Synopticæ.*
[5] *The Medical Language of St. Luke.*
[6] *Luke the Physician*, p. 122.
[7] *Luke the Physician*, p. 1.

Luke. And yet, even if they were right in their suppositions, the importance of the Acts of the Apostles at least still remains fundamental. However, I hope to have shown in the following pages that critics have gone astray in this question, and that the traditional view holds good. The Lukan writings thus recover their own excelling value as historical authorities." Harnack, as we shall see, does not rank Luke as high as Ramsay does, but he has definitely championed the Lukan authorship of both the Gospel and Acts. Renan felt the charm of Luke's Gospel as a literary production when he pronounced it "the most beautiful book ever written."

The historical worth of the Gospel and Acts comes up for formal discussion in succeeding chapters. Sanday thinks that Ramsay's "treatment of St. Luke as a historian seems too optimistic" when he ranks him as the foremost ancient historian, even above Thucydides. But, whatever view one holds of the Lukan writings, no serious student of the New Testament can neglect them. The author writes two books that interpret the origins of Christianity. How far has he been successful in this effort? He claims that he took pains to do it with care. Criticism has challenged his claims. One cannot complain of criticism *per se*. Carpenter[1] well says: "Let us by all means have historical criticism, but let it be genuinely historical." It is not best to prejudge the case before we examine the evidence, and Chase[2] sums the matter up thus: "But it may be safely said that the certain results of archæological research strongly confirm the accuracy and truthfulness of the author of the Acts." Let the facts speak for themselves.

2. *The Same Author for Both Gospel and Acts.*—The author of the Gospel and the Acts makes the distinct claim of identity in Acts 1 : 1: "The former treatise I made, O Theophilus, concerning all that Jesus began both to do and teach." Theophilus is clearly a proper name, "not an imaginary *nom de guerre* for the typical catechumen, nor a conventional title for the average Christian reader."[3] He was a Christian who had already been catechized[4] (Luke 1 : 4) and who wished further instruction. It is probable that Theophilus was a man of rank

---

[1] *Christianity According to S. Luke*, p. ix.
[2] *The Credibility of the Book of the Acts of the Apostles*, p. 8.
[3] Moffatt, *Introduction*, p. 262.
[4] κατηχήθης. Cf. Apollos in Acts 18 : 25.

because of the epithet "most excellent"[1] (Luke 1 : 3), which is "technical and distinctive"[2] for the equestrian rank (cf. Acts 24 : 3; 26 : 25). Ramsay doubts if a Roman officer in the first century would be willing to bear the name Theophilus, and suggests that it was his baptismal name which Luke employs because "it was dangerous for a Roman of rank to be recognized as a Christian." Be that as it may, identity of authorship is claimed by the address to Theophilus. It is hardly likely that there were two authors who used his name to prove identity. It has been suggested that Luke was a freedman brought up in the home of Theophilus, who was his patron, and who defrayed the expense of the publication of both of Luke's books.[3] Hayes[4] conjectures that Theophilus, who lived in Antioch, educated Luke at the university, and that he was also a schoolmate of Barnabas and Saul there.

We are not here arguing that the Acts shows unity of authorship. That point must be assumed for the present. The proof will be given later that the writer of the "we" sections is the author of the whole of Acts, though he used a variety of sources, as he did in the writing of the Gospel (Luke 1 : 1–4). The point that is now urged is that whoever wrote one book wrote the other. The same man wrote both Gospel and Acts. It is not necessary to argue that the author contemplated a third volume because of his use of "first"[5] in Acts 1 : 1. That nicety in the use of language was not common in the Koiné[6] where the dual form had nearly vanished. To-day we speak of first wife when a man had only two, and we talk of the first story of a two-story house. This item plays no real part in the argument one way or the other.

---

[1] κράτιστε. [2] Ramsay, *St. Paul the Traveller*, p. 388.
[3] One thinks of Mæcenas and Horace. "This was the recognized practice of the time." Moffatt, *Introduction*, p. 313.
[4] *The Synoptic Gospels and the Book of Acts*, p. 197.
[5] τὸν πρῶτον λόγον. Cf. Robertson, *Grammar of the Greek New Testament in the Light of Historical Research*, p. 280. Luke never employs πρότερος. The papyri nearly always use πρῶτος.
[6] The *Koiné* is the name given to the Greek current throughout the Greco-Roman world after the conquests of Alexander the Great. It was the language common to all classes and nations and it was the means of communication practically everywhere. It was employed in the vernacular, as is seen in the papyri of Egypt, and literary men like Polybius and Plutarch wrote in it also. The New Testament writers used the *Koiné* as a matter of course.

In spite of the variety of sources employed in both the Gospel and the Acts, there is the same general vocabulary and style in both books. This argument has been well developed by Friedrich.[1] It ought not to be necessary to argue this point, since "the linguistic and other peculiarities which distinguish the Gospel are equally prominent in the Acts."[2] The words peculiar to Luke in both Gospel and Acts are more numerous than those peculiar to any other New Testament writer, except Paul (counting the Pastoral Epistles).[3] The argument of Hobart in his *Medical Language of St. Luke* applies to both the Gospel and the Acts, as we shall see, and is proof of identity of authorship. There is little opposition among critics to the Lukan authorship of the Gospel. "If the Gospel were the only writing ascribed to his authorship, we should probably raise no objection against this record of ancient tradition; for we have no sufficient reason for asserting that a disciple of Paul could not have composed this work."[4] It is with the Acts that critics have trouble. De Wette doubted the Lukan authorship of the Gospel, and Scholten argued that the same man could not have written both Gospel and Acts. Harnack[5] grows facetious over this argument: "Seeing how one critic trustfully rests upon the authority of another, we may congratulate ourselves that some accident has prevented Scholten's hypothesis—that the third gospel and the Acts have different authors—from finding its way into the great stream of criticism and so becoming a dogma in these days." The line of attack has not been to show that Luke's Gospel and Acts are unlike, but that the Acts was not written by a companion of Paul. To the Acts, then, let us go. Who wrote the Acts?

3. *The Author of Acts a Companion of Paul.*—Here is where the real battle has raged. Very few critics have the hardihood

---

[1] *Das Lukas—Evangelium und die Apostelgeschichte Werke desselben Verfasser* (1890).

[2] *Supernatural Religion*, vol. III, p. 32. This concession is noteworthy.

[3] Cadbury, *The Style and Literary Method of Luke*, p. 3. Cf. also Vogel, *Zur Charakteristik des Lukas nach Sprache und Stil*, p. 11.

[4] J. Weiss, *Die Schriften des N. T.; das Lukas-Evangelium*, 1906, p. 378. So, then, J. Weiss argues still that "the Lukan writings as a whole are the work of a man of the postapostolic generation." But Loofs regards Luke as the author of the Acts (*What Is the Truth about Jesus Christ?*, p. 91).

[5] *Luke the Physician*, pp. 7, 21, n. 2.

to say that Luke did not write any part of the Acts. Schmiedel admits that the same man wrote the Gospel and the Acts, but denies that he was a companion of Paul. Holtzmann[1] holds Luke to be the author of the "we" sections only. Schleiermacher had credited the "we" sections to Timothy. A host of critics (Baur, Clemen, De Wette, Hausrath, Hilgenfeld, Holtzmann, Jülicher, Knopf, Overbeck, Pfleiderer, Schürer, Spitta, Von Soden, Wendt, J. Weiss, Zeller) have reached " the certain conclusion that tradition here is wrong—the Acts cannot have been composed by a companion and fellow worker of St. Paul."[2] But this judgment of critical infallibility has been reversed by the steady work of Blass, Credner, Harnack, Hawkins, Hobart, Klostermann, Plummer, Ramsay, Vogel, Zahn. Plummer[3] courageously says: "It is perhaps no exaggeration to say that nothing in Biblical criticism is more certain than the statement that the author of the Acts was a companion of St. Paul." There is no manner of doubt that the author of the "we" sections of Acts (16 : 10–40; 20 : 6–28 : 31) was a companion of Paul. There is no other way to explain the use of "we" and "us." It may have been a diary or travel document or travel notes, but the author was with Paul.

Is he the same writer as the author of the Acts as a whole? It is here that patient labor has borne results. Klostermann[4] has dealt carefully with the "we" sections. B. Weiss in his commentary on Acts and Hawkins in his *Horæ Synopticæ* have proven the unity of the Book of Acts. There may (or may not) have been an Aramaic source for the earlier part of Acts, as Torrey claims.[5] We shall look into that later. Harnack[6] with great minuteness has compared the Greek of the "we" sections with that of the rest of the Acts. He says:[7] "It has often been stated and often proved that the 'we' sections in vocabulary, in syntax, and in style are most intimately bound up with the whole work, and that this work itself (including the Gospel), in spite of all diversity in its parts, is distinguished by a grand unity of literary form." With great detail Harnack follows this line of argument in his *Luke the*

[1] *Einl.*, p. 383.   [2] Harnack, *Luke the Physician*, p. 6.
[3] *Commentary on St. Luke*, p. xii.
[4] *Vindiciæ Lucanæ*, 1866.
[5] *The Composition and Date of Acts*, 1916.
[6] *Luke the Physician*, pp. 26–120.   [7] *Ibid.*, p. 26.

Physician and *The Acts of the Apostles*. It is not merely agreement in words that we see, but the same syntax and style. He
returns to the subject in *The Date of the Acts and the Synoptic
Gospels* (1911), and meets the objections of Clemen and others
to the identity of the author of the "we" sections with the
author of the whole book. He had said that "a difference in
the authorship of the third gospel and the Acts can be alleged
with much more plausible reasons than a difference in the
authorship of the Acts as a whole and the 'we' sections."[1]
The upshot of the whole investigation is seen to be this: "In
the 'we' sections the author speaks his own language and
writes in his usual style; in the rest of the work just so much
of this style makes its appearance as was allowed by the nature
of the sources which he used and the historical and religious
coloring which he aimed at imparting."[2] Like a true artist
in style Luke reflects his sources in both the Gospel and the
Acts, but not to the obliteration of his own style and method.

It can hardly be maintained that a compiler of the Acts carelessly retained the "we" and "us" like slovenly mediæval
chroniclers. This author is no unskilled writer and knows
how to work over his material. Overbeck[3] prefers Zeller's
theory that the "we" is left designedly because the compiler
wished to create the impression that he was one of Paul's companions, so as to recommend his book. But Theophilus would
not be taken in by a subterfuge like that. The only other alternative is the view that the writer of the Acts is himself the
author of the "we" sections and the companion of Paul. Linguistic considerations give strong support to this view.[4] Even
in Luke's Gospel there are eighty-four words common to it
and Paul's Epistles that are not found in the other gospels.
In the Acts the number is much greater.

McGiffert in his *History of Christianity in the Apostolic Age*
(1897) argues with great ability for the compilation theory of
the Acts and vigorously assails the Lukan authorship. He
dissects the book mercilessly and regards it as a second-hand
work. But Harnack brushed aside McGiffert's criticisms.

---

[1] *Luke the Physician*, p. 7, n. 2.
[2] Harnack, *Date of Acts and Synoptic Gospels*, pp. 20 f.
[3] Cf. Zeller, I, 43 (English tr.), and S. Davidson, *Introduction to N. T.*,
II, 272.
[4] Hawkins, *Horæ Synopticæ*, p. 183.

Ramsay[1] says: "Doctor McGiffert has not convinced me; in other words, I think his clever argumentation is sophistical." In spite of McGiffert's attacks and Torrey's theory about the Aramaic document for the early part of Acts, the argument holds, as the result of this long conflict, that the same man is the author of both Gospel and Acts and he was a companion of Paul.

4. *This Companion of Paul a Physician.*—It can be stated in the words of Hawkins[2] that the linguistic argument for unity of authorship of Acts appears "irresistible." There is, then, "an immense balance of evidence" in favor of the view that the author of Acts was a companion of Paul, since he was the writer of the "we" sections.[3] The next step, and an inevitable one, is the fact that this companion of Paul, the author of Acts, was a physician. There is no such statement in the Gospel or in the Acts. But the cumulative linguistic evidence to that effect is compelling and quite conclusive to one who is open to the proof. Zahn[4] puts the matter tersely and strongly thus: "Hobart has proved for every one who can at all appreciate proof that the author of the Lukan work was a man practised in the scientific language of Greek medicine—in short, a Greek physician." The detailed proof of this claim must be reserved for Chapter VII. But at this point it is necessary for one to realize the force of the argument as a whole. The credit for this line of argument is due to Hobart's *The Medical Language of St. Luke* (1882), in which with utmost precision and minuteness the medical terms in the Gospel and Acts are examined in comparison with the writings of the leading Greek physicians (Galen, Hippocrates, Dioscorides, Aretæus, and the rest). Like most champions of a new line of argument, Hobart has claimed too much. Some of the words employed by Luke and the other physicians belong to the common speech of the time and have no technical sense. But some of these common words do acquire a technical significance with a physician. Thus in Acts 28 : 6 the natives in Malta expected that Paul "would have swollen," we read. This word[5] appears here only in the New Testament and is the technical medical term for

---

[1] "The Authorship of the Acts," in *Pauline and Other Studies*, p. 305.

[2] Hawkins, *Horæ Synopticæ*, p. 185.

[3] Hawkins, *Horæ Synopticæ*, p. 189.

[4] *Einl.*, II, 427.   [5] πίμπρασθαι.

inflammation in Galen and Hippocrates.[1] The writer of the Gospel shows a clear desire to avoid a reflection on physicians that appears in Mark's Gospel. In Mark 5 : 26, we read that the woman with an issue of blood "had suffered many things of many physicians, and had spent all that she had, and was nothing bettered, but rather grew worse." Now Luke (8 : 43) describes her as one "who had spent all her living upon physicians, and could not be healed of any." He took care of the physicians very neatly in his restatement of Mark's sly "dig" at the doctors. Hers was simply a chronic case that no physician could cure.

In the Acts we note the clear implication that the writer practised medicine in Malta. Paul "prayed, and laying his hands on him healed[2] him" (28 : 8); we read of the cure of Publius, an evident miracle that Luke reports. But he proceeds (verses 9–10): "And when this was done, the rest also that had diseases in the island came, and were cured."[3] It is to be noted that Luke employs a different Greek word for "were cured," a word that was common for medical cases. The natural implication is that Luke practised medicine here in Malta while Paul healed by miraculous power. The medical missionary and the preacher were at work side by side. Luke may have used prayer like Paul. One hopes that he did, as all physicians should. But he practised his medical art by the side of Paul. The people of Malta honored both Luke and Paul. Luke was no "wild enthusiast who cured diseases" but a "man who continued to practise his profession of physician with success, and who in it had earned the permanent esteem of a man of such high temper as St. Paul."[4] Harnack[5] is absolutely convinced by the arguments of Hobart: "The evidence is of overwhelming force; so that it seems to me that no doubt can exist *that the third Gospel and the Acts of the Apostles were composed by a physician*" (italics his). Deductions have to be made from Hobart's list of medical words in the Gospel and Acts. "But, when all deductions have been made, there remains a body of evidence that the author of the Acts naturally

---

[1] Hobart, *Medical Language of St. Luke*, p. 50.   [2] ἰάσατο.

[3] ἐθεραπεύοντο. Ramsay (*Luke the Physician*, pp. 16 f.) insists that ἐθεραπεύοντο means ("received medical treatment" whether "cured" or not.

[4] Harnack, *The Acts of the Apostles*, p. xl.

[5] *Luke the Physician*, p. 198.

and inevitably slipped into the use of medical phraseology, which seems to me irresistible."[1]   Chase[2] actually complained that for twenty years Hobart's work "remained unnoticed by the assailants of the traditional view of the third Gospel and Acts."   But this complaint can no longer be made.   Clemen[3] has endeavored to show that a physician could not have written the Gospel and Acts: "Truly the author of these writings employs some medical terms in their technical sense, but in a few cases he uses them in such a way as no physician would have done."   But it is very hard to prove a negative.   Hobart undoubtedly claimed too much, but Clemen has attempted the impossible.   "One cannot know to-day what an ancient physician could not have written.   Of course the absence of marked medical traits does not prove that a doctor did not write Luke and Acts."[4]   Cadbury's monograph is a reasoned attempt to prove that "the style of Luke bears no more evidence of medical interest and training than does the language of other writers who were not physicians."[5]   Cadbury claims that many of these medical terms belonged to the language of culture of the time and occur in the writings of Lucian, "the travelling rhetorician and show lecturer," quite as much as in the Gospel and Acts.   There is something in this point beyond a doubt, but Paul was just as much a man of culture as Luke.   So was the author of the Epistle to the Hebrews.   Yet these two New Testament writers of culture do not reveal a fondness for medical language.   It is difficult to make comparisons because of difference in subject-matter and length of books.   The mere tabulation of lists of words does not carry one very far.   Cadbury[6] admits that the selected lists of medical terms given by Harnack, Moffatt, and Zahn "have greatly strengthened the argument by selecting from Hobart only the most convincing examples."   Cadbury is wholly right in insisting that these examples need testing.   He undertakes to do it, though conscious of the difficulties in his way.   His method is merely one of tabulation, which means very little.   The upshot of the whole matter is that the impression of the most striking examples in the Gospel and Acts remains unshaken.   Hobart gives

---

[1] Chase, *The Credibility of the Acts*, pp. 13 f.   [2] *Ibid.*, p. 14.
[3] *Hibbert Journal*, 1910, pp. 785 f.
[4] Cadbury, *The Style and Literary Language of Luke*, 1919, p. 51.
[5] *Ibid.*, p. 50.   [6] *Ibid.*, p. 39.

the full quotations from the Greek medical writers so that one can see the context. We have the context in the Gospel and the Acts. The effect of Hobart's argument remains with me after a careful study of Cadbury's arguments. Most impressive of all is it to read Mark's reports of the miracles and then Luke's modifications. And then the reading of the Gospel and the Acts straight through leaves the same conviction that we are following the lead of a cultivated physician whose professional habits of thought have colored the whole in many subtle ways. This positive impression refuses to be dissipated, though Cadbury is quite right in saying that Luke could still be the author even if he does not betray by his language that he is a physician. Further details will be given in Chapter VII.

It ought to be added that the medical element is spread over the Gospel and the Acts and is another argument for the unity of Acts.[1]

5. *This Physician and Companion of Paul Is Luke.*—The writer does not say so. In fact, the absence of any mention of the name Luke in the Acts is one of the things to be explained. This "is just what we should expect if he himself were the author of the book." So Harnack argues.[2] But it is a bit curious that every other important friend of Paul, judging by his Epistles, except Luke and Titus, is mentioned in the Acts. Aristarchus, coupled with Luke (Col. 4 : 10, 14; Philemon 24), is mentioned in the Acts three times. Once (Acts 27 : 2) Aristarchus is mentioned as present with Paul and the author of the book (Luke). Three reasons occur for the omission of Titus. One, the view of Harnack,[3] is that Titus is not coupled with Luke in the Epistles and hence the omission of his name in Acts is not strange. This is not quite satisfactory. It is easy to see why Luke, though retaining "we" and "us" in his travel diary, declines to mention his own name. It would be known to Theophilus and thus to others. But why omit Titus? Lightfoot[4] denies that Titus was important enough to be mentioned in Acts, but Ramsay[5] rightly rejects that explanation. It has been suggested by A. Souter and others (cf. Origen's view of II Cor. 8 : 18) that Luke and

[1] Moffatt, *Introduction to Lit. of the N. T.*, p. 300.
[2] *The Date of the Acts and the Synoptic Gospels*, p. 28.
[3] *Ibid.*, p. 28, n. 2.   [4] *Biblical Essays*, p. 281.
[5] *St. Paul the Traveller*, p. 390.

Titus were brothers and that for this reason Luke does not call his name. It is possible to understand II Cor. 12 : 18 to be a reference to Titus's brother. This use of the Greek article is common enough.[1] "I exhorted Titus, and I sent his brother with him." The same translation is possible in II Cor. 8 : 18, "his brother." Who is this brother of Titus? One naturally thinks of Luke.

Paul had other companions, but they have to be eliminated one by one. Some are spoken of in a way that renders it difficult to think of them as writing the Acts. This is true of Aquila and Priscilla, Aristarchus, Mark, Silas, Timothy, Trophimus. Selwyn[2] argues at length, but not at all convincingly, that Luke and Silas are one and the same man. Crescens and Titus Justus are rather too insignificant. There remain only Titus and Luke. Curiously both names are absent in the Acts, as already noted. "The movements of Timothy, Silas and the others cannot be fitted in with the hypothesis that any one of them was the companion at the time in question. The hypothesis breaks down in every case. With the exception of Titus, for whose authorship there is no other evidence, each one of them can be shown to have been elsewhere at one or more of the times. Luke 'is with me' at them all."[3] No one seriously argues that Titus wrote the Gospel and Acts. Why not Luke? Titus was not a physician. Was Luke?

We know that Luke was with Paul in Rome (Philemon 24, "Mark, Aristarchus, Demas, Luke, my fellow workers")[4] during his first imprisonment. He is also called by Paul at this time "Luke the beloved physician"[5] (Col. 4 : 14). Harnack[6] argues quite plausibly that Paul means to call "Luke my beloved physician." At any rate it is quite possible, indeed probable, that Luke was Paul's physician as well as helper in the mission work. It is quite possible that Luke, called in as physician either at Antioch during Paul's stay there, or in Galatia during a sudden malarial attack (Gal. 4 : 13), or at Troas, where we first note his presence with Paul, was converted by his patient to the service of Christ. He is with

---

[1] Robertson, *Grammar*, p. 770.   [2] *St. Luke the Prophet.*
[3] Carpenter, *The Christianity of S. Luke*, p. 14.
[4] οἱ συνεργοί μου.   The "we" sections of the Acts show Luke's work with Paul.   Cf. Acts 16 : 10.
[5] ὁ ἰατρὸς ὁ ἀγαπητός.   [6] *Luke the Physician*, p. 3, n. 2.

Paul at the last. "Only Luke is with me" (II Tim. 4 : 11).
Luke, therefore, fulfils precisely the conditions called for by
the evidence unless there is positive external evidence to the
contrary.

But the external evidence is unanimously in favor of Luke
as the author of the Gospel and the Acts. "The unanimous
tradition that St. Luke is the author of the Acts of the Apostles has come to us with the book itself."[1] The Lukan authorship of both Gospel and Acts has been universally recognized
since 140 A. D.[2] Since it is all one way it is needless to cite
it. Specific statements of the Lukan authorship occur in
Irenæus, Tertullian, Clement of Alexandria and the Muratorian Canon.

The case seems to be made out. Certainly Kirsopp Lake
cannot be accused of partiality for traditional views any more
than Harnack. In the Hastings *Dictionary of the Apostolic
Church* (article "Acts of the Apostles") Lake concludes: "The
argument from literary affinities between the 'we-clauses' and
the rest of Acts remains at present unshaken; and, until some
further analysis succeeds in showing why it should be thought
that the 'we-clauses' have been taken from a source not written
by the redactor himself, the traditional view that Luke, the
companion of St. Paul, was the editor of the whole book is the
most reasonable one." That is cautious enough to suit any
timid soul and seems to express the rather reluctant admission
of Lake that is forced by the overwhelming evidence. Harnack[3] pays his respects to the "attitude of general mistrust
in the book, with airy conceits and lofty contempt; most of
all, however, with the fruits of that vicious method wherein
great masses of theory are hung upon the spider's thread of a
single observation." Moffatt[4] concludes that the Lukan
authorship of the Gospel and the Acts "has now been put
practically beyond doubt by the exhaustive researches of Hawkins and Harnack." As for myself, I am bound to agree to
this judgment of M. Jones.[5] "This author of Acts and the

---

[1] Harnack, *Date of the Acts and the Synoptic Gospels*, p. 28.
[2] Harnack, *Luke the Physician*, p. 2.
[3] *The Acts of the Apostles*, p. xlii.
[4] *Introduction to the Literature of the New Testament*, p. 295. See also
Burkitt, *Gospel History and Its Transmission*, pp. 115 f.
[5] *New Testament in Twentieth Century*, p. 231.

third gospel is to be identified with St. Luke the companion, friend, and physician of St. Paul." In the light of all the facts known to-day, after a generation and more of the most exacting criticism and research, the theory of the Lukan authorship holds the field, greatly strengthened by the new light that has come. Scholarship can point with pride to what has been done in this field of Biblical investigation. The picture of Luke now stands before us in sharp outline.

CHAPTER II

A SKETCH OF LUKE'S CAREER

"Only Luke is with me" (II Tim. 4 : 11)

If Luke, the physician and friend of Paul, really wrote the Gospel and Acts, as is now proven as clearly as a literary fact can be shown, one naturally has a keen desire to know something about him. He was evidently a modest man and kept himself in the background in both Gospel and Acts, save in the incidental allusions in the "we" sections of Acts. Indeed, the anonymous author of *Supernatural Religion* seeks to obscure the items that are given and to befog the picture of Luke that has survived. "Let it be remembered that with the exception of the three passages in the Pauline Epistles quoted above, we know absolutely nothing about Luke."[1] The writer then proceeds to throw doubt on the identity of the Luke in Col. 4 : 14 and Philemon 24 and II Tim. 4 : 11. He speaks of "this literary labyrinth" (p. 41) of the "we" passages in Acts and throws Luke into the waste-basket. But modern scholarship, thanks to Lightfoot, Hawkins, Hobart, Ramsay, Harnack and others, has thrown aside the three able volumes on *Supernatural Religion* that were expected to destroy the New Testament. Let us piece together the known facts concerning Luke.

1. *The Name Luke.*—It is now known for a certainty that Loukas[2] is an abbreviation or pet-name (*Kosennamen*) for Loukios.[3] There used to be a deal of speculation on the subject. Lucanus, Lucilius, Lucianus, Lucius were all suggested. Lucanus is common in inscriptions.[4] Several Old-Latin manuscripts of the fifth century read *secundum Lukanum* instead of the usual *secundum Lucam*, probably "due to learned speculation and discussion about the origin of the form"[5] Loukas.

---

[1] *Supernatural Religion*, vol. III, p. 39.
[2] Λουκᾶς.
[3] Λούκιος.
[4] Plummer, *Comm. on Luke*, p. xviii.
[5] Ramsay, *Bearing of Recent Discovery*, p. 371.

"We have to ask whether or not the Greek name Loukios, borrowed from the Latin Lucius, could according to Greek custom have as a familiar by-form the *Kosennamen* Loukas."[1] It is purely a matter of evidence. The proof has been found. On the walls of the peribolos which surrounded the sanctuary of the god Men ·Askænos in Antioch are written a number of dedicatory vows to the god. Some of them are in Latin, but most of them "are the work of Greek-speaking people, who bore Roman names."[2] One of these dedications in Greek is by Loukas Tillios Kriton and Noumeria Venusta (evidently his wife). Both names are Roman, and Loukas appears as Greek for the Latin Lucius. In another instance the same man makes two dedications. In one instance the name of his son occurs as Loukios, in the other as Loukas.[3] There is no longer room for dispute on this point. The vernacular Koiné did employ Loukas as a pet-name (cf. Charlie and Charles) for the Latin Lucius (Greek Loukios). We find this in Antioch. It may have been true anywhere. In Acts 13 : 1 we read of "Loukios the Cyrenian," but it is quite unlikely that he is the same person as our Luke, the author of the book, though it is the same name, as has just been shown. If Luke is the author of the Acts, he would hardly refer to himself as "Loukios the Cyrenian." The use of abbreviated names is common in the New Testament (cf. Silas and Silvanus, Prisca and Priscilla, Apollos and Apollonius) as in the papyri and inscriptions.[4] Plummer[5] terms it "a caricature of critical ingenuity" to make Lucanus = Silvanus because lucus = silva. Selwyn in his *St. Luke the Prophet* argues for this identification in most inconclusive fashion. A name may count for nothing, it is true, and then again a name may stand for much. "The name of a contemporary and eye-witness guarantees the truth of a probable story, provided there is no other reason for raising objections."[6]

[1] *Ibid.*

[2] *Ibid.* · See article in *Journal of Hellenic Studies*, 1912, pp. 144 ff., by Mrs. Hasluck, where the evidence is given in full.

[3] Ramsay, *Bearing of Recent Discovery*, pp. 376–380.

[4] Robertson, *Grammar*, pp. 171–3.

[5] *Comm. on Luke*, p. xviii. Moulton (*Grammar of N. T. Greek*, vol. II, part I, p. 88) quotes Λεύχιος for Latin Lucius in *P. Tebt.*, I, 33, 3 (B. C. 112). Nachmanson (*Beiträge zur Kenntnis der altgriechischen Volkssprache*, p. 61) notes other instances and considers it a different name from Λούχιος.

[6] Harnack, *Luke the Physician*, p. 146.

Fortunately Luke is no longer an obscure name and we can "picture to ourselves the personality which stands behind the name Luke."[1]

2. *A Gentile, Probably a Greek.*—In Col. 4 : 12–14 Paul separates Epaphras, Luke and Demas from Aristarchus, Mark and Jesus Justus, "who are of the circumcision" (4 : 10 f.). Paul here seems to imply that Luke was not a Jew. This is the view of commentators generally, though Hofmann, Tiele and Wittichen argue that Paul's language does not necessarily mean this. It is possible that Luke could have been a proselyte (a tradition mentioned by Jerome), but there is no hint of such a thing in Acts or the Epistles. In Philemon 23 f., Paul draws no such line of cleavage between those who send greetings. In Romans 16 : 21 Paul calls "Loukios and Jason and Sosipater, my kinsmen." As in Acts 13 : 1, so here the name Loukios, as we have seen, could be the formal spelling of the familiar Loukas. But this kinsman[2] of Paul was a Jew and is ruled out by the distinction drawn in Col. 4 : 10–14. The knowledge of Aramaic shown by Luke's use of Aramaic sources in Luke 1 and 2 and in Acts 1–15 does not show that he was a Jew. Indeed, Torrey[3] argues that Luke did not always understand his Aramaic document, if he had one. *Per contra*, the classic introduction to the Gospel (1 : 1–4) seems quite impossible for a Jew to have written, even if he were a man of culture. It ranks with the introductions of Herodotus and Thucydides for brevity, modesty and dignity. It is couched in purest literary Koiné. Other things in his writings confirm the view that he was originally a heathen and not a Jew. He has the wide sympathy of a Gentile of culture and approaches Christianity from the outside. If he is a Gentile, as seems most probable, he is the only writer of the New Testament (or the Old) of whom this is true.

It is probable also that Luke was a Greek rather than a Roman, since in Acts 28 : 2, 4 he speaks of the inhabitants of Malta as "the barbarians," quite in the Greek fashion. The

[1] Harnack, *ibid.*, p. 146.

[2] Ramsay suggests that these six kinsmen of Paul in Romans. 16 : 7–21 are fellow tribesmen and fellow citizens of Tarsus. Cf. *The Cities of St. Paul*, p. 177.

[3] *The Composition and Date of the Acts.* Kirsopp Lake ("Luke," *Hastings's Dict. of the Apostolic Church*) holds that the facts about Luke can be met on the hypothesis that he was a Hellenistic Jew. But not so easily.

Greek antithesis was "Greeks and barbarians," as Paul used it in Romans 1 : 14.   But Miss Stawell in a paper on "St. Luke and Virgil" at the International Medical Congress in Oxford in 1913 argued that Luke was a Roman and not a Greek.   She argues that some of the greatest medical authorities of the day were Romans, like Celsus (about 50 A. D.), who were familiar with the Greek medical writers, as was Luke.   She pleads that Luke lived in Philippi, a Roman colony, and had a fondness for Rome, as the close of the Acts shows.   She argues, also, that Luke is a Latin name, "a surname in the *gens Annæa* to which Seneca, Gallio, and Lucan all belonged."[1]   His apparent liberty in Rome while Paul was a prisoner may be due to his being a cadet of that house.   She draws a parallel between the Æneid and the Acts.   Jones agrees that the suggestion is "both instructive and picturesque" (p. 235).   Ramsay[2] allows as one of the possibilities about the name Luke that "the evangelist might have been a Hellene bearing the simple name Loukios."   In that case he was not a slave and not a Roman citizen, not a Roman at all, but "an ordinary free Hellene."   His full name thus was Loukios, without *nomen* or *cognomen*.   He says that the other alternative is that "Lucius may have been his *prænomen* as a Roman citizen; and in that case it would follow almost certainly that the physician Loukios was a freedman, who acquired the full Roman name when he was set free."   But in neither case would Luke be a Latin by birth.   We seem, therefore, shut up to the idea that Luke was a native Greek, not Latin.   Whether he acquired Roman citizenship is uncertain, though possible.   The use of Roman names was very common and does not of itself prove that Luke was not Greek.

3. *Possibly a Freedman.*—It has already been suggested by Ramsay that "physicians were often freedmen; and freedmen were frequently addressed by their *prænomen*, which marked their rank."[3]   And Loukios (Latin Lucius) could be the *prænomen* of our Luke (Loukas) as a Roman citizen.   Ramsay adds that "the custom of society would make it probable that this physician, who led for many years the life of a companion of Paul, was not born a Roman citizen (as perhaps Silvanus

[1] M. Jones, *N. T. in Twentieth Century*, p. 233.
[2] *Bearing of Recent Discovery*, p. 382.
[3] *Bearing of Recent Discovery*, p. 382.

was)."[1] Ramsay notes, however, that "a *libertus* usually remained in close relation to his former master, who continued to be his *patronus*."[2] But there were exceptions. There seems no way to reach a positive conclusion on this point. Paul had a Roman name (besides the Hebrew name of Saul) and also Roman citizenship. Paul was not a freedman, but free born (Acts 22 : 28). Luke's ready pen, his versatility and his interest in the sea are Greek traits,[3] whether Luke was a free Hellene or a Greek slave set free with Roman citizenship and a Roman name.

Ramsay declines to express an opinion as to whether Luke was a freedman. Dean Plumptre[4] has made the interesting suggestion that the Roman poet Lucanus, born A. D. 39 in Corduba, Spain, was named after the physician Luke. It was a common practice for children to be named after a beloved physician. Hayes[5] is quite taken with the idea. He thinks that Luke "was born a slave in the household of Theophilus, a wealthy government official in Antioch."[6] If so, Theophilus set him free, after educating him as a physician. Luke then won Theophilus to Christ and Theophilus continued Luke's patron. Gallio and Seneca were uncles of the poet Lucanus. If Luke told Lucanus about Paul, it is easy to think that he may have told Gallio and Seneca about the Apostle. Thus the kindness of Gallio to Paul in Corinth is explained, and the traditional friendship between Paul and Seneca has some possible foundation.[7] It is a pleasing fancy, but that is all one can say.

4. *Probably the Brother of Titus.*—There are other conjectures about Luke that may be dismissed at this point. If he was either a Greek or a Roman, free or freedman, he was not one of the Seventy (Epiphanius) or the unnamed disciple with Cleophas (Luke 24 : 13) according to "Theophylact's attractive guess, which still finds advocates."[8] Not being a Jew, he is ruled out *ipso facto*. That is not true of the conjecture that

---

[1] *Ibid.*   [2] *Ibid.*, p. 383.

[3] Rackham, *Comm. on Acts*, p. xxviii.
[4] *Books of the Bible, N. T.*, pp. 74 f.
[5] *The Synoptic Gospels and the Acts*, pp. 179 f., 197 f.
[6] *Ibid.*, p. 197.
[7] Cf. Lightfoot's *Essay on St. Paul, and Seneca, Comm. on Philippians*, pp. 207–333.
[8] Plummer, *Comm.*, p. xix.

he was one of the Greeks who came to Philip (John 12 : 20). It is possible in itself, but there is no proof for it and it seems to be ruled out by the implication in Luke 1 : 1–4 that the author is not one of the eye-witnesses. But it is possible that Origen and Chrysostom are correct in thinking that Luke was "the brother whose praise in the gospel was spread through all the churches" and who was the companion of Titus (II Cor. 8 : 18; 12 : 18).[1] This can be true even if he is not the brother of Titus, as is probable. If he is the brother of Titus, as the Greek idiom naturally implies, then Luke is a Greek, not a Roman by birth; for Titus is a Greek (Gal. 2 : 3). And if a Greek, he is possibly, though not necessarily, a freedman. Thus far we seem to be quite within the range of probability. It may be added that in some manuscripts (of II Cor.) Luke is mentioned in the subscription as one of the bearers of the Epistle along with Titus.

5. *Luke's Birthplace.*—This matter is still in dispute. There is something to be said for Antioch in Syria, for Philippi and for Antioch in Pisidia. "The Clementines tell us that Theophilus was a wealthy citizen of Antioch."[2] If Luke had been the slave of Theophilus and was now a freedman, this would indicate that he was born in Antioch, though the argument is wholly hypothetical. But there are other considerations. The Codex Bezæ[3] after Acts 11 : 27 has the following peculiar reading: "And there was great rejoicing; and when we were gathered together one of them stood up and said." This may be a mere Western addition, but it represents an early tradition that Luke was associated with Antioch during the stay of Barnabas and Saul there. Blass[4] is confident that it is the insertion of Luke himself in the revision: "Now this *we*, which is also attested by St. Augustine, clearly shows that the author was at that time a member of the church at Antioch, which is the tradition given by Eusebius (*Hist. Eccl.* 3 : 4, 7) and others." Eusebius speaks of "Luke being by birth of those from Antioch."[5] This certainly means that Luke's family

[1] See 5. in Chapter I.

[2] Hayes, *Synoptic Gospels and Acts*, p. 194.

[3] This remarkable reading in the B text is ἦν δὲ πολλὴ ἀγαλλίασις. συνεστραμμένων δὲ ἡμῶν ἔφη εἰς ἐξ αὐτῶν κτλ.

[4] *Philology of the Gospels*, p. 131. Cf. also Blass, *Acta Apostolorum*, p. 137; "*Lucuntissimum testimonium, quo auctor sese Antiochenum fuisse monstrat.*"

[5] Λουκᾶς τὸ μὲν γένος ὢν τῶν ἀπ' 'Αντιοχείας.

came from Antioch, but it hardly "amounts to an assertion that Luke was not an Antiochian," as Ramsay[1] argues. The expression of Eusebius is "awkward," but not "obviously chosen in order to avoid the statement that Luke was an Antiochian."[2] In fact, Jerome[3] plainly speaks of "Luke the physician of Antioch." Likewise Euthalius[4] describes Luke as "being by birth an Antiochian." Once more the *Præfatio Lucæ* (placed in third century by Harnack) speaks of "Luke, by nation a Syrian of Antioch." Plummer[5] concludes that "this is probable in itself and is confirmed by the Acts. Of only one of the deacons are we told to which locality he belonged, 'Nicolas a proselyte of Antioch' (6 : 5): and we see elsewhere that the writer was well acquainted with Antioch and took an interest in it (11 : 19–27; 13 : 1; 14 : 19, 21, 26; 15 : 22, 23, 30, 35; 18 : 22)." Antioch in Acts is the new centre of Christian activity. It cannot be said that this evidence is absolutely convincing, but it renders it probable that Luke was born and reared in Antioch in Syria, though he spent his later years elsewhere, as in Philippi, Cæsarea, Rome.

But Ramsay, like Renan, argues for Philippi as the place of Luke's nativity. He suggests that, since Antioch was a Seleucid foundation, there was a Macedonian element in the population. "Thus it may very well have happened that Luke was a relative of one of the early Antiochian Christians; and this relationship was perhaps the authority for Eusebius's carefully guarded statement." Ramsay[6] even suggests that "perhaps Titus was the relative of Luke; and Eusebius found this statement in an old tradition attached to II Cor. 8 : 18, 12 : 18, where Titus and Luke (the latter not named by Paul, but identified by an early tradition) are associated as envoys to Corinth." But in II Cor. 12 : 18 "the brother" can naturally mean "his brother," but not "his relative," though it can mean "cousin," as Ramsay[7] notes. If Titus and Luke were brothers, they were naturally born in the same city. Ramsay admits that "there is not sufficient evidence to justify

[1] *St. Paul the Traveller*, p. 389.   [2] Ramsay, *ibid.*

[3] *De Vir. Ill.*, vii. *Lucas Medicus Antiochensis.*

[4] Migne, *Patr. Gk.*, vol. LXXXV, p. 633. Ἀντιοχεὺς γὰρ οὗτος ὑπάρχων τὸ γένος

[5] *Comm. on Luke*, p. xxi.   [6] *St. Paul the Traveller*, p. 390.

[7] *Luke the Physician*, p. 18, n 1.

an opinion." He exaggerates the difficulty about Eusebius and increases the problem in II Cor. 12 : 18. Ramsay urges, also, the civic pride shown by Luke in pointing out that Philippi is the first city of that division of Macedonia. But his long residence in Philippi would amply explain such pride. Ramsay also argues that in Acts 16 : 9-10 "the man from Macedonia" is Luke who had been speaking with Paul about Macedonia the day before the vision. This is plausible and quite possible, though Luke, if now a resident of Philippi, may have gone there from Antioch, either before his conversion or afterward. There is nothing in Acts 16 : 9-10 to indicate that Luke and Paul have met for the first time. Rackham[1] holds that "it is extremely unlikely that S. Luke met S. Paul for the first time at Troas," though Ramsay[2] argues this view. Carpenter[3] thinks that "the two views may be combined by supposing that he was an Antiochian who was in medical practice at Philippi."

Rackham[4] urges Antioch in Pisidia as the place of Luke's birth. He accepts the South Galatian theory that Paul wrote to the churches founded in the first mission tour. He holds that Luke met Paul first at Antioch in Pisidia, where he preached "because of an infirmity of the flesh" (Gal. 4 : 13), when Luke was called in as physician. He suggests that Luke descended from an old Philippian family that had settled here. His theory is that Luke went to Antioch in Syria when Paul came to the help of Barnabas, having been converted at Tarsus by Paul before going to Antioch. It can only be said that this view is possible, though nothing like so plausible as the tradition that Luke is a native of Antioch in Syria. The question cannot be settled yet. Some day we may know.

6. *Luke's Education.*—It is plain enough that the man who wrote the Gospel and the Acts was a man of genuine culture. As a physician he "belonged to the middle or higher plane of contemporary culture. To this plane we are directed not only by the prologue of the Gospel, but by the literary standard attained in the whole work."[5] "This man possessed the higher culture in rich measure,"[6] as his use of his materials in the

[1] *Comm. on Acts*, p. xxx.   [2] *St. Paul the Traveller*, p. 201.
[3] *The Christianity According to S. Luke*, p. 20.
[4] So Rendall on the basis of ἡμᾶς in Acts 14 : 23.
[5] Harnack, *Luke the Physician*, p. 13.   [6] *Ibid.*

Gospel and the Acts proves. "He had at his command an average education, and possessed a more than ordinary literary talent."[1] If a freedman of Theophilus at Antioch, he would receive a good education in the schools there. As a physician, he would be sent by Theophilus either to Alexandria, Athens or Tarsus, the great universities of the time. Alexandria seems unlikely in the absence of any allusion to the city.[2] We know that Luke seems familiar with Athens (Acts 17), but Tarsus is much more likely. Hayes[3] considers it almost certain that Luke was sent to Tarsus and at the same time with Paul and Barnabas, while Apollos was in the Alexandrian university. If Apollos wrote Hebrews, it is easy to see what a great part was played in early Christianity by these college or university men who became fast friends. In Tarsus Luke would receive a good classical education, and would study medicine "where the great masters in that profession, Aretæus, Dioscorides and Athenæus, had been educated. Just a few miles away, at Ægæ, stood the great Temple of Æsculapius, which furnished the nearest approach to the modern hospital to be found in the ancient world. From the university lectures Luke got the theory of medicine; in the Temple of Æsculapins he got the practice and experience needed." Thus Hayes[4] indulges his fancy in reproducing the probable educational environment of Luke. Plummer agrees that it is more than probable that Luke studied in "Tarsus, where there was a school of philosophy and literature rivalling those of Alexandria and Athens," for "nowhere else in Asia Minor could he obtain so good an education." [5]

And yet Ramsay[6] quotes Strabo as saying that no students ever came from outside Tarsus to the university, in this respect falling behind Athens and Alexandria and other schools that drew students to their halls. So one has to pause before concluding that Luke went to Tarsus. Of course Strabo may mean that not many outsiders came. The city of Tarsus was dominated by the university of which they were proud. It

---

Ibid., p. 147.   [2] Rackham, *Comm. on Acts*, p. xxviii.
[3] *Synoptic Gospels and Acts*, p. 197.
[4] *Synoptic Gospels and Acts*, p. 197.
[5] *Comm. on Luke*, p. xxi.   Cf. Strabo, XIV, 5, 13, φιλοσοφίαν καὶ τὴν ἕλλην παιδείαν ἐγκύκλιον ἅπασαν.
[6] "The Cities of St. Paul" (*The University of Tarsus*, p. 232).

was a great university in the eagerness of the students for knowledge, and in the great ability and experience of some of the teachers and in the Hellenic freedom for teacher and pupil.[1] Strabo "praises highly the zeal for philosophy and the whole range of education which characterized the people of Tarsus in his time. In this respect they surpassed Athens and Alexandria and every other seat of learning."[2]   Their students went to other great universities for further study, but were rich in the heritage of Athenodorus, the Stoic philosopher, who spent his closing years in the University of Tarsus.   Seneca, in Rome, quotes Athenodorus, and Paul must have felt the influence of this "greatest of pagan Tarsians."   Ramsay[3] suggests that Athenodorus's influence on both Seneca and Paul is the probable explanation of the likeness in their phraseology.   Athenodorus "was long worshipped as a hero by his country," and he influenced the university life long after his death.   If Luke went to Tarsus, he entered into an atmosphere of great traditions, young as the school was in comparison with some others. Of one thing we may be sure.   Luke received a liberal education at one or more of the great technical schools of the time and probably at Tarsus.

7. *Luke's Conversion.*—Here we are wholly in the field of speculation. It seems clear that Luke was not a follower of Jesus in the flesh. The Muratorian Canon says: "But neither did he see the Lord in the flesh." It also states that Luke became a follower of Paul after the Ascension of Christ.   Jerome mentions a tradition that Luke became a proselyte to Judaism before he became a Christian, but it is unsupported. The Western reading (Codex Bezæ) of Acts 11 : 28 (the "we" section at Antioch) "would require that his conversion to Christianity take place before St. Paul met him."[4]   This might have been under the influence of the "men of Cyprus and Cyrene, fleeing from Jerusalem; and Luke was among the first to hear it and to accept it.   He told his master, Theophilus, about it, and Theophilus himself became interested and at last converted.   Then about the first thing that Theophilus did as a Christian was to give Luke his freedom "[5]   This is possible

---

[1] *Ibid.*, p. 233.   [2] *Ibid.*, p. 232.   [3] *Ibid.*, p. 223.
[4] Bebb, "Luke the Evangelist," Hastings's *D. B.*
[5] Hayes, *Synoptic Gospels and Acts*, p. 197.

and plausible. The *Præfatio Lucæ*[1] speaks of Luke as "a disciple of the apostle, and afterward a follower of St. Paul." This could mean that Luke was a convert before he met Paul, but that does not necessarily follow. Tertullian,[2] however, speaks of Paul as Luke's *magister* and *illuminator*. Plummer[3] thinks that by these words "Tertullian perhaps means us to understand that Luke was converted to the Gospel by Paul, and this is in itself probable enough." If so, then Luke may have been already converted when Paul came to Antioch at the call of Barnabas. Rackham[4] argues that, as the Bezan text for Acts 11 : 28 shows that Luke was in Antioch at this time, it is probable that Luke had already been won to Christ. "We can suppose that after much travel in the study and practice of medicine he paid a visit to Tarsus and its famous university. There he met and was converted by S. Paul; and when Barnabas came from Antioch and took back Saul with him about the year 42 (11:25–26), S. Luke accompanied them." Once more, one can only say that it is possible. If the Bezan text for Acts 11 : 28 does record a fact, then Barnabas, Paul and Luke are together in Antioch as early as A. D. 42. Once more, if they were college mates at Tarsus, one can understand afresh the new tie that now knit them together. "In all probability it had begun at a most impressionable age in college life."[5] Luke met other men of prominence in Christian work, we know; Silas, Timothy, James, Mark, Aristarchus and others.

Harnack[6] sees no light on this phase of the subject: "We have no knowledge where and by whose influence he became a Christian, nor whether he had previously come into sympathetic touch with the Judaism of the Dispersion; only one thing is certain—that he had never been in Palestine."

Furneaux[7] thinks that the likelihood that Luke and Paul had been fellow students at Tarsus explains "the absence of any record of their first meeting. It is further possible that they had worked together at Antioch; or that Paul, when stricken down by illness in Galatia, had sent for 'the beloved

---

[1] *Discipulus apostolorum, postea Paulum secutus.*
[2] *Adv. Marcion*, IV, 2.   [3] *Comm. on Luke*, p. xx.
[4] *Comm. on Acts*, p. xxxi.
[5] Luckock, *The Special Characteristics of the Four Gospels*, p. 119.
[6] *Luke the Physician*, p. 146.   [7] *Comm. on Acts*, p. 258.

physician.' The 'us' of verse 10 shows that he was not a new convert." It would be pleasing to think that Luke was won to Christ when called in by Paul as his physician. This, to be sure, could be true, whether at Antioch, in Galatia (4 : 13) or at Troas. If Luke saved Paul's life in the frequent attacks of malaria, Paul in turn saved his soul by leading him to Christ.

Ramsay[1] is positive that, though Luke was probably already a Christian, he and Paul met for the first time at Troas. "Luke became known to Paul for the first time here." Ramsay suggests that Luke was a resident of Troas at this time and that Paul called him in as a physician for one of his malarial attacks. What is certain is that at this point Luke injects himself purposely into the narrative, probably by using his own travel diary. It may well be that Luke had been to Macedonia and spoke to Paul about the need there. But that is not certain. Least certain of all is Ramsay's insistence that Luke and Paul had never met before the incident at Troas. If they had never met before, it might be that here Paul won Luke to Christ but for the implication in the context that Luke is already a Christian. Knowling considers it probable that Luke and Paul were friends before. Whether Luke was Paul's trophy for Christ or not, he is now ready to follow Paul in the service of Christ.

8. *The Medical Missionary.*—It seems plain that in the passage before us the succeeding words in verse 10 lead to the natural inference that Luke, too, was a preacher of the Gospel, and had already done the work of an evangelist. "We sought to go forth into Macedonia, concluding that God had called us to preach the Gospel unto them." This call to preach in Macedonia was answered by Luke as well as by Paul, Silas and Timothy. At the place of prayer by the riverside near Philippi "we sat down and spake to the women that were come together" (Acts 16 : 13). The poor girl with the spirit of soothsaying said: "These men are servants of the Most High God, who proclaim unto you the way of salvation" (Acts 16 : 17). Luke was left in charge at Philippi, when Paul and Silas departed, and he apparently remained there over six years till Paul comes back from Corinth on the third tour on his way to Jerusalem (Acts 20 : 5). Thence he is with Paul to the close of Acts. So he is Luke the Evangelist because he preached as well as because he wrote the Third Gospel. He had probably travelled

[1] *St. Paul the Traveller*, pp. 200-5.

a good deal for the study and practice of his medical profession. Now he kept up his work as a physician and added that of a preacher of the Gospel. Like the Great Physician, he went about doing good to the souls and the bodies of men. The Romans did not rank the physician high, but the Greeks placed him on a par with the philosopher.[1] Certain it is that "his medical skill would be of use in gaining an opening for preaching the Gospel, as modern missionaries often find."[2] We have already seen that in Acts 28 : 9–10 Luke seems to mean that he practised his profession as physician during the three months in Malta. It is also plain that "his history owes much to the fact that he joined Paul at the critical moment when a special revelation led him to Europe."[3] Various traditions report Luke as preaching in Dalmatia, Gallia, Italy, Achaia, Macedonia, Africa, Bithynia. They are all of no value save that they testify to his work as a preacher of Christ. One report is that he became the second bishop of Alexandria. His presence with Paul we do know. In Philemon 24 Paul calls him a "fellow worker," but not a fellow prisoner, with him in Rome. At the same time (Col. 4 : 14) he alludes to him as "the beloved physician." In Rome he was both preacher and physician. He was Paul's friend and companion and trusted physician. It is evident that Paul had frail health for many years. We probably owe Paul's living to old age, under God, to the skill of Luke, his physician, who watched over him with tender solicitude. Luke is probably one of "the messengers (*apostles;* literally, missionaries) of the churches, the glory of Christ" (II Cor. 8:23). If so, he is one of the agents in the great collection for the poor saints in Jerusalem, and Paul demands that the Corinthians show unto them in the face of the churches the proof of their love (8 : 25). "He was beloved for his medical skill and for his ever-aggressive and ever-attractive Christianity. He might well be a model for all in the medical profession."[4] He was "a doctor of the old school," the first scientific physician who laid his skill at the feet of Jesus. Thousands have followed in his steps and, like Luke, have

---

[1] Rackham, *Comm.*, p. xxviii.   [2] Furneaux, *Comm.*, p. 259.

[3] *Ibid.* Canon G. W. Whitaker ("Barnabas, Luke and Bithynia," *The Expositor*, December, 1919) seeks to connect Luke with Bithynia. The *Præfatio vel argumentum Lucæ* does say that Luke *obiit in Bithynia.*

[4] Hayes, *Synoptic Gospels and Acts*, p. 188.

taken Christ with them into the sick-room. Doctor W. T. Grenfell, the "Labrador doctor" and missionary, is a modern example of what Luke was in the first century.

9. *Loyal to the Last.*—We have Paul's own words to prove that Luke was true when others fled from Paul as if he had the pestilence. That is, if we credit II Tim. to Paul, as I do. Paul is now in the second and last Roman imprisonment. He is facing certain death and he knows it. Nero is persecuting followers of Jesus for the crime of Christianity. Since the burning of Rome in A. D. 64 the whole atmosphere has changed. Before then Paul was allowed his own hired house and much liberty (under guard), and his friends came and went at will. Finally Paul was set free, as the case against him fell through. But now the air is black with death. Many Christians have already forfeited their lives for the faith. Paul is the next victim. Now Paul's old friends in Asia, when they come to Rome, avoid his dungeon for fear of death. Onesiphorus dared all and apparently lost his life (II Tim. 1 : 15–17). A faithful band in Rome are firm (4 : 21), but most of Paul's companions have left him—Demas, Crescens, Titus; probably for good reasons, but they are gone. "Only Luke is with me." Luke alone stood fast. Paul longs for Timothy and for Mark, even Mark. Let us hope that they came before Paul was executed, and were able to go with Paul and Luke to the execution. Luke, doubtless, saw to the burial of the body of his great friend.

And then what? Who knows? Gregory Nazianzen ranks Luke with Stephen, James and Peter as a martyr under Domitian after a long and useful career after Paul's death. Another story is that he died a natural death in Achaia or Bithynia. He was loyal to Paul. He was loyal to Christ both as preacher and physician. Irenæus speaks of Luke as *inseparabilis a Paulo.* Jüngst actually denies any trace of Pauline influence in the Gospel and the Acts. That would be amazing and is not true. However, Luke does not copy Paul. He interprets Paul and Peter as he interpreted Christ out of fulness of knowledge and with largeness of view. Examination of the Lukan books shows no undue Pauline influence. Indeed, the portrait of Christ in the Gospel is distinctly drawn from pre-Pauline sources. The picture of Paul in the Acts is not taken from the Pauline Epistles. And yet Luke's very soul was knit to Paul's in loving affection. Paul was one of his heroes to the last.

CHAPTER III

THE DATE OF THE GOSPEL AND THE ACTS

"And he abode two whole years in his own hired dwelling, and received all that went in unto him, preaching the kingdom of God, and teaching the things concerning the Lord Jesus Christ with all boldness, none forbidding him" (Acts 28 : 30–31).

1. *The Atmosphere of the First Century.*—It may now be stated definitely that the second-century date for the Gospel and Acts has been abandoned save by a small number of exceedingly radical critics. The general acceptance of the Lukan authorship of the two books disposes of the Baur theory that it was a religious romance written for the purpose of reconciling the opposition between Peter and Paul. The notion that Luke's Gospel made use of that of Marcion has been given up. It is now known that Marcion used a mutilated edition of Luke's Gospel. Blass[1] holds that Marcion had the Western text of Luke's Gospel. The arguments for the second century (105–130) are given at length by Schmiedel (*Enc. Biblica*) and by Holtzmann.[2] It is argued that the author made use of Paul's Epistles, of Josephus, that he imitated Plutarch's *Lives* in his picture of Peter and Paul, that he reflects the atmosphere of second-century ecclesiasticism and takes interest in the political side of the Roman Empire. It must be confessed that these are not very weighty or very serious arguments. It is by no means certain that he used Paul's Epistles, but what if he did? Certainly the political outlook of the Acts is precisely that of Paul's Epistles (Headlam, Hastings's *D. B.*, art. "Acts"), but surely that argues for the early date. As to Josephus, that is more important and will call for discussion a bit later. But that can be true and the author still be Luke. The possible use of Josephus bears on the date of the Acts, not on the Lukan authorship. "In this event he must have been about seventy when he wrote Acts, which is

[1]*Philology of the Gospels*, pp. 145 f.   [2] *Einl.,*[3] 1892, p. 405.

30

by no means impossible or even improbable."[1] Ramsay[2] pointedly says: "We must face the facts boldly. If Luke wrote *Acts* his narrative *must* agree in a striking and convineing way with Paul's: they *must* confirm, explain and complete one another." The writings of both stand that test. The genuineness of nearly all of the Pauline Epistles is now admitted by the mass of modern scholars. The Lukan authorship of the Gospel and the Acts now carries the weight of modern opinion. Ramsay's researches show in innumerable ways how Luke's knowledge of first-century details can only be explained on the view that he was a contemporary of these events. The frequent changes in the Roman provinces (from imperial to senatorial, and *vice versa*) make pitfalls for the unwary. Luke steps with sure tread because he was on the ground and knew the facts. He has been triumphantly vindicated, as will be shown in future chapters.

2. *The Date of the Acts.*—The book was written after the Gospel (Acts 1:1) and before Luke's death. Lightfoot declined to discuss the date of the Acts in his article on the Acts.[3] Plummer[4] states that Lightfoot regarded the question of the date of Acts as dependent on the date of Luke. So it is in so far as determining the date before which the Acts can be located. But it is equally true that the date of the Acts determines the time beyond which the Gospel cannot go. Lake[5] puts the case fairly: "The evidence for the date is very meagre. If the Lucan authorship be accepted, any date before the last events chronicled, *i. e.*, a short time before A. D. 100, is possible." Both books must come within the lifetime of Luke. There is no way to tell how much time elapsed between the two books. Probably it was not long. On the whole, it is simplest to take up the Acts first. There are three dates that are at present argued for both the Gospel and the Acts as they hang together. But we shall confine the argument here to the Acts.

(a) *A. D. 94 to 100.*—Those who hold to this date for Acts, do so on the theory that Luke made use of Josephus. As already stated, Luke need not have been more than seventy

---

[1] Moffatt, *Intr. to Lit. of the N. T.*, p. 312.
[2] *St. Paul the Traveller*, p. 14.   [3] Smith's *D. B.*,[2] pp. 25–43.
[4] *Comm.*, p. xxix.
[5] Hastings's *Dict. of Ap. Ch.*, article "Acts."

at the end of the century, if a young man when he first became associated with Paul. Burkitt[1] and Peake[2] accept the view that Luke drew on the writings of Josephus. Stanton[3] concludes that Luke made use of the *Jewish War*, but not the rest of the works of Josephus. If this is true, the late date is not necessary. The date of the *Antiquities* is 94 A. D. It may be said at once that most of the arguments employed to prove that Luke knew the writings of Josephus are utterly inconclusive. Some of the arguments of Clemen[4] and Krenkel[5] are criticised sharply by Belser[6] and Plummer,[7] who calls them "childish." By like arguments of common Greek words one may show that Luke was influenced by Thucydides. Some of the likenesses are due to the use of the Septuagint by both Luke and Josephus. The only matter of serious import is the fact that both Josephus (*Ant.* XX., v. 1 f.) and Luke (Acts, 5: 36 f.) speak of Theudas and Judas the Galilean in this order as if Theudas lived before Judas. The two are mentioned in Josephus some twenty lines apart. The name Theudas is a common one. It is quite possible that another man is meant, as in the case of the tetrarch Lysanias in Luke 3 : 1. The discrepancy only exists in case the same man is meant. Even then it is the discrepancy of Gamaliel and not of Luke, unless Luke wrote the speech. There are more divergences than likenesses in the two reports that suggest independent narratives, as in the two reports of the death of Herod Agrippa I. Lake[8] considers the use of Josephus by Luke too doubtful to be decisive: "The decennium 90–100 seems, on the whole, the most probable, but demonstrative proof is lacking." M. Jones[9] thinks these inferences about the use of Josephus too "precarious" to be conclusive. Plummer[10] holds this hypothesis "highly improbable." "Moreover, where the statements of either can be tested, it is Luke who is commonly found to be accurate, whereas Josephus is often convicted of exaggeration and

---

[1] *The Gospel History and Its Transmission*, ch. iv.
[2] *Introduction to the N. T.*, p. 135.
[3] *The Gospels as Historical Documents*, part II, pp. 263–273.
[4] *Die Chronologie der paulin. Briefe* (1893).
[5] *Josephus und Lukas* (1894).
[6] *Theol. Quartalschrift*, *Tübingen* (1895, 1896).
[7] *Comm.*, p. xxx.   [8] Hastings's *Dict. of Ap. Ch.*, article "Acts."
[9] *New Testament in the Twentieth Century*, p. 255.
[10] *Comm.*, p. xxix.

error." The supposed use of Josephus by Luke cannot, therefore, be held to be certain or, as I think, even probable. We must look elsewhere for decisive evidence on this subject. Harnack (*Luke the Physician*, p. 24, n. 2) says: "The time of Josephus need not be taken into consideration; for the theory that the author of the Acts had read that historian is quite baseless."

Besides, there are strong arguments against the date 94–100, which Plummer[1] summarizes forcibly. The use of "the Christ"[2] as the Messiah instead of a proper name Christ would be hard to explain. The use of "the Lord" for Jesus, not in Matthew or in Mark save in the disputed appendix, would have been more common. Besides, would Luke have kept 21 : 32 if written after "this generation" had passed away? The historical atmosphere of Acts is not that of 95–135 A. D. Besides, what could have induced a companion of Paul to remain quiet so long after his death? These arguments are very strong.

(b) A. D. 70–80.—The majority of modern critics date the Acts here. But nothing of a very positive nature can be adduced for this date. Ramsay[3] thinks that he has found "a clew, though in itself an uncertain one, to suggest the date when Luke was at work" on the Acts. The reign of Titus was reckoned from association with his father on July 1, A. D. 71. Hence, Ramsay argues, Luke wrote the Gospel (and the Acts) about that time, because he speaks of the reign of Tiberius (Luke 3 : 1–2) in the fifteenth year, reckoning from A. D. 12, when Tiberius was associated with Augustus in the empire. But this is too precarious an argument for so solid a conclusion. The chief argument relied upon for the date shortly after A. D. 70 is Luke 21 : 20. It is argued by Sanday, B. Weiss and others that Luke here changes the language of Daniel 9 : 27 in Mark 13 : 14 and Matt. 24 : 15 ("the abomination of desolation") to the definite statement about Jerusalem being "encompassed with armies." It is held to be a *vaticinium post eventum*. The omission of scripture quotation makes it necessary also to omit the explanatory notes: "Let him that readeth

---

[1] *Comm.*, pp. xxx, xxxi.
[2] ὁ χριστός. Cf. Luke 2 : 26; 3 : 15; 4 : 41; 9 : 20; 20 : 41; 22 : 35, 39; 24 : 26, 46.
[3] *St. Paul the Traveller*, p. 387.

understand." But the mention of armies is very vague.
Furneaux[1] is very positive and says that "the Third Gospel
cannot have been written earlier than A. D. 70, the year of the
destruction of Jerusalem. Hence, the Acts cannot have been
written much before A. D. 75." But such a vigorous pronounce-
ment carries little weight. "Savonarola foretold, as early as
A. D. 1496, the capture of Rome, which happened in 1527,
and those sermons of 1496 were printed in 1497."[2] Surely
Jesus could foretell as much as Savonarola, and Luke cannot be
charged with writing this prophecy after the destruction of
Jerusalem. Lake,[3] who holds to the late date, as we have
seen, sees very little in the idea that the Gospel of Luke must
be after the destruction of Jerusalem: "It is doubtful if there
are really any satisfactory proofs that this was the case."
Torrey (Composition and Date of Acts, p. 70) holds that all the
items in Luke's report of the prediction occur in Old Testament
prophecies and denies that the passage in Luke can be called a
vaticinium ex eventu. Plummer[4] makes much of the idea that
the date A. D. 70–80 allows time for the "many" to draw up
narratives about Christ, but there was time enough between
A. D. 30 and 55 for that. Harnack[5] had already given up this
argument in his Acts of the Apostles. He had himself[6] in 1897
argued for A. D. 78 as the earliest possible date for Acts. Now
in 1909 he writes "to warn critics against a too hasty closing
of the chronological question." He concludes:[7] "Therefore,
for the present, we must be content to say: St. Luke wrote at
the time of Titus or in the earlier years of Domitian, but perhaps even so early as the beginning of the seventh decade of
the first century." So astonishing a surrender on the part of
Harnack created consternation among many critics. It was
clear that the matter could not rest thus.

　(c) About A. D. 63.—The early date for the Acts has always
nad able advocates. Men like Alford, Blass, Ebrard, Farrar,
Gloag, Godet, Headlam, Keil, Lange, Lumby, Maclean,
Oesterzee, Resch, Schaff, Tholuck, Wieseler, have reasoned that
Luke closes the Acts as he does and when he does for the simple

---

[1] Comm., p. x.　　　　　　[2] Blass, Philology of the Gospels, p. 42.
[3] Hastings's Dictionary of Ap. Ch., art. "Acts."
[4] Comm., p. xxxi.　　　　[5] Engl. tr., 1909, p. 291.
[6] Chronologie der alt-christl. Litt. I., pp. 246–250, 718.
[7] Acts of the Apostles, p. 297.

reason that events have proceeded no farther with Paul. "In investigating the date of a book, the first step is to look for the latest event mentioned."[1] And yet after A. D. 63 some of the most stirring events in Christian history occurred, like the burning of Rome in A. D. 64 with the persecution of Christians which is reflected in 1 Peter, the martyrdom of Peter and Paul, and the destruction of Jerusalem and the Temple in A. D. 70. How are we to explain the absence of any allusion to these great events? There are three ways of doing so. One is the view already stated. Rackham[2] puts the argument clearly. It seems incredible that Luke should betray no knowledge of Paul's death if he had known it. That would be the natural climax to the Acts. The martyrdom of Stephen and of James would have been crowned with that of Paul. Besides, Acts is a joyful book and Paul remains full of cheer to the very end. If Luke knew that Paul went back to Ephesus, would he have left the prediction in Acts 20 : 25 that he did not expect to see their faces again? Besides, in the Acts the attitude of Rome toward Christianity is still undecided, whereas after A. D. 64 it became openly hostile. It was clear that Harnack must continue his studies on the date of Acts. This he does in his *Date of the Acts and the Synoptic Gospels* (tr. 1911). In 1909 he pleads for fresh investigation. After an exhaustive survey of the whole question, he says:[3] "We are accordingly left with the result: that the concluding verses of the Acts of the Apostles, taken in conjunction with the absence of any reference in the book to the result of the trial of St. Paul and to his martyrdom, make it in the highest degree probable that the work was written at a time when St. Paul's trial in Rome had not yet come to an end." With this conclusion I heartily agree and I had long held and taught it before Harnack reached it. Maclean[4] considers this view "the more probable." Blass,[5] indeed, would place the Acts as early as A. D. 59.

Lake[6] says that all this important argument is weakened by two other possibilities. One is that Luke contemplated a third volume in which he meant to go on with the story of Paul,

[1] Rackham, *Acts*, p. 1.
[2] *Ibid.*, pp. li ff.
[3] *Date of the Acts and Synoptic Gospels*, p. 99.
[4] Hastings's *One Volume D. B.*, art. "Acts."
[5] *Philology of the Gospels*, pp. 33 ff.
[6] Hastings's *Dict. of the Ap. Ch.*, art. "Acts."

though, he adds, this theory is not very probable. Ramsay
argues for it, but it is a mistaken notion to press Luke's use of
"first" in Acts 1 : 1, as we have seen. The current Koiné gives
no support for such an idea. The other consideration advanced by Lake against the sudden and apparent abrupt ending of Acts is that Luke really implies that the case fell through
and that Paul was released by his mention of "two years." A
passage in Philo's *in Flaccum* tells of a certain Lambon who
was kept in prison for two years, which Philo calls the longest
period. The idea seems to be that, if the case did not come to
trial in two years, dismissal came as a matter of course. This
is by no means certain, but even if it is, it would still not prove
that Luke did not write the Acts just at the close of the period
when there was prospect of Paul's release. Rackham, like
Harnack, is impressed with the joyous and optimistic note of
the Acts.

Bartlet in his *Apostolic Age* and article on "Acts" in the
Standard Bible Dictionary argues that Luke closed the Acts
with Paul's arrival in Rome for artistic and literary reasons.
This event marked the grand consummation of the Gospel in
the early age. *Paulus Romæ apex evangelii.* This natural
climax would be spoiled by the fruitless story of Paul's release,
journeys, arrest, trial and death. Certainly something can
be said for this interpretation. E. J. Goodspeed[1] presses this
argument against the force of Harnack's conclusion for the
early date of Acts, which "carries with it important consequences for early Christian literature." "If the subject of
Acts is the Rise and Progress of the Greek Mission, it has
reached in Paul at Rome a climax beyond which it could not
go."[2] "When Acts is written Paul is a hallowed memory,
and already the sects are beginning to appear."[3] Possibly so,
but one feels that all this is too subjective for Luke. He shows
literary skill and great ability as an historian, but he does not
write like a novelist for artistic effect by concealing important
facts. In the case of the Gospel he carries the story on to its
actual climax, the Resurrection and Ascension of Jesus. It is
hard to believe that, knowing of Paul's death, Luke avoided
mention of the subject for fear of spoiling his story. Believe
it who can. Headlam[4] notes that the arguments against the

[1] *The Expositor*, London, May, 1919, p. 387.   [2] *Ibid.*, p. 388.
[3] *Ibid.*, p. 391.   [4] Hastings's *D. B.*, art. "Acts."

early view are not very strong, while it is the obvious way to treat the close of Acts. Besides, if Luke wrote after the destruction of Jerusalem, why did he not change "flee to the mountain" in Luke 21 : 21 when the Christians fled to Pella? On the whole, the early date has the best of it. We, therefore, date the Acts about A. D. 63 and in Rome. Torrey[1] puts the date for the supposed Aramaic Document (Acts 1–15) A. D. 50, and the translation of it by Luke and the writing of Acts 16–28 not later than A. D. 64 and in Rome. It is needless to discuss Ephesus, Corinth, and the other places alleged in place of Rome as Luke's abode when he wrote the Acts.

3. *The Date of the Gospel.*—Our conclusion concerning the date of the Acts carries with it the early date of the Gospel. We have seen that Lake admitted as much. "It has usually been assumed that this (the date of the Lukan Gospel) must be posterior to the fall of Jerusalem in A. D. 70, but it is doubtful whether there are really any satisfactory proofs that this was the case."[2] We have seen that there are no such proofs. The date of the Gospel turns on that of the Acts. The earliest evidence for the date of Luke's Gospel is Acts 1 : 1. Here Luke definitely refers to the book. Harnack[3] states the matter succinctly: "Hence, it is proved that it is altogether wrong to say that the eschatological passages force us to the conclusion that the Third Gospel was written after the year 70 A. D. And since there are no other reasons for a later date, it follows that the strong arguments, which favor the composition of the Acts before 70 A. D., now also apply in their full force to the Gospel of Luke, *and it seems now to be established beyond question that both books of this great historical work were written while St. Paul was still alive*" (italics Harnack's). I do not think that Harnack has put the matter more strongly than the evidence justifies. He expects that some critics will be slow to accept so firm a conclusion after a century of turmoil and dispute. The rapid conversion of Harnack to the early date is viewed with suspicion by some as unscientific. Lake[4] admits that "Harnack's powerful advocacy has turned the current of feeling in favor of the traditional view, but he has really dealt

[1] *Composition and Date of Acts*, p. 67.
[2] Hastings's *Dict. Ap. Church*, art. "Acts."
   Date of Acts and Synoptic Gospels, p. 124.
[4] Hastings's *Dict. of Ap. Ch.*, art. "Luke."

adequately with only one side of the question and dismissed the theological and (to a somewhat less extent) the historical difficulty too easily." The theological argument strongly confirms the early date, for the picture of Christ in the Gospel of Luke is distinctly more primitive than that of Paul in the Epistles of the first Roman imprisonment (Philippians, Colossians, Ephesians, Philemon), A. D. 61–63. Indeed, the same thing is true of Acts, particularly of the first half of the book. The historical question is dealt with in great detail by Ramsay in his various books. It cannot be said that the proof here argues strongly for 63 as against 75 A. D., but there is nothing that is hostile to the 63 date. The historical argument is decidedly against A. D. 95 to 100 A. D. Lake wishes to leave the question of the date *sub judice* for the present. Jones[1] gives a fair résumé of Harnack's arguments for A. D. 63, but still holds to A. D. 75–80 as "on the whole more satisfactory." But the facts brought out concerning A. D. 63 as the date for Acts will meet with increasing acceptance from scholars, in my opinion.

If Luke wrote Acts while Paul was alive and in Rome, then he wrote the Gospel either before that, while in Cæsarea (two years), or he finished it after reaching Rome, before he wrote the Acts. Torrey[2] argues, naturally, that the Book of Acts was an afterthought when Luke wrote the prologue to the Gospel. But Chase[3] is positive that Luke had the Acts in mind and meant the same prologue for both books. It matters little. The extreme brevity of the address to Theophilus in Acts with the reference to the prologue in the Gospel argues for a short period between the two volumes. Torrey therefore suggests A. D. 61 as the latest date for the Gospel. Moffatt[4] thinks it unsafe to contend that nine or ten years should elapse between the two books.

There remains only one further difficulty of importance in the way of dating the Gospel of Luke so early as 59 or 60 in Cæsarea or 61 in Rome. It is certain that Luke used the Gospel of Mark as one of his many sources for his Gospel. Synoptic criticism has proved this as clearly as seems possible.[5]

---

[1] *N. T. in Twentieth Century*, p. 260.

[2] *Composition and Date of Acts*, p. 68.

[3] *Credibility of the Acts*, p. 16.   [4] *Intr. to Lit. of N. T.*, p. 313.

[5] See Sanday *et alii*, *Oxford Studies in the Synoptic Problem* (1911); Hawkins, *Horæ Synopticæ*[2] (1911); Robertson, *Studies in Mark's Gospel* (1919).

Can the Gospel of Mark be dated before A. D. 59? Jones[1] is convinced that Mark's Gospel does not stand in the way. Edmundson[2] holds that Luke had an earlier recension of Mark "for the use of Greek-speaking converts in Judea." But this hypothesis is by no means necessary. Luke made use of the Logia of Jesus (Q) as did Matthew, but no trouble arises from this source. It probably belongs to the period before 50 A. D. I have discussed the date of Mark's Gospel at some length in my *Studies in Mark's Gospel* and need not repeat the arguments here. Tradition and internal evidence combine to show that Mark wrote the Gospel while Peter was still alive. There is good ground for thinking that Mark[3] was in existence by A. D. 50. Both the Gospel of Matthew and the Gospel of Luke make use of Mark's Gospel. We know from Col. 4 : 10, 14 that Mark and Luke were with Paul in Rome. Harnack[4] finds that the latest recension of Mark's Gospel must come in "the sixth decade of the first century at the latest." It is therefore quite possible that Luke either in Cæsarea or in Rome saw a copy of Mark's Gospel. Nolloth[5] places the Gospel of Luke 57 or 58 A. D.

4. *The Historical Worth of the Lukan Writings.*—The remainder of the present volume is an investigation of the reliability of Luke as a historian and the credibility of his works. The evidence must be discussed in detail. The proof will be cumulative and varied. But at this stage of the discussion the point can be justly made that the early date of both Gospel and Acts gives a strong presumption in favor of the historical value of the books. There was less time for legends to grow. The author was nearer to his sources of information. The historian who is a near contemporary is not always able to give a true and large perspective for his facts, though Thucydides did it. But, at any rate, since Luke the physician, the friend of Paul, wrote these two books, they cannot be thrown aside as second-century romances written to deify Jesus and to idealize Peter and Paul.[6] The writer is so close to the facts of which he

[1] *N. T. in the Twentieth Century*, p. 258.
[2] *The Church in Rome During the First Century*, p. 67, n. 4.
[3] Nolloth, *The Rise of the Christian Religion*, 1917, p. 18.
[4] *The Date of Acts and Synoptic Gospels*, p. 133.   [5] *Op. cit.*, p. 15.
[6] The Tübingen view has been abandoned. Cf. Chase, *Credibility of the Acts*, p. 9. Jülicher (*Einl.*, p. 355) still speaks of "a genuine core" in Acts which is "overgrown with legendary accretions."

writes that he has to receive serious consideration to see if, after all, he has not drawn his characters to the life.

Even Harnack[1] balks at the miraculous element in Luke's Gospel and the Acts. He ranks Luke far above Josephus in historical worth,[2] but his prejudice against anything supernatural explains his reluctance to rank Luke among the very highest historians. "The book has now been restored to the position of credit which is its rightful due. It is not only, taken as a whole, a genuinely historical work, but even in the majority of its details it is trustworthy."[3] That is all true, but Harnack fails to appraise Luke's work as highly as it deserves. But his witness is remarkable when one considers how far Harnack has come.

But Ramsay has made the same journey, only he has been longer coming and has come farther. Let him tell his own story:[4] "I began with a mind unfavorable to it (the value of the Acts), for the ingenuity and apparent completeness of the Tübingen theory had at one time quite convinced me. . . . It was gradually borne in upon me that in various details the narrative showed marvellous truth." The leaven worked in Ramsay's mind as he kept up his researches in Asia Minor. He came to the study of Luke and Paul from the side of classical scholarship and the archæology of the Græco-Roman civilization. The whole drift of modern criticism is reflected in Ramsay's own experience. "The question among modern scholars now is with regard to Luke's credibility as a historian; it is generally conceded that he wrote at a comparatively early date, and had authorities of high character, even when he himself was not an eye-witness. How far can we believe his narrative? The present writer takes the view that Luke's history is unsurpassed in respect of its trustworthiness."[5] This testimony of Ramsay is of the greatest value. Ramsay is not infallible, but he is sincere and able, and relates with immense power his own conversion to the high estimate of Luke as a historian. "The first and the essential quality of the historian is truth."[6] "The more that I have studied the nar-

---

[1] Cf. his "Primitive Legends of Christendom" in his *Date of the Acts and the Synoptic Gospels*, pp. 136–162.

[2] *The Acts of the Apostles*, pp. 203–229.

[3] *Ibid.*, p. 298. [4] *St. Paul the Traveller*, p. 8.

[5] *The Bearing of Recent Discovery*, p. 81. [6] *St. Paul the Traveller*, p. 4.

rative of the Acts, and the more I have learned year after year
about Græco-Roman society and thoughts and fashions and
organizations in those provinces, the more I admire and the
better I understand.   I set out to look for truth on the border-
land where Greece and Asia meet, and found it here.   You
may press the words of Luke in a degree far beyond any other
historian's, and they stand the keenest scrutiny and the hardest treatment, provided always that the critic knows the subject and does not go beyond the limits of science and justice." [1]
That judgment will be found to be true if one looks at all the
facts with an open mind.

There is hardly need to say more, but for one thing.   No
plea is made that Luke could not make any mistakes because
he was inspired.   He himself makes no direct claim to inspiration.   That is a matter of opinion.   We know very little about
the nature of inspiration.   It is a fact as life is a fact, but we
understand neither one.   The writings of Luke are just as
much inspired after research has confirmed them as they were
before;   no more, no less.   Luke is entitled to be trusted like
any other ancient historian.   It is not necessary to show that
he never made a mistake or to be able to solve every difficulty
raised by his writings in order to form an intelligent opinion
about the value of his works.[2]   Ramsay[3] puts the case justly:
"Our hypothesis is that Acts was written by a great historian,
a writer who set himself the task to record the facts as they
occurred, a strong partisan indeed, but raised above partiality
by his perfect confidence that he had only to describe the facts
as they occurred, in order to make the truth of Christianity
and the honor of Paul apparent."   Ramsay, after a lifetime of
research, ranks Luke as the greatest of all historians, ancient
or modern.   The Gospel stands the same test that the Acts
has undergone.   It is not only the most beautiful book in the
world, but it is written with the utmost care and skill.   Luke
himself tells us his methods of work upon this book, methods
that he undoubtedly applied also to his work upon the Acts.
We are now in a position to let Luke speak for himself concerning his habits and motives as a historian.

[1] *Bearing of Recent Discovery*, p. 89.
[2] Ramsay, *St. Paul the Traveller*, p. 16.   [3] *Ibid.*, p. 14.

CHAPTER IV

LUKE'S METHOD OF RESEARCH [1]

"It seemed good to me also" (Luke 1 : 3)

1. *The Habits of a Literary Man.*—Luke alone has a literary prologue to his Gospel (1 : 1–4) that answers also for the Acts, whether he meant it to do so at the time or not. It is immaterial whether or not Luke consciously imitated the prefaces of Herodotus, Thucydides and Polybius, or that of Dioscorides, the famous medical writer on plants (*materia medica*), and of Hippocrates. There are verbal parallels to one or all of them and Luke's does not suffer by comparison with any one of them. The preface of Luke's Gospel "is modelled on the conventional lines of ancient literature," [2] as is natural for one who undertakes to write a history. "Luke's method is historical, but his object, like that of John (20 : 31), is religious." [3] The point to note here is that it is "Luke's intention to write history, and not polemical or apologetic treatises." [4] Hence he reveals his method of work in these opening verses of the Gospel in a clear manner. All that we really know about the composition of early narratives concerning the life of Christ we obtain from these verses. [5] Their value is therefore inestimable. With utter frankness Luke lays bare his literary plan, method and spirit. "Great historians are the rarest of writers." [6] Ramsay undertakes to show that Luke measures up to the standard of Thucydides, and in some respects surpasses him. It is important, therefore, to see what Luke has to say about himself and his habits of work.

The preface is not only literary in structure and vocabulary, but it is also periodic in form. It is written in the grand style. Blass[7] would call it Atticistic, but it is enough to say that it is in the literary *Koiné*. The sentence[8] is composed of six mem-

[1] *The Biblical Review*, April, 1920.
[2] Moffatt, *Intr. to Lit. of N. T.*, p. 263.　　[3] *Ibid.*
[4] Plummer, *Comm. on Luke*, p. xxxvi.
[5] Plummer, *Comm. on Luke*, p. 2.
[6] Ramsay, *St. Paul the Traveller*, p. 3.
[7] *Philology of the Gospels*, p. 9.　　[8] *Ibid.*, p. 10.

42

bers, three in the protasis and three in the apodosis, and they correspond with each other in the style of the finished literary writer. The language is ornate rather than colloquial. But, withal, it is precise and there is not any display of rhetoric. There is literary skill beyond a doubt, that no one but a man of real culture can show. Luke nowhere else in his writings employs just this style, because elsewhere he follows more or less closely his sources.

But we are fortunate in this glimpse of the historian in his study. It is not hard to see the pile of notes of conversation or of investigation lying near at hand. Here are papyri rolls of previous monographs on various phases of the life of Christ. Luke himself sits by his own small desk with his own roll spread out before him. He writes after he has gotten ready to write and with all available data at hand. The papyri discovered in Egypt[1] help us to reproduce the workshop of Luke, who proved to be the greatest of all historians, by the skill that he displayed in the use of his materials. Renan[2] rightly terms the Gospel of Luke "the most literary of the Gospels," as well as the most beautiful book in the world. Sanday[3] says: "St. Luke has more literary ambition than his fellows." The prologue has the aim of an educated man with scientific training and habits. "Something of the scholar's exactness is included in the ideal of Luke."[4] The writer undoubtedly employs the same literary methods for the Acts that he mentions in the preface to the Gospel.[5]

Luke has taken great pains to make himself understood in his prologue and has given a great deal of valuable information

---

[1] Not all students have access to the great printed collections of papyri like the *Amherst Papyri* by Grenfell and Hunt (*P. Amh.*), the *Ægyptische Urkunden aus den Kœniglichen Museen zu Berlin* (*B. G. U.*), *Greek Papyri in the British Museum* (*P. Brit. Mus.*), *Fayum Towns and their Papyri* by Grenfell and Hunt and Hogarth (*P. Fay.*), the *Hibeh Papyri* by Grenfell and Hunt (*P. Hib.*), the *Oxyrhynchus Papyri* by Grenfell and Hunt (*P. Oxy.*). There are convenient handbooks that give valuable information concerning the papyri like Milligan's *Greek Papyri*, Deissmann's *Bible Studies* and his *Light from the Ancient East*, Milligan's *New Testament Documents*, Cobern's *The New Archæological Discoveries and Their Bearing upon the New Testament*, Souter's *Pocket Lexicon of the Greek New Testament*, and in particular Moulton and Milligan's *Vocabulary of the New Testament*. Abbott-Smith's *Manual Lexicon of the Greek N. T.* is in press.

[2] *Les Evangiles*, chap. XIII.   [3] *Book by Book*, p. 401.
[4] Hayes, *Synoptic Gospels and Acts*, p. 217.   [5] Furneaux, *Acts*, p. 1.

in condensed form, but he has been seriously misunderstood at several points as will be shown.[1] Luke knows that what he says must be trustworthy, but he is entitled to be judged by what he undertook to do, not by our theories of what he ought to have done. "It is necessary to study every historian's method, and not to judge him according to whether or not he uses our methods."[2] So then we must study Luke's method, not that of the modern critic of Luke. Let Luke himself speak to us. What does he say of his own qualifications for his great task?

2. *Stimulated by the Work of Others.*—"Forasmuch as many have taken in hand to draw up a narrative . . . it seemed good to me also." The reason is stated in a formal manner, but with perfect directness. The grammatical construction[3] is like that in Acts 15 : 24, 25: "Forasmuch as we have heard . . . it seemed good unto us." How "many" had made such "attempts"? No one knows, but "this preface gives a lively picture of the intense, universal interest felt by the early Church in the story of the Lord Jesus: Apostles constantly telling what they had seen and heard; many of their hearers taking notes of what they said for the benefit of themselves and others: through these gospelets acquaintance with the evangelic history circulating among believers, creating a thirst for more and yet more; imposing on such a man as Luke the task of preparing a Gospel as *full, correct* and *well-arranged* as possible through the use of all available means—previous writings or oral testimony of surviving witnesses."[4] Cicero employed shorthand in the trial of Catiline and shorthand was much in vogue in the first century A. D. Salmon[5] thinks that the Logia of Jesus (Q) was written down in notes during the life of Jesus. The discovery of Sayings of Jesus in the Oxyrhynchus Papyri illustrates how this was done.

There is no real objection to thinking of a considerable number of fragmentary reports of the life and words of Jesus.

[1] Blass, *Philology of the Gospels*, p. 7.

[2] Ramsay, *St. Paul the Traveller*, p. 17.

[3] Plummer, *Comm.*, p. 2. The word ἐπειδήπερ (ἐπεί, δή, πέρ) is common in ancient Greek and the Lxx, but not elsewhere in the N. T. In Acts 15 : 24 it is ἐπειδή.

[4] Bruce, *Expositors' Greek Test.*, on Luke 1 : 4.

[5] *Human Element in the Gospels*, p. 274. So Ramsay, *The Expositor*, May, 1907.

Only the so-called apocryphal Gospels are ruled out because they belong to a much later time. "Probably all the documents here alluded to were driven out of existence by the manifest superiority of the four canonical Gospels." So Plummer[1] argues, unless, forsooth, Luke included Mark's Gospel and the Logia of Matthew in the list, as now seems certain. The Logia of Matthew is largely preserved by the Gospel of Matthew and the Gospel of Luke. Mark's Gospel, used by both Matthew and Luke, has survived intact save for the ending. But the other sources have disappeared.

Does Luke mean to disparage the other attempts at writing accounts of Jesus? He certainly does not mean censure since he brackets himself, "me also," with the other writers.[2] The word[3] for "attempted" literally means "to take in hand, to undertake," and does not of itself imply failure or error. There is nothing in this context to suggest that previous efforts were heretical or unreliable. Luke does imply that they were incomplete and so inadequate for the needs of Theophilus and for others like him. Theophilus had received instruction[4] of a more or less formal nature, like a catechumen, concerning Jesus, but Luke wishes him to have a fuller and more comprehensive story. Bruce[5] suggests that there was a widespread impulse to preserve in writing the evangelic memorabilia that stimulated Luke to do likewise. His active mind was seized with the desire to make a more adequate and orderly presentation of the words and deeds of Jesus while it was still possible to do so. In doing this great service he was conscious of meeting a widespread demand, the author's usual sense of filling a long-felt want, that sometimes is true, though publishers cannot always know it.

There was, therefore, "extensive activity in the production of rudimentary gospels," Bruce[6] argues. It was a time of literary activity concerning Jesus. Great literature is usually produced under the incentive of some great impulse or excitement, like love, war, discovery. New ideas spur the mind to fresh effort. The years at Cæsarea offered Luke an opportunity for new research and for first-hand knowledge that set his soul aflame. Luke, instead of being deterred by the mul-

---

[1] *Comm.*, p. 2.

[2] Plummer, *Comm.*, p. 2.

[3] ἐπεχείρησαν.

[4] κατηχήθης, 1 : 4.

[5] On Luke 1 : 1.

[6] *Ibid.*

tiplicity of efforts, was the rather incited to one more attempt on a more ambitious scale, one that would conserve the best in all of them and thus give a richer and a more exact portrayal of Christ than had yet been drawn. That he accomplished this purpose is plain in respect to Mark's Gospel, which has fortunately survived. It seems true, also, of the Logia (Q). It was all the more true of the others that have perished precisely because Luke did his work so well.

It is certain that Luke is not hostile to the Twelve in the writing of his Gospel. The book itself refutes that idea.[1] It is open to him to improve upon the words of others if he can. It is certain, also, that though Luke is the friend and follower of Paul, he is not a narrow partisan of Paul. He cannot in the Acts be accused of distorting history in the interest of Paul or of Peter or of promoting a reconciliation between them.[2] In spite of the fact that Paul is Luke's hero in the Acts, Ramsay[3] can say: "It is rare to find a narrative so simple and so little forced as that of Acts. It is a mere uncolored recital of the important facts in the briefest possible terms." The same thing is true of the Gospel. Luke is a master artist in his grouping of the facts, but they are facts. "St. Luke remains unconvicted of the charge of writing party pamphlets under the cover of fictitious history."

3. *A Contemporary of the Events, but a Participant in None Save Part of the Acts.* In the "we" sections of Acts Luke was an eye-witness and a fellow-worker. But in the rest of the Acts and all of the Gospel he has to rely upon others for his information. This is the natural implication of his language about the Gospel. "Eye-witnesses and ministers of the word have delivered unto us" the story of "the things that have been fulfilled among us." The "us" here, occurring twice, is clearly not the literary plural, which Paul sometimes employs, but "among us Christians," "to us Christians." "Christendom is the sphere in which these facts have had their accomplishment."[4] The use of "delivered"[5] shows that some time has elapsed since the events took place. Plummer[6] says: "If these things were

---

[1] Plummer, *Comm.*, p. xxxvi.
[2] Moffatt, *Intr. to the Lit. of N. T.*, pp. 301-2.
[3] Ramsay, *St. Paul the Traveller*, p. 20.
[4] Plummer, *Comm.*, p. 3.
[5] παρέδοσαν. Cf. παράδοσις for tradition.   [6] Ibid.

handed down to Luke, then he was not contemporary with them." Not in the strictest sense, to be sure, and yet, if Luke was only forty years old in A. D. 60, he was ten years old in A. D. 30, old enough to hear echoes of what was going on in Palestine if he was within reach. He was more likely fifty than forty. Luke comes in between the first generation of eye-witnesses and the second generation, whose lives come wholly after the great era of the life of Christ on earth. For the life of Paul he is both contemporary with all and partici-pant in much of it.

But he looks backward quite distinctly upon the story of Jesus "concerning those matters which have been fulfilled among us." The perfect tense[1] emphasizes the idea that the story has been preserved as well as finished. It is not clear what the sonorous verb means. Eusebius takes it in the sense of "convince," as Paul does in Rom. 14 : 5; Col. 4 : 12. But Paul uses it of persons, not of things. Others take the word in the sense of "believe," "surely believed" (A. V.), following Tyndale, but that hardly seems suitable. Others make it "fully proved." Bruce[2] suggests "fulness of knowledge," but that is a bit strained. The natural way is to take it in the sense of "fulfil," "complete" as in II Tim. 4 : 5, 17.[3] This is Jerome's translation "*completæ sunt.*" Luke writes after the close of Christ's earthly ministry and yet it is not in the dim past.

If Luke is writing in Cæsarea, he includes himself naturally among the "us." He is in the midst of the atmosphere of the life of Jesus, At every turn he finds fresh reminders of word and deed of Jesus. The Christian community in Judea still recall the wonderful words of the matchless teacher.[4] He could not be insensible to his environment. Though a Greek of An-tioch, let us say, yet he was now a Christian, and everything that concerned Jesus interested him. Through the centuries since men have made pilgrimages to Palestine to get the proper orientation for the study of the life of Christ. Luke had time enough to gratify his eagerness for details and his scholarly desire for accuracy. He had come to Christ from the heathen fold and had looked upon Christianity as a great moral and

---

[1] πεπληροφορημένων.
[2] *Comm.*, p. 458.
[3] Like πληρόω (Acts 19 : 21).
[4] Blass, *Philology of the Gospels*, p. 14.

spiritual revolution. It is difficult for a contemporary to get the right perspective. But Luke is a man of ability, culture and wide sympathy. He has a large horizon and draws his picture upon a large canvas. He knows that he is discussing the life story of the Man of the Ages. It is important that he be sure of his facts.

4. *Talks with Eye-witnesses.*—One would feel sure that Luke would make it his business while in Palestine to seek interviews with important persons who could add bits of color to his narrative about Christ, if he had any idea of writing the story of Jesus. He would listen to those talk who saw and heard Jesus. But we are not left to conjecture. These "eye-witnesses" [1] were primary authorities and spoke from personal experience and knowledge. They saw with their own eyes and gave their own interpretations of what took place. People would be eager to tell what they knew of this or that incident, whether they knew of Luke's purpose or not. A few questions would draw out much information which Luke would be quick to jot down. But the public preaching of the word consisted largely in the recital of the great events in the life and death of Jesus, as we can see from the sermons of Peter and Paul in the Acts. Luke had only to make notes as he listened to these "ministers of the word," [2] many of whom were also eye-witnesses, to add to his store of oral testimony.

They not only had personal experience, but they had also practical experience of the power of the preached word on human lives.[3] Many of them had followed Christ from the start and were thus able to speak with authority. They knew the outstanding facts connected with the ministry of Christ from the beginning. Some of them may have known the still earlier details of the childhood, though it is almost certain that the preaching of the time began with the ministry of Jesus (Acts 10 : 36–43). Luke later (Acts 1 : 1) explains that his Gospel treated "all that Jesus began to do and to teach."

---

[1] αὐτόπται. In II Peter 1 : 16 we have ἐπόπται for the eager beholders of the majestic glory on the mount of transfiguration. Cf. ἐποπτεύοντες in I Pet. 2 : 12.

[2] ὑπηρέται τοῦ λόγου. It is hardly likely that Luke here employs λόγος in the Johannine sense of the personal Word. These "under-rowers" had much to tell that was worth while. Cf. Luke 4 : 20; Acts 13 : 5.

[3] Plummer, *Comm.*, p. 3.

The Jews lay great store by oral witness. Books were expensive and scarce in spite of the remark in Ecclesiastes about the making of so many books. People had to rely largely on the memory for the retention of knowledge. The Jews themselves developed a vast system of oral law in elucidation of the written law, and finally came to think more of it than they did of the Mosaic law. Westcott and A. Wright look to the oral teaching as the main, if not the only, source of the gospels. In this they are not sustained by modern research. But we must not overlook the fact that, when Luke wrote his Gospel, he had easy access to eye-witnesses whose testimony was of inestimable value. He himself speaks (Acts 21 : 16) of "one Mnason of Cyprus, an early disciple, with whom we should lodge." There were many more. Philip and his four daughters were in Cæsarea, and had but recently entertained Paul and his party (Acts 21 : 8 f.). James, the brother of the Lord, and all the elders met Paul and Luke in Jerusalem (21 : 18). Harnack (*Luke the Physician*, p. 122) thinks that Luke did not at this time know the Twelve Apostles. He certainly knew Mark and his mother Mary, whose home was the centre of the Christian life in Jerusalem (Acts 12 : 12). It is possible that Mary, the mother of Jesus, was still alive. She may have lived in Jerusalem with James, now that he is a firm believer and leader. But, if Mary was no longer living, James may have had her narrative of the great events that she alone knew. Each one would have his own story to tell. Each would supplement the other. The true historian knows how to prize and to weigh oral testimony. That Luke did not follow old wives' fables and foolish legends is proven by a comparison of his books with the apocryphal lives of Jesus.

5. *Examination of Documents.*—Luke expressly says that "many have taken in hand to draw up a narrative." It is not perfectly clear what Luke means by "draw up a narrative." [1] The word for "narrative" "implies more than mere notes or anecdotes." [2] It is a carrying through a connected story to the end (cf. Sirach, 6 : 35; II Mac. 2 : 32). Luke draws a distinction between the oral testimony of eye-witnesses in verse 2 and the written documents in verse 1. [3] Both verb and substantive occur here alone in the New Testament. The verb is

---

[1] ἀνατάξασθαι διήγησιν.   [2] Plummer, *Comm.*, p. 3.
[3] Blass, *Philology of the Gospels*, p. 16.

a rare one in Greek literature.[1] In both instances the notion of repetition or practice is present. Plutarch has an elephant practising by moonlight from memory what his keeper taught him. Irenæus describes Ezra as restoring from memory the words of the prophets. Blass,[2] therefore, plausibly argues that Luke's meaning must be this: "Since many writers have undertaken to restore from memory a narrative of the things which have come to pass among us." The oral tradition was liable to pass into oblivion unless it were written down while still a living memory. This is probably the true idea.

It may well be that some of the "many" themselves had access to written documents. Luke uses a general expression. But he undoubtedly means to affirm that he had access to a number of written documents concerning the life of Jesus. This statement, as already shown, effectually disposes of the idea that our Gospels relied entirely upon oral testimony. But the next verse shows plainly that Luke employed oral testimony, also. He made use of both kinds of testimony, as any sensible man in his position would do. He has before him, as he writes, some of these narratives which have incited him to his task.

But it is not enough to be in possession of priceless historical treasures, absolutely essential as this fact is for all historical research. The true historian cannot and dare not "invent" his facts save in the etymological sense of that word. He must find his facts before he writes. Research is the first step, long and patient gathering of the data. I may be excused a personal word at this point. My first book, *The Life and Letters of John A. Broadus* (1901), was written after reading some twenty-five thousand letters, besides other biographical material. Before anything else was done, these letters had to be read, all of them. A selection of all that threw light upon the life of Broadus was made and placed in chronological order. This was the first step, but it was not all. What was the relative value and importance of this varied assortment of material?

6. *Sifting the Evidence.*—We can picture Luke in his study with his papers piled around him, papyrus rolls and scraps at

---

[1] Plutarch (*De Soll. Animal.* xii), Irenæus (III, 21 : 2), and v. 1 in Eccles. 2 : 20.

[2] *Phil. of the Gospels*, p. 15. The Latin and English versions vary greatly in the translation of this word.

every turn. But he is not yet ready to write his book. He himself tells what his next step was. He only began to write after "having traced the course of all things accurately from the first." [1] Eusebius[2] takes "all" as masculine, a reference to the eye-witnesses and ministers. Epiphanius[3] expressly says that Luke followed closely the eye-witnesses and ministers of the word. This is the literal meaning of the verb, following closely by one's side. Certainly Luke was not a constant follower of the Twelve from the beginning or of other eye-witnesses of Christ, though he probably knew some of them. Besides, this literal sense of this compound verb occurs nowhere else in the New Testament. "But Polybius and other Hellenistic authors employ the verb in the sense of studying, and there can be no doubt that Luke's use is the same." [4] Luke means that he had instituted a process of research in his inquiries concerning the life of Christ that covered "all things." It was, therefore, a thorough and careful investigation that began at the beginning, "from the first," [5] meaning with the birth of John the Baptist, as the sequel shows. "He has begun at the beginning, and he has investigated everything." [6] Bruce [7] thinks that Luke made this research "long antecedent to the formation of his plan." The tense of the verb is perfect and naturally bears that meaning, if by "plan" is meant the outline of the Gospel, not the purpose to write it. The idea of Luke seems to be that, having decided to write another and a fuller narrative than those in existence, he first made an investigation of all the available material that he could lay his hands upon.

But he adds one other word[8] that is quite pertinent. He has done it "accurately." There is no idle boast in these three qualifications for his task.[9] In a straightforward way Luke reveals his literary method. He has aimed at full research and accurate use of his material. He has not dumped it all out in anecdotal form with no appraisement of its value. He

---

[1] παρηκολουθηκότι ἄνωθεν πᾶσιν ἀκριβῶς. Cf. Demosthenes, *De Corona*, ch. LIII, 344 (p. 285) παρηκολουθηκότα, τοῖς πράγμασιν ἐξ ἀρχῆς.

[2] III, 24, 15. So the Syrian Translation.   [3] *Ag. Her.*, 51, 7.

[4] Blass, *Philology of the Gospels*, p. 18.

[5] *a principio*, the Vulgate has it.

Plummer, *Comm.*, p. 4.   [7] *Comm.*, p. 459.

[8] ἀκριβῶς.   [9] Plummer, *Comm.*, p. 4.

has weighed the worth of the information before he told it. He has tried to tell it as it happened. Accurate writing can only follow accurate investigation. In a word, Luke has sifted the evidence and has given us the wheat, not the chaff. This is a necessary task for the historian if he is to be more than a mere romancer. Even Harnack,[1] though championing the Lukan authorship of Gospel and Acts, is still skeptical about his use of his authorities. "He certainly believes himself to be an historian (see the prologue) and so he is; but his powers are limited, for he adopts an attitude toward his authorities which is as distinctly uncritical as that which he adopts towards his own experiences, if these admit of a miraculous interpretation." Harnack here charges Luke with giving a miraculous coloring to natural occurrences, when he was probably less disposed to do that than any man of his day. Luke distinctly claims accurate research. It is quite compatible[2] with this historical research and love for the truth that one should have a sense of decorum and reverence. But Luke is not the man to be charged with mere credulity without proof.

Luke does not say that the previous writers were not accurate. He only claims that he has covered the whole field and has done it in harmony with the facts as he could ascertain them after careful investigation. "And, in spite of the severest scrutiny, his accuracy can very rarely be impugned."[3] And the results of modern research confirm the justice of Luke's claim wherever his works can be tested by new discoveries. This will be shown to be true in detail in succeeding chapters in a most astonishing degree.

Ruskin[4] has a good word about misjudging a writer: "Be sure that you go to the author to get at *his* meaning, not to find yours and to judge it afterwards, if you think yourself qualified to do so; but ascertain it first. And be sure, also, if the author is worth anything, that you will not get at his meaning all at once; nay, that at his whole meaning you will not for a long time arrive in any wise." Luke, like any other writer, is entitled to be credited with his own conception of his task. He disclaims being a slipshod writer in the use of his material. He has the Greek love for clarity and for truth. He has the physician's skill in diagnosis that will stand him in

---

[1] *Luke the Physician*, p. 123.
[2] Bruce, *Comm.*, p. 460.
[3] Plummer, *Comm.*, p. 4.
[4] *Sesame and Lilies*, p. 15.

good stead as he dissects the data before him. He has traced the story of Jesus from its origin with historical insight and balanced judgment. He is already in possession of the evidence before he begins to write, as the perfect tense shows. He does not jot down scraps of information in a haphazard way as he gets hold of it. "Luke claims to have studied and comprehended every event in its origin and development."[1] He has gotten ready to write before he begins to write.

7. *Orderly Arrangement.*—"To write unto thee in order," Luke declared to be his purpose. What kind of "order"[2] is it? He does not say that it is chronological order, though one naturally thinks of that. Papias[3] states that Mark's Gospel was not "in order," but he employs a different word,[4] which suggests military order. Luke's word occurs in Acts 11 : 4 concerning Peter's discourse in Jerusalem about the events in Cæsarea which Blass[5] interprets to be a full recital without important omissions, a complete series rather than chronological sequence. Ramsay[6] takes it to be "a rational order, making things comprehensible, omitting nothing that is essential for full and proper understanding." Such an order would be chronological in its main features. That is true of the great turning points in the Gospel, most assuredly. As a matter of fact, both Luke and Matthew follow the general order of Mark's Gospel. Matthew departs from it mainly in the first part and Luke in the last part, where each introduces new material on a large scale. Plummer[7] thinks that Luke generally aims at chronological order and on the whole attains it without, however, slavishly following chronology in every detail. In the Acts the chronological order is plain, as a rule. But there is no proof that Luke deliberately formed a scheme of theological development in the life of Christ and then selected his material to illustrate it.[8] Luke sometimes prefers another order to the chronological, but it is always a systematic treatment and not a mere hotch-potch.

He has a proper proportion, also, in his use of his material,

---

[1] Ramsay, *Was Christ Born at Bethlehem ?*, p. 11.
[2] καθεξῆς. Peculiar to Luke in the N. T.
[3] Eus., *Hist. Eccl.*, 3 : 39, 151.   [4] τάξει.
[5] *Philology of the Gospels*, pp. 18 f.
[6] *Was Christ Born at Bethlehem ?*, p. 14.
[7] *Comm.*, p. xxxvii.   [8] *Ibid.*

and writes the story with due regard to scale and space.[1] Each event receives treatment according to its importance in relation to the whole. "The historian who is to give a brief history of a great period need not reproduce on a reduced uniform scale all the facts which he would mention in a long history, like a picture reduced by a photographic process."[2] He must omit a great deal, he must seize the critical points, he must interpret the great personalities, he must make the whole vivid, and give a true perspective. The outstanding feature of Luke's Gospel is its completeness. It charms one with its sheer beauty and power.

There is no discounting the artistic skill of Luke in his literary workmanship. He must be attacked on some other ground. But there is no trace of literary affectation or artificial whimsicalities. Lieutenant-Colonel G. Mackinlay[3] makes out an interesting case for his theory that Luke is fond of "triplications" in his Gospel. But one wonders if Luke made conscious use of such a literary device. He is writing a serious history, not mere memoirs, not a biographical puzzle. He is full of the historic spirit and sets forth the grand development of the life of Christ toward the great Tragedy and the grand victory of the Resurrection.

Luke's Gospel is the nearest approach to a biography[4] that we have, since he begins with the birth and carries on, at intervals, to the grand close. It is not only the most comprehensive, but it is also the longest of the gospels. If we think of the whole course of Christian history in the Gospel and Acts the work is chronological.[5] The figures are drawn with lifelike power and the greatest drama of human history is set forth with supreme literary skill. The book is a scholar's attempt to picture and to interpret the life of Christ for the world at large. Theophilus is the representative of this outside world beyond Palestine. Luke has supreme equipment for such an undertaking by birth, education and diligence. As a scientific physician he learned to make generalizations from specimens. So as the historian he knows how to make the miracles and parables of Jesus picture the Great Physician and Teacher.

[1] Ramsay, *Was Christ Born at Bethlehem ?*, p. 14.
[2] Ramsay, *St. Paul the Traveller*, p. 7.
[3] *The Literary Marvels of St. Luke* (1919).
[4] Plummer, *Comm.*, p. xli.   [5] Chase, *Credibility of the Acts*, p. 17.

8. *Reliable Results.*—Luke is able to assure Theophilus, who had already received technical instruction[1] in the matters pertaining to the life of Christ, and whose deep interest in the subject can be assumed, that he can feel confident concerning "the certainty" of the new narrative. Luke wrote pointedly "that thou mightest know the certainty concerning the things wherein thou wast instructed." Theophilus had received many details[2] about the various events which the ministers of the word had related to Luke.[3] Now he will have the same full knowledge[4] that the Christians in Judea have enjoyed, with the advantage that he will have it in a comprehensive and unified treatise that will preserve in written form much that would else be perishable.[5] Luke may not have perceived what a treasure for mankind he had prepared, but he wishes Theophilus to understand "that the faith which he has embraced has an impregnable historical foundation."[6]

There is a solemn emphasis in the conclusion of Luke's preface. Harnack[7] admits, as we have seen, that Luke "certainly believes himself to be an historian." Ramsay[8] has a luminous chapter on "Luke's History: What it professes to be" in his *Was Christ Born at Bethlehem?* He shows that it is distinctly uncritical to accept the Gospel and Acts "as the work of the real St. Luke, the follower and disciple and physician and intimate friend of Paul," and then "to write about the inadequacy of his authorities, the incompleteness of his information, the puzzling variation in the scale and character of his narrative according as he had good or inferior authorities to trust to."[9] Certainly Luke would repudiate that estimate of his work. "He claims to state throughout what is perfectly trustworthy. It may be allowed, consistently, that his information was not everywhere agreeably good and complete."[10] Ramsay[11] presses the argument of Luke to a conclusion: "Either an author who

[1] κατηχήθης. This verb is used in 21:21 of wrong information, but that is not the essential idea, as Blass (*Philology of the Gospels*, p. 20) seems to think. The verb κατηχέω means to sound down or din into the ears.

[2] λόγοι in verse 4, not πράγματα of verse 1.

[3] Plummer, *Comm.*, p. 5.

[4] ἐπιγνῷς. Additional (ἐπι-) knowledge.

[5] Blass, *Philology of the Gospels*, p. 20.

[6] Plummer, *Comm.*, p. 5.   [7] *Luke the Physician*, p. 123.

[8] Pp. 3–21.   [9] *Was Christ Born at Bethlehem?* p. 16.

[10] *Ibid.*   [11] *Ibid.*, p. 18.

begins with a declaration such as that (in his preface) had mixed freely with many of the eye-witnesses and actors in the events which he proceeds to record, or he is a thorough impostor, who consciously and deliberately aims at producing belief in his exceptional qualifications in order to gain credit for his History." "If the author was an impostor, his work remains one of the most incomprehensible and unintelligible facts in literary history."

Luke has made his bold claim. It has been viciously attacked by various critics. Nothing but "the demonstration of hard facts" will clear the issue. Who is right, Luke or his modern critics? Enough has been discovered to test Luke's accuracy in crucial and important points, in the very points where he has been attacked. Meanwhile, we shall assume that Luke has made a careful use of his material and is entitled to make his confident claim to Theophilus. He aims to give a record of the truth in both Gospel and Acts.[1]

9. *The Stamp of Luke's Personality.*—Luke was no mere chronicler of dry details. He was not a scrap-book historian who simply spliced together documents. He used literary sources as every real historian must. They influenced his style, in certain parts more than in others, but he put his own stamp upon all the material that he incorporated. Luke, unlike Shakespeare, reveals his personality in the Gospel and the Acts. "Carlyle could not write another man's biography without writing his autobiography between the lines. No more could Luke." [2] Hence we can rejoice all the more that Luke felt impelled ("it seemed good to me also") to write. "It was such a book as a lover of men could write for a lover of God." [3] But it is the self-revelation of a soul that was humble and Christ-like. "There are times when one wishes that he had never read the New Testament Scriptures—that he might some day open the Gospel according to Luke, and the most beautiful book in the world might come upon his soul like sunrise." [4]

He was called a painter by the ancients. Plummer[5] traces it to the sixth century to Theodorus Lector, reader in the Church in Constantinople. He states that the Empress

---

[1] Rackham, *Acts*, p. xxxvii.
[2] Hayes, *The Synoptic Gospels and Acts*, p. 265.
[3] *Ibid.*　　　　[4] Ian Maclaren.　　　　[5] *Comm.*, p. xxii.

Eudoxia found at Jerusalem a picture of Mary the mother of Jesus, painted by Luke. There is, at least, this much of truth in the legend. Luke has exerted a profound influence upon Christian art by his lifelike portrayals of character in the Gospel and the Acts. He painted with his pen, if not with hi brush. His pictures are drawn to the life and glow with life.

It is interesting to note that all the early writers assign the ox or calf to Luke, though differing greatly concerning the other three symbolical figures for the other Gospels (the man, the lion, the eagle). It is probable that Luke's Gospel was so called[1] because it is the Gospel of propitiation, of sacrifice. The priesthood of Christ comes to the fore in the Gospel of Luke and Jesus is pictured with the priestly attributes of sympathy, compassion and mercy.[2]

The most astonishing trait in Luke's style is his versatility. He is not only the most versatile writer in the New Testament, but one of the most versatile of all historians. "He can be as Hebraistic as the Septuagint, and as far from Hebraisms as Plutarch."[3] Certainly he is Hebraistic because of his Aramaic sources in Luke 1 and 2 and Acts 1–5, but it is at least open to one to think "that he has here allowed his style to be Hebraistic because he felt that such a style was appropriate to his subject-matter."[4] The contrast is sharpest in Luke 1 : 1–4 and the rest of chapter 1 and all of 2, but we see it also in the Acts. Moffatt[5] sees "the literary finish of the third Gospel" in the careful rhythm of the prologue, his versatility in using the "archaic semi-Biblical style" and in "leaving the rough translation of an Aramaic source practically unchanged for the sake of effect." But the unity of Luke's style is preserved throughout both Gospel and Acts in his characteristic freedom of expression and in the range of his vocabulary.[6] Luke exhibits the science of the trained student and the skill of the artist in giving "an harmonious picture"[7] by the use of varied material. "St. Luke exhibits constant proof of his Greek origin in the substitution of more cultured terms for the

---

[1] *Ibid.*
[2] Luckock, *Special Characteristics of the Four Gospels*, pp. 166–181.
[3] Plummer, *Comm.*, p. xlix.   [4] *Ibid.*
[5] *Intr. to the Lit. of the N. T.*, p. 278.   [6] *Ibid.*, p. 279.
[7] Milligan, *N. T. Documents*, p. 151.

colloquialisms of the other synoptists, while his treatment of Q is marked by various stylistic alterations." [1]   In a number of passages in the Gospel and the Acts "the phraseology seems to be purposely varied for no other reason than that of imparting a certain literary elegance to the narrative " [2]   Luke employs some 750 words in the Gospel and Acts not found elsewhere in the New Testament.   Some of these are due to the medical terminology of Luke and some to the nautical terms in Acts 27.   A few occur nowhere else, so far as known.   Norden[3] and Blass[4] see Atticistic influence in Luke's style, but this is not necessary.   Certainly he has a fine command of the literary *Koiné* as well as of the vernacular.[5]   He is fluent, but not prolix.   His style reveals the same finish that we saw in his research.

Hayes[6] describes Luke as a musician because he is the first great Christian hymnologist.   He has preserved the psalms of praise from Elizabeth, Mary, Zacharias, the angels and Simeon. We do not have to think that Luke composed these noble songs of praise and prayer.   But he alone has preserved them because he had a soul for music and for poetry.

Carpenter[7] has a chapter on "S. Luke the Artist."   By this expression he means that he was "a master of style."   Style is difficult of definition.   Style is the man, to be sure, but style varies with the subject, and style varies with one's age. Stalker says that style is shaped by full knowledge of the subject.   Certainly Luke's "supreme delineation of the Saviour of the world" rests primarily on fulness of knowledge on the part of the man of culture whose heart is loyal to Jesus as Lord.   There are abundant proofs of Luke's artistic skill. He has touches that would please cultured Gentiles like "the good and honest heart" in 8 : 15.[8]   Carpenter[9] suggests that Luke's fondness for "table-talk" (Luke 7 : 36 f.; 11 : 37 f.; 14 : 1 f.) may be due to his knowledge of the *symposia* of Greek

---

[1] *Ibid.*, p. 149.   [2] Milligan, *N. T. Documents.*

[3] *Kunstprosa*, II, pp. 485 ff.

[4] *Die Rhythmen der asianischen und römischen Kunstprosa*, p. 42.

[5] Robertson, *Grammar of the Greek N. T.*, p. 122.

[6] *Synoptic Gospels and Acts*, pp. 188 f.

[7] *Christianity According to S. Luke*, pp. 189–202.

[8] καρδίᾳ καλῇ καὶ ἀγαθῇ.   Plato and other Greek writers use καλὸς κἀγαθός as the equivalent of "gentleman."   Carpenter, *op. cit.*, p. 190.

[9] *Ibid.*, p. 191.

literature. Luke knows how to make a cumulative effect by contrast as in parables in rapid succession in chapters 14-18. Carpenter[1] shows that Luke is "a master of tragic irony." He knows how to make the climax tell by saying just enough and no more. The intellectual surprise is complete and abiding. The story of the two disciples going to Emmaus in Luke 24 is the most beautiful story in all the world. It is told with consummate skill. Luke can depict a situation with supreme art.

As a painter of short portraits Luke also excels. He has drawn the pictures of Jesus, Peter and Paul on large canvas with the master's hand. Luke has made his story vivid both in the Gospel and the Acts by the use of the power of personality. He understood the true principle of dealing with so vast a subject. He found the secret in personality.[2] "His short pen pictures of Zacharias, the Virgin Mother, Martha and Mary, Zacchæus, and the repentant robber are masterly." [3]

But, scholar as Luke is, he is also a mystic of the true kind. "Strange and unexpected touches occur in Luke's narrative, corresponding to the astonishing and inexplicable psychological experiences of ordinary life." [4] The proofs are many. "They yet believed not for joy" (Luke 24 : 41). "What a natural touch that was! They believed it, and yet it was too good to be true." [5] Carpenter[6] devotes a whole chapter to "S. Luke the Psychologist." It is not only fine workmanship that Luke gives us. He exhibits insight into human nature. He knows also the ways of God's Spirit with man. Carpenter[7] quotes a theologian who said to him that Luke was the Evangelist that he should like most to meet. "S. John was a saint, but I think I know the kind of thing that he would say to me. But S. Luke is different. He was not a saint. He was a psychologist. I should like to meet him." Loisy[8] finds the chief charm of Luke in "a certain psychological note, a profound sense of the things of the soul." So Luke is a psychologist among the saints for the benefit of the saints.

---

[1] Ibid., p. 194. [2] Rackham, Acts, p. xl.
[3] Carpenter, Christianity according to S. Luke, p. 195.
[4] Hayes, Synoptic Gospels and Acts, p. 225.
[5] Ibid. [6] Op. cit., pp. 177–188.
[7] Op. cit., p. 177.
[8] Les Évangiles Synoptiques, I, p. 260.

He is certainly a lover of mankind who fell in love with Jesus. "From being interested in the singular case of one Paul, a travelling sophist, whose restless zeal begins to play havoc with the constitution, he passed to the consideration of 'one Jesus, who was dead, whom Paul affirmed to be alive' (Acts 25 : 19)." [1] He had the devotion to Jesus that Plutarch calls *pietas*, when a biographer loves his subject. Luke was not a formal theologian, but he had the sense of mystery in the presence of Christ's overwhelming personality. Chesterton[2] says: "Christ had even a literary style of his own, not to be found, I think, elsewhere; it consists in an almost furious use of the *a fortiori*. His 'how much more' is piled one upon another like castle upon castle in the clouds." Carpenter[3] notes that in the use of this figure Luke's Gospel is in affinity with the Epistle to the Hebrews.

Carpenter[4] observes also how Luke understood the loneliness of Jesus. "One of the penalties of greatness is loneliness. The great artist is, perhaps, never understood by his contemporaries. The consummate Artist has twelve pupils, but they do not understand him. And the Evangelist, himself an artist, has not failed to indicate this in his picture. One of the chief impressions taken from the Gospel is that Our Lord lived alone." As one instance, note that "it came to pass as he was praying by himself" (Luke 9 : 18). Carpenter[5] does not claim that Luke "understood all the pathos and the glory of Our Lord's life, that he was fully sensitive to the whole wonder of its sweetness and its tragedy and its triumphs," but in Luke we learn how Jesus "experienced in the days of His flesh something of that which may be called, perhaps unworthily and foolishly, but not altogether inexcusably, the loneliness of God." [6] The humanity of Jesus in Luke is not the deity of humanity so much as the humanity of deity.

[1] Carpenter, *Op. cit.*, p. 178.   [2] *Orthodoxy*, p. 269.
[3] *Op. cit.*, p. 184.   [4] *Ibid.*, p. 186.
[5] *Op. cit.*, p. 187.   [6] *Ibid.*, p. 188.

CHAPTER V

THE SOURCES OF THE GOSPEL

"Even as they delivered them unto us" (Luke 1 : 2).

Luke tells us frankly that he used sources of information in writing his Gospel which were of two kinds, oral and written. It is possible to tell in a broad way some of these sources and how he used them.

1. *Assimilation rather than Quotation.*—This was the method of the ancients. It is a fine exercise to read First Maccabees in the translation Greek in which we have it, an evident translation from a Hebrew or Aramaic original, and then turn to the corresponding passage of the *Antiquities* of Josephus where the same ground is covered as in the story of Judas Maccabeus. It is perfectly manifest that Josephus has followed the narrative of First Maccabees. He has written his account in flowing, idiomatic Greek of the literary *Koiné*, at times really Atticistic in conscious imitation of the Attic literary models. He has avoided the frequent Hebraisms in First Maccabees, but has used the material freely and faithfully, without any mention of his source. That is his usual practice. Occasionally Josephus does allude to some of the writers whom he consulted, but there is little formal quotation. Josephus did not consider himself a copyist, but a historian, and used his data with freedom.

Luke employed the literary devices of men of his age. "In using his materials Luke's methods are in the main those of other writers of the same period. They are quite unlike those of modern writers. A writer of the present day seeks to tell his story in his own words and in his own way, giving references to, and, if necessary, quotations from, his sources, but carefully avoiding all confusion between traditional fact and critical inference, and certainly never altering the direct statement of the earlier document without expressly mentioning the fact. The method of antiquity was, as a rule, almost the reverse. The author of a book based on earlier materials strung together a series of extracts into a more or less coherent whole, giving no indication of his sources, and modifying them freely in order to harmonize them." In this paragraph Lake[1] has given a fair statement of ancient usage. There was no idea of plagiarizing in failing to give credit. It was simply a different literary habit. Lake thinks that it is "obviously inferior to modern procedure," but he agrees that Luke used it well. That is putting it mildly when critics treat the Gospel as a work of consummate literary skill. And yet Luke does make quotations from the Old Testament, though nothing like so frequently or so formally as Matthew's Gospel. There were regular formulas for scriptural quotations, but these were not always employed. The early Christian writers, as J. Rendel Harris[2] shows, were fond of quoting *Testimonia* or strings of quotations like what Paul has in Romans 3.

And yet Luke was not a slavish copyist. The stamp of his own personality is on all his work. Sanday[3] has some wise and true words on the folly of complaining at the Gospels for freedom in the use of their sources: "The Evangelists thought of themselves not merely as copyists but as historians. They are not unconscious of a certain dignity in their calling. They are something more than scribes tied down to the text which they have before them. They considered themselves entitled to reproduce it freely and not slavishly. They do not hesitate to tell the story over again in their own words." Luke does not hesitate to use what others have written, if it suits his purpose, but he does not confine himself to any one source. He is writing his own book. His Gospel is more elaborate than the other Gospels. "Accordingly, there is perhaps in his case a little more of the blending or fusion of different authorities. He has a somewhat higher ambition in the matter of style. In a word, he approximates rather more nearly to the ancient secular historian."[4] "It was very much their (secular historians') ideals which guided his hand."[5] But, with all the freedom in the use of their sources, it is amazing how much alike the picture of Jesus is in all the Synoptic Gospels. "Verse after verse, saying after saying, might be quoted to you from the three

[1] Art. "Luke," Hastings's *Dict. of Ap. Church*, pp. 771 f.
[2] Various articles in *The Expositor*
[3] *Oxford Studies in the Synoptic Problem*, p. 12.
[4] *Oxford Studies in the Synoptic Problem*, p. 13.   [5] *Ibid.*, p. 14.

Synoptic Gospels, and, unless you happened to have special knowledge or had given special attention to such matters, you would be unable to say to which Gospel they really belonged." [1]

Sanday[2] reminds us that the physical difficulties in the way of quoting books played a large part in their literary method. The ancients used tables for eating, not for writing, and for paying out money. They had desks, "but they were not like our desks, on a writing-table. They were quite small, like the reading-desks that we attach to the arm of an armchair. As a rule they are affixed to a raised stand, which is independent of other furniture." One can easily see that the roll was not a convenient form for a book or for such a little desk. The pictures of early writers, as of Virgil,[3] represent one as sitting with the open roll on his knees and the desk at his side. The ancient writer had great difficulty in keeping one roll open from which he was copying, and the other open on which he was writing. There would be the constant tendency to trust one's memory, as in oral transmission, though the habits of writers would vary.

Luke's habit was to give a series of separate pictures with local color. He individualized the separate incidents and gave "editorial notes," as A. Wright calls them, that gave the finishing touches to the story.

We must remember, moreover, that we do not know all the sources that Luke employed nor his precise method in the use of all of them.

2. *Primitive Semitic Sources.*—Where did Luke get his information for 1 : 5–2 : 52 of his Gospel? Wellhausen drops this portion from his edition of Luke's Gospel as not worthy of consideration by the modern historian. At once, therefore, we see Luke put on the defensive in the use of his sources, when he finishes his prologue. The instant change in his style shows that he is using Semitic material unless he is inventing the whole story of the infancy narratives, and by supreme literary skill is giving them a Semitic flavor to create the impression of their genuineness. It is possible to think that Luke has been influenced by reading the Septuagint, and that there may be intentional imitation by Luke, though a Greek.

---

[1] Burkitt, *The Gospel History and Its Transmission*, p. 216.

[2] *Oxford Studies in the Synoptic Problem*, pp. 16 ff.

[3] Birt, *Die Buchrolle in der Kunst*, p. 178.

But, if so, why did he not keep the Aramaic or Hebrew coloring throughout? There are scattered Hebraisms in the Gospel, but not to the extent that we see them in Chapters I and II. Allen[1] is confident that "conscious imitation of the Septuagint will quite adequately account for" these Hebraisms. Dalman[2] thinks that Luke "does not shrink from using those Hebraisms which are most foreign to the feeling of the Greek language." Bartlet[3] holds that "he consciously writes his Gospel on the lines of the Greek Bible." Probably so, but one can hardly think of so careful and faithful a writer as Luke consciously using Hebraisms to give a sacred flavor to his narrative. To me Luke seems quite incapable of such a literary artifice. Least of all can one think of the Greek Luke inventing the hymns of Mary and of Zacharias.

If Luke "is a historian of the first rank" and worthy of being "placed along with the very greatest historians," as Ramsay[4] argues, then he meets a severe test at once in these opening chapters. He has just claimed that his narrative is trustworthy and reliable in its use of the sources. The very first instance that we have is the story of the infancy. Certainly Luke means his report of the birth of Jesus to be taken seriously.[5] We have seen already that "Luke did not rest his narrative on unsifted traditions." [6] We cannot except the opening chapters from this statement. Indeed, "the author must have regarded this part of his work with special interest, and been impelled to work it up with peculiar care, on account of the authority on which it rested." [7] It is urged by some that this section was a later addition, because Marcion omits Chapters 1–4 from his edition of Luke, but the Lukan characteristics are in these early chapters. Wright[8] holds that

[1] "Aramaic Background of the Gospels" (*Oxford Studies in the Synoptic Problem*, p. 293).

[2] *The Words of Jesus*, p. 83.

[3] "Sources of St. Luke's Gospel" (*Oxford Studies in the Synoptic Problem*, p. 317). Aramaisms in Luke's style here are seen in such constructions as ἀφείς, ἤρξατο, εὐθύς, the use of εἰμί with the participle, while genuine Hebraisms appear in ἐν τῷ and the infinitive, καὶ ἐγένετο, ἀποκριθείς εἶπεν, ἐπιθυμίᾳ ἐπεθύμησα. Cf. Dalman, *Words of Jesus*, pp. 17 ff.

[4] *Bearing of Recent Discovery*, p. 222.

[5] Ramsay, *Was Christ Born at Bethlehem ?*, p. 73.

[6] Moffatt, *Intr. to Lit. of N. T.*, p. 263.

[7] Ramsay. *Was Christ Born at Bethlehem ?*, p. 73.

[8] *Gospel According to St. Luke in Gk.*, pp. viii f.

Luke wrote it, but added it last to the book. We have noted that it is unlikely that Luke would have written a free composition in archaic style.

The remaining hypothesis is that Luke used Semitic sources for the infancy narrative. It is not certain whether Luke's authority here was oral or written, Hebrew or Aramaic. Plummer (Comm., p. xxiii) thinks that "we need not doubt the first two Chapters are made up of written narratives, of which we can see the conclusions at 1 : 80, 2 : 40 and 2 : 52." It is argued that Luke had a written source in original Hebrew.[1] Dalman[2] holds that a Greek like Luke could not have known Aramaic. But that is not certain. There is no real reason why Luke could not know enough Aramaic to translate it himself.[3] There are some traces of an Aramaic original.

But Ramsay argues at great length that the Aramaic source was oral and not written, and that Mary herself was that source, either directly or indirectly. The story "is an episode of family history of the most private character."[4] Sanday[5] thinks that Joanna, the wife of Chuza, Herod's steward, was probably Mary's confidante, and told Luke the wonderful story. We may take it as certain that Luke did not record "the narrative of the birth and childhood of Christ from mere current talk and general belief: he had it in a form for which Mary herself was in his opinion the responsible authority."[6] The story is told from the standpoint of Mary, as in Matthew the birth of Jesus is given from the standpoint of Joseph. Luke himself says that Mary "kept all these sayings hid in her heart" (2 : 19), and once more he states that "Mary kept all these sayings, pondering them in her heart" (2 : 21). "The historian, by emphasizing the silence and secrecy in which she treasured up the facts, gives the reader to understand that she is the authority." [7] With this judgment Harnack[8] agrees: "Indeed, from 2 : 19, 51 it follows that the stories are intended to be regarded in the last instance from Mary herself." "His

[1] "Aramaic Background of the Gospels" (Oxford Studies in the Synoptic Problem, p. 292).
[2] Words of Jesus, pp. 38 f.
[3] Moffatt, Intr. to Lit. of N. T., p. 267.
[4] Was Christ Born at Bethlehem ?, p. 74.
[5] Expository Times, XIV, p. 299.
[6] Ramsay, op. cit., p. 80.   [7] Ramsay, op. cit., p. 75.
[8] Date of the Acts and the Synoptic Gospels, p. 155.

practice elsewhere as an historian proves that he could not have himself invented a fiction like this." [1]   The physician is brought into close relation with the inner life of women, who will reveal to him what they would shrink from mentioning to other men.   There is no known reason why Luke could not have seen Mary herself if she was still living.   Certainly the current oral Gospel (see Mark) would not contain the birth narrative.   The delicate tact and restraint with which Luke gives the story, add to the impression of genuineness and remove the narrative entirely from the mythological stories of the gods and goddesses of Babylon and Greece. [2]

The story of John's birth was matter of common talk (Luke 1 : 65 f.).   It is not hard to understand how Luke could get the data for his narrative.   It may have come from the circle of the disciples of John. [3]   Luke presents John as the forerunner and the inferior of Jesus. [4]

The genealogy in Luke 2 : 23–38 would come, of course, "from some legal or tribal or temple document." [5]

There is every reason to conclude that Luke had solid ground for his narrative in the early chapters of his Gospel.

3. *Mark's Gospel.*—It is now practically demonstrated that Luke and Matthew made use of the Gospel of Mark.   One can test this for himself, even in the English translation, by a use of a harmony of the Gospels.   Thus we are able to test Luke's literary method.   If one reads Mark 2 : 9–11 and then Matt. 9 : 5–6 and Luke 5 : 23–24, it is obvious that both Matthew and Luke had Mark's text before them, for both preserve the parenthetical clause ("He saith to the paralytic," "Then saith he to the paralytic," "He said to the paralyzed man") and both follow Mark in placing the clause at the same place in the midst of a saying of Jesus.   The oral theory will not explain a case like this.   Both Matthew and Luke had a document before them.   That document is our Mark.   It is not absolutely certain that Matthew and Luke had Mark's Gospel in precisely the form in which we have it, or in the same form for each.   Holdsworth [6] suggests that Mark edited three edi-

---

[1] *Ibid.*   [2] Harnack, *op. cit.,* p. 156.   [3] *Ibid.,* p. 154.
[4] Cf. Wilkinson, *A Johannine Document in the First Chapter of S. Luke's Gospel* (1902).
[5] Hayes, *Synoptic Gospels and Acts,* p. 199.
[6] *Gospel Origins,* pp. 109–129.

tions of his Gospel. The first form was used by Luke, the second by Matthew, and the third is our canonical Mark. Stanton[1] follows the same line of argument. N. P. Williams[2] thinks that Mark's earlier edition omitted Chapter XIII, and the so-called great interpolation (Mark 6 : 45–8 : 26). But, apart from this, Williams will have no " Ur-Marcus" after the theory of Wendling.[3] Sanday[4] sees no necessity of either an " Ur-Marcus" or of a threefold edition of Mark's Gospel. He calls attention to the fact that Luke did not have to make a slavish use of Mark or of any of his sources. He felt free to make minor variations at will. There were probably variations in the text of Mark as used by Matthew and Luke. M. Jones[5] is inclined to agree with Sanday. Hawkins[6] thinks that a later edition may have added a few details, but sees no need of an appeal to various editions. Swete sees no cause for such editions, but is willing to consider some editorial revision.[7] It is clear that Luke had Mark before him and practically in the form in which we possess it to-day.[8] We know that Luke was with Mark in Rome about A. D. 63 (Col. 4 : 10; Philemon 24).

Mark is one, but only one, of Luke's sources. Luke follows Mark's general order of events, especially in the first part of the Gospel. One needs a deal of common sense in matters of criticism to avoid one-sided and erroneous conclusions. Rather more than half of Luke's material is now found in his Gospel alone.[9] The rest is divided between what Mark has and the non-Markan matter common to Luke and Matthew. But in a broad view of the material about two-thirds of Luke's Gospel follows the track of Mark, while three-fourths of Matthew's Gospel uses Mark's Gospel as a framework.[10] Apart from a few transpositions, Matthew and Luke do not desert Mark's

---

[1] *The Gospels as Historical Documents*, part II, p. 203.

[2] *Oxford Studies*, p. 421.

[3] *Urmarcus* (1905); *Die Entstehung des Marcusevangeliums* (1908).
     Oxford Studies, pp. 11–22. See also my *Studies in Mark's Gospel*, pp. 14 f.

[5] *N. T. in the Twentieth Century*, p. 203.

[6] *Horæ Synopticæ*, p. 152.

[7] *Commentary*, p. lix.   [8] Plummer, *Comm.*, p. xxiii.

[9] Bebb, art. "Luke," in Hastings's *D. B.*

[10] Hawkins, "Three Limitations to St. Luke's Use of St. Mark's Gospel" (*Oxford Studies*, p. 29).

order, except in Matt. 7 : 13 and Luke 9 : 51–18 : 14. Luke uses three-fourths of Mark's Gospel, but Luke does not always follow Mark in matters of detail. Sometimes Matthew reproduces Mark, where Luke takes another turn. Harnack[1] thinks that Luke is somewhat prejudiced against Mark and "wrote his Gospel in order to supplant Mark." I doubt that, but it is remarkable that Mark has survived, since Matthew and Luke incorporated nearly all of Mark, all but some fifty verses.

Mark's Gospel has the vivid touches of Peter's picturesque portrayal which gives the lifelike coloring of an eye-witness.[2] Luke cares less for these delicate nuances and has dropped Mark's "green grass" and "flower-beds" (Mark 6 : 39 f.; Luke 9 : 14 f.). Luke has a more polished style and smoothes out apparent roughnesses or lack of exactness in Mark. In Mark 1 : 4 we have the picture of digging through[3] the roof of a Palestinian hut, and the picture describes what actually occurred. Luke (5 : 19) seems rather to have the picture of a Roman house with a tile roof.[4] Carpenter[5] thinks that nearly all of the changes and omissions in Luke can be explained. Both Matthew and Luke largely avoid Mark's frequent use of the historical present. There are a few other instances, probably due to textual variations, in which Matthew and Luke agree against Mark, but they are unimportant.[6]

It seems unlikely that Luke made any use of Mark at all for 2 : 51–18 : 14. Here, as we shall see, Luke had other sources. But Luke did not use Mark 6 : 45–8 : 26, what is termed the great omission. It is not clear why Luke made no use of this portion of Mark. It may have been accidental, but it is more likely intentional on Luke's part, because he had so much other matter which he desired to use.[7] Hawkins[8] thinks that the material was such that Luke would not be indisposed to

---

[1] *Luke the Physician*, p. 158.

[2] Robertson, *Studies in Mark's Gospel*, ch. IV.   [3] ἐξορύξαντες.

[4] διὰ τῶν κεράμων. Cf. Ramsay, *Luke the Physician*, p. 46.

[5] *Christianity According to S. Luke*, p. 130. Cadbury (*The Treatment of Sources in the Gospel*, p. 96) thinks that in some instances Luke misunderstood Mark.

[6] Hawkins, *Horæ Synopticæ*, pp. 201 f.; Carpenter, *op. cit.*, pp. 130 f. In Luke 5:19 Klostermann (*Handbuch zum N. T.*, 1919, *in loco*) calls καθῆκαν "lukanisch" for χαλῶσιν.

[7] See Hawkins, "The Great Omission" (*Oxford Studies*, pp. 60–74).

[8] *Op. cit.*, p. 74.

pass it by. Holdsworth, Williams, and Wright say that Luke's edition of Mark did not contain this section.

In the Passion narrative (Luke 22 : 14–24 : 10) Luke follows Mark, but with more freedom than elsewhere, and apparently with other sources at hand. Hawkins[1] has a thorough discussion of the subject and seems to prove the point. In Luke 22 : 15–22 reference to the betrayal by Judas comes after the supper, and there are two cups in Luke's account of the supper. What other source or sources did Luke possess? It is clear that he had at least one other document, besides oral witnesses, almost certainly two, and possibly more. He used Mark in common with Matthew. Did Matthew and Luke have any other document that both show signs of using?

4. *The Logia (Q)*.—About one-sixth of Luke's Gospel agrees with Matthew's Gospel in non-Markan material. Whence did they get it? This matter consists mainly of sayings of Jesus. Hence, it is supposed that there was a collection of such sayings, called *Logia of Jesus*. Indeed, we know that such was the case, for scraps of such collections have been found in the papyri of Egypt.[2] Besides, Papias[3] expressly says that "Matthew composed the oracles[4] in the Hebrew[5] language, and each man interpreted them as he was able." To what does Papias, as quoted by Eusebius, refer? It is hard to think that Papias is describing our present Gospel of Matthew, which does not seem to be a translation from Aramaic or Hebrew.[6] True, the term "oracles" need not be confined to discourses, though that is the natural way to take it. "One or two critics suppose it to be the *Gospel according to the Hebrews*. Professor Burkitt and some others believe it to have been a collection of *Testimonia* or Messianic proof-texts from the Old Testament. But the most probable view is that which identifies the Logia with Q."[7] Now what is Q? Q stands for the German word for source (Quelle) and simply acts as a symbol for the non-

[1] *Op. cit.*, pp. 76–95.

[2] Lock and Sanday, *Two Lectures on the Oxyrhynchus Sayings of Jesus* (1889); Taylor, *The Oxyrhynchus Logia* (1899); Taylor, *The Oxyrhynchus Sayings of Jesus* (1905).

[3] Eusebius, *Hist. Eccl.*, III, 39.   [4] τὰ λόγια.

[5] Probably Aramaic, as in Paul's case (Acts 22 : 2).

[6] See Introduction to my *Comm. on Matt.* (*Bible for Home and School*) for discussion.

[7] Carpenter, *Christianity According to S. Luke*, p. 140.

Markan matter common to both Matthew and Luke. It is
not hard to see what this material is. Hawkins[1] gives a careful list of the passages where Matthew and Luke agree in the
use of the non-Markan matter. Harnack[2] gives the Greek
text of these passages with critical notes and appraisement.
It is possible, even probable, that Matthew himself wrote this
collection of Logia which critics call Q.[3] But Q is used to
avoid begging the question on that subject.[4] Only the use of
Q must not be allowed to prejudice one against the idea that
Matthew did write it.[5] The use of so many parallel passages
of considerable length seems to prove a common written source.[6]
It would be possible[7] to explain these passages on the theory
that Luke made use of our present Gospel of Matthew but for
the great divergence between Luke and Matthew in the birth
narrative, the genealogy and various matters of detail. It is
not necessary to decide here whether Matthew himself wrote
in Greek the present Gospel of his name, as is quite possible,
as well as the Logia (Aramaic or Greek or both). What is certain is that Luke had access to the same source for this material
that our present Matthew had.[8] Streeter[9] thinks that "had
Matthew written, it would have been a book like this." The
hope has been expressed that a copy of Q may yet be found,
but Carpenter[10] considers it "exceedingly unlikely." J. H.
Moulton[11] has pointed out that "in no soil outside of Egypt
could a papyrus copy of Q have lain hid and yet safe from
inevitable decay." It may be thought possible that such a
copy was made and taken to Egypt.

As to the date of Q, it is clear that it is earlier than Mark.
Streeter[12] makes a good case for the view that Mark knew and
made some use of Q. Certainly Q is older than Mark. "Nothing prevents it from being assigned to the year fifty, or even

[1] *Horæ Synopticæ*, pp. 107–113.   [2] *Sayings of Jesus* (1908).
[3] Harnack, *ibid.*, p. 249.
[4] Robinson, *Study of the Gospels*, pp. 69 f.
[5] Hawkins, *op. cit.*, p. 107.   [6] *Ibid.*, p. 66.
[7] As Holtzmann, Simons, Wendt and others do in fact.
[8] B. Weiss, *Intr. to the Lit. of N. T.*, II, p. 294.
[9] *Oxford Studies*, p. 216.
[10] *Christianity According to S. Luke*, p. 141, n. 3.
[11] *Expositor*, July, 1917, p. 17.
[12] *Oxford Studies*, pp. 165–183.

earlier."[1]   Streeter[2] adds: "If our characterization of Q above is correct, it was probably written twenty years before Mark, and might well have reached Rome before him."   Ramsay[3] thinks that Q was written down during the life of Jesus and did not include the account of the death and resurrection of Jesus. Ramsay[4] has developed this contention with great plausibility that Q is "a document practically contemporary with the facts, and it registered the impressions made on eye-witnesses of the words and acts of Christ" (p. 89).   Streeter[5] suggests that Mark wrote to supplement Q as Luke wrote to supplement both Q and Mark.   He makes much of the point that Q is close to the living oral tradition.   "At that period and in that non-literary society of Palestine only that was written down which one would be likely to forget."[6]   All this would suit the idea that Matthew, the publican, took down notes of the sayings of Jesus, if necessary in shorthand, which was in common use at that time.   Allen[7] agrees with Ramsay that Harnack's notion of Q forbids its circulation in the early years of Christian history, and holds, at any rate, that Harnack abbreviates Q too much.   But Harnack only presents a minimum.

As to the original extent of Q, Streeter[8] shows it was almost certainly larger than the non-Markan material common to Luke and Matthew.   But Matthew and Luke differ in their use of Mark.   The common Markan material amounts to only two-thirds of our Mark.   Each uses portions of Mark not used by the other.   Precisely this situation probably exists as to Q.   If so, we must greatly enlarge our idea of the extent of Q.   Besides, Hawkins[9] shows that Matthew and Luke put three-fourths of Q, as used by them, in different places.   It must be still further admitted that Q may have contained matter not used by either Matthew or Luke.

Streeter [10] thinks it possible that Matthew and Luke had different editions of Q.   Bartlet [11] takes up this idea and carries it still further.   He holds that, when Luke got hold of Q, it had

---

[1] Harnack, *Date of the Acts and the Synoptic Gospels*, p. 125, n. 1.

[2] *Oxford Studies*, p. 219.   [3] *Expositor*, May, 1907.

[4] "The Oldest Written Gospel" (*Luke the Physician*, pp. 71–101).   So Salmon, *The Human Element in the Gospels*, p. 274.

[5] *Oxford Studies*, p. 219.   [6] *Oxford Studies*, p. 215.

[7] *Ibid.*, p. 239.   [8] *Ibid.*, p. 185.

[9] *Oxford Studies*, p. 120.   [10] *Ibid.*, p. 205.

[11] "The Sources of St. Luke's Gospel" (*Oxford Studies*, pp. 313–363).

already been combined with another special source, so that Bartlet can talk of QM, QMk, QL. Stanton[1] agrees with Bartlet in this view of Luke's special source. This is a special two-document theory for Luke. The commonly accepted two-document hypothesis is that both Matthew and Luke used Mark and Q. Both Matthew and Luke had, of course, other sources of information, but these two explain most of what we find in them. Sanday[2] assumes this "Two-Document Hypothesis" and cannot follow Bartlet in his special interpretation.[3]

Before we proceed to the discussion of Luke's special sources it is pertinent to inquire what view of Christ is given in Q. Harnack[4] discusses "the Personality of Our Lord" in Q and seeks to give a depreciated view of Christ in our oldest known Gospel record. But the facts do not justify this interpretation, as I have shown in *The Contemporary Review*[5] in an article on "The Christ of the Logia." The Christ of Q is in essence the Christ of Mark, of Matthew, of Luke, of Paul, of John. The earliest known picture of Christ is drawn on the same scale and plan as the latest. Jesus of Nazareth is pictured in Q as the Son of God as well as the Son of Man.

5. *Other Sources of Information.*—It is plain that Luke had special sources of knowledge beyond Mark and Q and beyond the infancy narrative. Bartlet would make his second source cover practically the whole of what Luke gives us, parallel even with Mark's narrative.[6] But that theory is not likely to win a foothold. Bartlet thinks that Luke's second source came to him in oral form and was first written down by him. It is not surprising that we are not able to find all of Luke in Mark and Q, though we must admit that some of what we discuss at this point may well have been in Q. It is worth saying that Luke probably had sources that can never be traced. He said that he had "many," both oral and written. The facts seem to justify his statement. Kirsopp Lake[7] holds that Luke used only Mark, Q, the LXX and possibly Josephus. But our failure to find all of Luke's sources does not of necessity limit his resources. The misfortune is ours, not Luke's.

[1] *Gospels as Historical Documents*, II, pp. 239 f.
[2] *Oxford Studies*, p. 2. [3] *Ibid.*, pp. xx f.
[4] *The Sayings of Jesus*, pp. 233–246.
[5] August, 1919. [6] *Oxford Studies*, p. 323.
[7] Hastings's *Dict. of the Ap. Church.*

The "Two-Document Hypothesis" does not undertake to refer all of Luke's Gospel to Mark and Q. There is a large residuum outside, or apparently outside, for we are bound to note that we do not know the limits of Q. Luke 9 : 51–18 : 14 is generally called the Great Interpolation, because in this section Luke fails to follow the Markan material. Hawkins[1] terms it "the Disuse of the Markan Source." Burton[2] calls it "the Peræan Document." But Streeter[3] objects to this designation and notes that of the block 9 : 51–12 : 59, "nearly four-fifths, as occurring also in Matthew, is *verifiably* Q, as in the case, also, with all but a few verses of 13 : 18–35." Certainly, then, a large part of the so-called Great Interpolation comes from Q. It is in this section that many of the "doublets" in Luke's Gospel occur. Sanday[4] urges strongly that "allowance should, however, be made for the possibility of what may be called real doublets as well as literary doublets. I believe that similar sayings were spoken by Our Lord more than once." This is certainly true, as every popular preacher or teacher knows in his own experience. Repetition is not only common with the public speakers to different audiences in different localities, but to the same audience, if one is to be understood. Not only may one use similar sayings, but he must repeat the same sayings to drive the point home. Those critics forget this fact who insist that Luke has here dumped together a mass of material that he did not know what else to do with, material that really belongs elsewhere, as we see from Matthew. But such criticism forgets, also, Luke's express claim to an orderly discussion. It is just as easy to think of repetition of similar incidents and like sayings in the life of Jesus. It is precisely in the Great Interpolation that the great parables in Luke occur. "The more we consider his collection, the more we are entranced with it. It is the very cream of the Gospel, and yet (strange to say) it is peculiar to Luke." [5] Wright terms this a "Pauline collection," not because he derived it from Paul, but because it breathes Paul's cosmopolitan spirit. But Jesus was cosmopolitan before Paul and more so. Haw-

---

[1] *Oxford Studies*, pp. 29–59.
[2] *Some Principles of Literary Criticism and Their Application to the Synoptic Problem*, p. 49.
[3] *Oxford Studies*, pp. 189 f.   [4] *Oxford Studies*, p. xvii.
[5] Wright, Hastings's *Dict. of Christ and the Gospels*.

kins[1] calls it "The Travel-Document," but cannot believe that Luke was one of the seventy sent forth by Jesus. He thinks that Luke may even have drafted this document himself before he began the Gospel narrative. He may have obtained first-hand information from one of the eye-witnesses who was with Jesus, possibly one of the seventy. So the matter must rest for the present. Only we must note that Luke may well have had a special source (written or oral) for the later Peræan and Judean Ministry, which parallels in many respects the great Galilean Ministry. It is possible that in John's Gospel we have a parallel to the three journeys of Jesus to Jerusalem in this section. John describes three journeys to Jerusalem in the later ministry (7:2; 11:17; 12:1). These may correspond[2] to Luke's journeys (9:51; 13:22; 17:11).

Did Luke have any other special sources? It has already been noted that in Luke's account of the Passion Week Luke "does not abandon Mark, but uses him with freedom, and makes a number of additions." [3] Did Luke have another written record of the Passion of Christ, or did he supplement Mark from oral tradition? Some hold that the copy of Q that Luke used had received this narrative addition. It is to be noted that Luke uses much more freedom in the arrangement of his material here than in the early parts of his Gospel. But Hawkins[4] holds that here, beyond a doubt, Luke makes use of oral material, and probably as a result of Paul's preaching. Paul preached largely about the death and resurrection of Jesus. The account of the institution of the Lord's Supper in Luke 22:19 f. is almost precisely the language of Paul in I Cor. 11:23-25. Luke was a fellow worker with Paul (Philemon 24). Moulton has suggested that Paul was in Jerusalem before the Crucifixion and collected evidence against Jesus, that he had witnessed the death of Christ and that the face he saw on the road to Damascus he had first seen on the Cross. All this is quite possible, but Luke was not confined to Paul's preaching and Mark's Gospel. He knew James, the

---

[1] *Oxford Studies*, pp. 55 ff.

[2] See Broadus's *Harmony of the Gospels*, p. 251.

[3] Carpenter, *Christianity According to S. Luke*, p. 145. McLachlan (*St. Luke: The Man and His Work*, p. 19) holds that Luke shows the same "decided literary ability" in the use of these unknown sources.

[4] *Expositor*, July, 1911.

brother of Jesus (Acts 21 : 18), Manaen, a foster-brother of Herod (Acts 13 : 1), Joanna (Luke 8 : 3; 24 : 10), the wife of Herod's steward Chuza, who could tell much about the trial before Herod as well as before Pilate. Luke knew Philip and his daughters at Cæsarea (Acts 21 : 8). During the two years at Cæsarea, Luke had abundant opportunity to secure full and precise information for his Gospel. Harnack[1] seeks to discredit these eye-witnesses of the word: "These we must think of as 'ecstatics.' Altogether wanting in sober-mindedness and credibility, like Philip and his four prophesying daughters who came to Asia." "Papias, who himself saw the daughters, expressly states that they transmitted stories of the old days." But why discredit them? They may, indeed, partly explain Luke's interest in the work of women for Christ, but that fact throws no shadow on his record as a historian. In the Galilean section of the Gospel, Luke adds various items (Luke 4 : 3-13, 16-30; 5 : 1-11; 6 : 21-49; 7 : 1-8) to Mark's narrative. Burton would suggest a special Galilean document for these variations, but Wright thinks "anonymous fragments" sufficient to explain the phenomena. We cannot claim that we have traced all of Luke's sources for his Gospel. It is not necessary to do so. Enough is now known to justify Luke's claim to the use of "many" records and reports of eye-witnesses and others who told the story of Jesus by voice or pen. "The conclusion to which we must come is that S. Luke's Gospel, as has been often pointed out, is a new work."[2] He has not been a mere annalist or copyist. He has made careful research for the facts and has taken equal pains to write a narrative that is more complete than any in existence and that is accurate and reliable. He has done it with the skill of the literary artist and with the stamp of his own style and personality at every turn. He has woven the material together into a unified whole that is to-day the joy of all lovers of Jesus and the despair of all imitators. Luke has made the whole world see Jesus as he saw him, in the vivid stories and narratives that made his own soul glow with the Light of the ages.

[1] *Luke the Physician*, p. 153.
[2] Carpenter, *op. cit.*, p. 147. Mr. Lummis (*How Luke Was Written*, p. 46) thinks that Luke was a young man when he began the Gospel.

CHAPTER VI

THE SOURCES OF THE ACTS

"We sought to go forth into Macedonia" (Acts 16:10)

1. *Both Oral and Written Sources.*—There is no formal statement of Luke's method of study in the Acts, but one is entitled to believe that what Luke said in the Gospel applies to the Acts.[1] Certainly he would be no less industrious and painstaking. He would use all available material that would help him in his laudable ambition to picture the growth of Christianity in the Roman Empire. Luke has not told us what his aim is in the Acts, and modern scholars differ greatly about it. It is clear that the book is not a history of the work of all the apostles nor of all the work of any one of them. It is not a biography of Paul, for great gaps exist in the story of Paul's work, as we can see from Paul's Epistles. It is not a sketch of Peter and Paul for the purpose of reconciling two factions in Christianity that followed these leaders. And yet it is true that "the most superficial examination of Acts shows that it is divided most obviously into a 'Peter' part and a 'Paul' part."[2] But this is true because in the stages of the apostolic period Peter was the chief figure, while Paul took the leadership later on. So in chapters 1–12 Jerusalem is the centre of Christian activity, while in Chapters 13–28 the centre has shifted to Antioch. An elaborate "source-criticism" has arisen on the basis of the outstanding facts. A complicated system of "redactions" for the result has been worked out that is theoretical and unsatisfactory. Moffatt[3] gives a careful sketch of the theories of Blass, Briggs, Clemen, Harnack, Jüngst, Sorof, Spitta, B. Weiss. Headlam[4] thinks that the statement of most of the speculations refutes them. Harnack thinks that for the

---

[1] Luke probably had both books in mind when he wrote the Gospel. Certain it is that both books at first circulated together, parts of one whole. Chase, *Credibility of the Acts*, p. 16.

[2] Lake, Hastings's *Dict. of Ap. Church.*

[3] *Intr. to Lit. of N. T.*, pp. 286–9.   [4] Hastings's *D. B.*, art. "Acts."

first twelve chapters of Acts Luke has no written documents, while C. C. Torrey holds that Luke translated an Aramaic document for Chapters 1–15. So the doctors differ. We do not have the benefit of actual comparison of Acts with the original sources to help us, as was true of the Gospel of Luke with Mark and Q. Hence the result is more inconclusive. But some broad facts are clear. One is the use of both oral and written sources. Another is that Luke himself is a participant in a large part of the story. Another is the fact of Paul's presence and Epistles. Another is the stay of Luke in Cæsarea and Palestine, when he had opportunity to learn much about the earlier stages of the history before he became a Christian. It is plain, therefore, that Luke had exceptionally good opportunities for obtaining historical data for the Acts. And yet the trustworthiness of the Acts has been more severely criticised than has that of the Gospel. It is precisely the Acts that has been more helped by recent discovery and criticism than any other book of the New Testament. The Gospel of Luke, as we shall see, was sharply criticised in 3 : 1–3 for alleged historical blunders, but the Acts was attacked in scores of places. Luke has been vindicated in nearly all of these instances where once he stood alone and is entitled to respectful consideration in the rest.

Ramsay[1] holds that the Acts has been the victim of a false interpretation of the relation of Roman history and Christianity. For long it was assumed that Christianity was not persecuted by the state before Trajan's famous "Rescript" about A. D. 112. Hence all documents, like Acts, which showed evidence of such persecution, were relegated to the second century. But it is now plain that Pliny and Trajan are discussing a standing procedure, not a new order or attitude. "Yet a long series of critics misunderstood the documents, and rested their theory of early Christian history on their extraordinary blunder."[2] Ramsay[3] makes it clear how important this point really is: "This change of view as regards the attitude of the Roman state toward the Christian Church, while it affects the whole New Testament, has been the turning-point in the tide of opinion regarding the Acts. That is the history of Christianity in the Roman Empire; there were indubitably some attempts to propagate Christianity toward

[1] *Pauline and Other Studies*, p. 195.   [2] *Ibid.*
[3] *Ibid.*, pp. 195 f.

the east and south, beyond the limits of the empire, but the' author of Acts regards these efforts as unimportant, and omits them entirely from his view." So, then, "what is urgently required at the present time in early Christian history is a completely new start, free from all assumptions, whether on the 'critical' or on the 'traditional' side." [1] Paul (Acts 19:21) had an ambition to evangelize the Roman Empire, and Luke is seized with this conception and carries Paul to Rome, the capital, where they both are at the time of writing the Acts. Ramsay[2] explains how his studies in Roman provincial history in Asia Minor compelled him to see how the Acts "must have been written in the first century and with admirable knowledge. It plunges one into the atmosphere and the circumstances of the first century; it is out of harmony with the circumstances and spirit of the second century."

The Acts as a whole bears the stamp of one mind, in spite of the variety of sources, as truly as does Luke's Gospel. We must think of Luke as drafting the plan of the book to suit his purpose and using the material that suited his aim. He first gathered his data and then went to work on his facts. The result is one of the great books of all time.

2. *Personal Experiences of the Author.*—It is best to begin with the "we" sections of Acts (16:9–40; 20:5–28:31), for here Luke himself was an eye-witness (cf. Luke 1:2) of the story which he tells. He is Paul's companion and minister for that part of the second journey from Troas to Philippi, and on the return trip in the third tour from Philippi to Jerusalem, in Cæsarea for two years (most of it), on the voyage to Rome and for two years there. Here Luke was a participant in the events and could speak from personal knowledge. We do not have to think that Luke remained constantly with Paul during the whole of the two years and more in Cæsarea, but he evidently made Cæsarea headquarters and probably heard Paul make his several defenses in Jerusalem and Cæsarea. Thus we can best understand the great fulness of detail for these parts of Acts. Luke had the glowing interest of one who lived through those exciting days. The style is in all essentials the same in the "we" sections as in the rest of the Acts, but with an added freedom and vividness.

It is probable that Luke kept a diary for the time that he

[1] *Ibid.*, p. 197.   [2] *Ibid.*, p. 199.

was with Paul and is rewriting that for the Acts. For this reason Luke retains the "we" and "us." Luke was too careful a writer to retain the pronoun if he was using the travel diary of another person. He was too honest a historian to seek to create the impression that he was present when he was not.[1] He was not the kind of man to pose as an eye-witness. Some preachers are accused of appropriating illustrations and applying them to their own experiences for rhetorical effect. Carpenter[2] aptly says: "If he had wanted to pretend, he would have been clever enough to do it more efficiently. He would have stated roundly that he had been there. It is true that he was a literary artist. But one of the first duties of a literary artist is to use language that will convey his meaning and be understood by those for whom he writes." It is not necessary to repeat the arguments that prove conclusively that the "we" sections of Acts are written in the same style as the rest of the Acts and of the Gospel. Harnack[3] sums the matter up by saying: "In no other part of the Acts of the Apostles are the peculiarities of vocabulary and style of the author of the twofold work so accumulated and concentrated as they are in the "we" sections.

Blass[4] thinks that, whatever is true of the Gospel, for the Acts there is no need to raise any question concerning the sources, least of all for the "we" sections. He argues that Luke was so constantly with various participants in the events. Ramsay[5] has no patience with the idea that Luke had access to reliable sources here and there, but not as a whole: "That way of juggling with the supposed authorities of Luke, too, has been abandoned since then by all competent scholars. The idea that the writer of the Acts had good authorities to rely on for one or two details alone would not now be suggested or tolerated. That writer had a certain general level of knowledge and information and judgment. He has to be estimated as a whole." That is obviously true, and yet it is pertinent to show, where possible, the nature of the sources at Luke's disposal. It is important that we do not expect too much of the Acts. It is not a biographical monograph with exhaustive

---

[1] Carpenter, *Christianity According to S. Luke*, p. 13.
[2] Ibid., p. 14. [3] *Date of the Acts and the Gospels*, p. 12.
[4] *Acta Apostolorum*, p. 10.
[5] *Bearing of Recent Discovery*, p. 80.

details concerning any one character.[1] From Acts 13:1 on the book "becomes practically a biographical sketch of some phases of Paul's life and work."[2] Note the careful language of Moffatt. Luke does not aim at a complete narration of all events about Paul, but he tells what falls in with his purpose. Von Soden[3] notes that it was a common custom for distinguished travellers to have a diary kept by some member of the party as an aid to memory and for future use. It has been suggested that Xenophon did this for his *Anabasis*. It is noteworthy that Luke had the historical insight to keep such a diary while with Paul. In particular, Luke may have made notes of Paul's speeches which he heard (see later). Hayes[4] thinks that Luke is a hero-worshipper of the first order, and but for his devotion to Paul he might never have written the Acts.

3. *Paul.*—It is certain that Luke was with Paul some five or six years (at Troas, Philippi, the journey to Jerusalem, Jerusalem, Cæsarea, voyage, Rome), most of the time, if not all the time. It would have been very strange if Luke did not consult Paul at all about matters relating to their companionship and fellowship. It is here assumed, of course, that Luke wrote the Acts in Rome before Paul was set free from the first Roman imprisonment. Paul may have had notes of some of his speeches on which Luke could draw for the course of his argument if his own notes were deficient. He could ask Paul to fill in a gap here or there. He could use Paul's recollection to supplement and to check his own memory concerning details. It is incongruous to think that Luke was with Paul while writing the book and yet failed to avail himself of Paul's store of knowledge. This remark applies not only to Paul's supplementing Luke's diary or recollection of the "we" sections, but also to the rest of the Paul narrative.

On the hypothesis that Luke was Paul's companion, Lake[5] sees clearly that "if this be so, we have for the rest of the 'Paul' narrative a source ready to our hand in the personal information obtained by Luke from St. Paul himself, or from other companions of St. Paul whom he met in his society. This

---

[1] Chase, *Credibility of the Gospel and Acts*, p. 24.
[2] *Intr. to Lit. of the N. T.*, p. 293.　　　[3] *Intr. to N. T.*, p. 243.
　Synoptic Gospels and Acts, p. 335.
[5] Hastings's *Dict. of Ap. Church.*

may cover as much as Acts 9 : 1–30; 11 : 27–30; 12 : 25–31, or even more." Most assuredly, and we must include the story of the first mission tour (13 and 14), since Luke was not present, and the great conference in Jerusalem and after events in Antioch (15). It is inconceivable that Luke would fail to get the benefit of Paul's first-hand knowledge of all this period if Paul was at hand in Rome with him. Paul may not have been Luke's only source for this period, but he did have Paul as a reservoir of information on all disputed points. Carpenter feels that "a certain amount is surely from Paul himself." [1] We do not have to know how much. The important thing is for us to recognize that Luke wrote in the very atmosphere of his hero. Out of the Pauline environment then came both the Gospel of Luke and the Acts.[2] Luke was with Paul during the time when he was finishing the Judaizing controversy and was full of the Gnostic controversy. He saw Paul at the height of his powers. It is small wonder that in the Gospel and the Acts Luke reflects the Pauline conception of Christ. And yet Luke preserves the historical perspective. The early chapters of Acts faithfully preserve the primitive Christology, in essence the same as that of Paul. Carpenter[3] thinks that Luke the physician would be deeply interested "in the enthusiastic conversation of the friend, who was so bad a patient, so lovable a man." He would note the power of the Spirit in Paul, his fondness for the fellowship of his friends, his doctrine of Christ, his world outlook, his doctrine of the Kingdom, his eschatology.

Paul could be of service to Luke for the work in Thessalonica, Athens, Corinth, Ephesus (Acts 17–19). We do not have to think that Luke simply gives Paul's view of things. He used various sources. Silas and Timothy could supplement much for this period. And there was Titus for the Corinthian troubles, with whom Luke seems to have been associated (brother and delegate). Aristarchus was with Luke and Paul for the journey to Jerusalem and to Rome (Acts 19 : 29; 20 : 4; 27 : 2; Col. 4 : 10; Philemon 24). Luke had all these to reinforce Paul and himself for much of the Acts. Ramsay[4] is willing to admit that in Acts 19 : 2–16 Luke drops from his high

---

[1] *Op. cit.*, p. 11.   [2] *Ibid.*
[3] *Op. cit.*, p. 16. Harnack (*Acts of the Apostles*, p. 232) thinks that Luke relied on oral testimony for all this part of the Acts.
[4] *St. Paul the Traveller*, p. 272.

standard and reports "a popular tale," but he is not sure. Better give Luke the benefit of the doubt for the present, at any rate.

Did Luke have the help of Paul's Epistles? Some of them were written before Acts. If Acts appeared in A. D. 63 or 64, certainly I and II Thessalonians had been written (A. D. 51–53); I and II Corinthians, Galatians, Romans (55–57) were also accessible to Luke. Philippians, Philemon, Colossians, and Ephesians (61–63) were written from Rome, apparently while Luke was there, though he seems to have been absent when Philippians was despatched (2:20). But scholars are not agreed as to whether Luke knew Paul's Epistles or not. Lake[1] bluntly says: "There is no reason to suppose that Luke was acquainted with any of the Pauline Epistles. There is nothing in the Acts which resembles a quotation, and in relating facts alluded to in the Epistles there is more often difference than agreement, even though it be true that the difference is not always serious." This is the opinion of most scholars—that Luke had not read Paul's Epistles. It is only insisted here that he could have done so in so far as the date is concerned. His own movements would play some part in the matter. Ramsay,[2] however, says: "But personally I am disposed to think that Luke knew the letters, though he does not make them his authority, because he had still higher and better, viz., Paul's own conversation." With this opinion I cordially agree. Luke had probably read the Epistles (not the Pastorals), but he did not have them with him as he wrote. He made no effort to copy them or to square his narrative with them.

Some difficulties exist (cf. Gal. 2:1–10 and Acts 15:1–30), which will come up for discussion later. One must always bear in mind the purpose of Luke in Acts and the aim of Paul in his Epistles. In Gal. 2 Paul is discussing his independence of the Twelve, not his visits to Jerusalem. He is describing a private interview with the great Trio (Peter, James and John) in Jerusalem, not the public meetings of the whole Conference, as in Acts 15. Thus the two accounts can be reconciled if the same meeting is intended in both passages. Some take Gal. 2:1–10 to refer to another visit. Harnack[3] finds a special Antiochian source for Acts 15:1–30.

[1] Hastings's *Ap. Church.*   [2] *Bearing of Recent Discovery*, p. 52.
[3] *Acts of the Apostles*, p. 199.

But there is no denying the light that the Acts and the
Epistles throw upon each other, as Paley long ago showed in
his *Horæ Paulinæ*. "Acts rightly understood is the best commentary of the letters of Paul, and the letters on the Acts. If
Luke had never known or read these letters, then all the more
remarkable is it as a proof of the truth and historicity of both
that the agreement is so perfect."[1] Harnack[2] has shown
thirty-nine striking coincidences between Paul's Epistles and
Acts 1-14 in the section before Luke came into contact with
Paul. The agreement, Harnack argues, "is so extensive and
so detailed as to exclude all wild hypotheses concerning those
passages of the Acts that are without attestation in those
Epistles."[3] And yet Luke has remained himself everywhere.[4]
His style is his own, his intellectual independence is maintained, he is not obsessed by Paul so as to lose his perspective.
"One of the most assured results of recent research is that he
was not a Paulinist masquerading as a historian."[5] The spirit
of Paul is in the Acts and Paul's picture is drawn on bold canvas, but Luke has drawn the portrait in his own manner.

4. *Other First-Hand Reporters.*—It is certain that Luke was
Paul's companion and so had his own notes and recollections
for that portion of the history. It is certain, also, that he
enjoyed the benefit of Paul's own suggestions for the same
period and for the Paul narrative, where Luke was not a participant. Besides, Luke had access to others of the Pauline
circle, Aristarchus, Silas, Erastus, Timothy, Titus, Gaius,
Sopater, Tychicus, Trophimus, Mark, Demas, Epaphras,
Mnason, and possibly Barnabas, Symeon Niger, Lycius of
Cyrene, and Manaen. We are certain of all in this Pauline
group save the names beginning with Barnabas. If the Bezan
text is correct in Acts 11 : 28, then Luke knew Barnabas and
all those named in Acts 13 : 1. Thus we can see Luke's sources
for two-thirds of the Acts, for nearly all of chapters 9–28 (ex-
cepting Peter's ministry in Lydda, Joppa, Cæsarea, and Jerusalem). That of Barnabas in Cæsarea and Jerusalem could
have come from Paul, if not from Barnabas.

So far so good. But what about the rest? "The problems

[1] Ramsay, *Bearing of Recent Discovery*, p. 52.
[2] *Acts of the Apostles*, pp. 264–274.
[3] *Ibid.*, p. 272.   [4] *Ibid.*, p. 274.
[5] Moffatt, *Intr. to Lit. of N. T.*, p. 281.

presented by the earlier chapters are much more complicated."[1] Here again we are confronted with the problem of oral or written sources. Lake[2] holds that it "seems quite impossible to say whether he was using written sources." There is, undoubtedly, an Antiochian tradition and a Jerusalem tradition for the material that Luke employs for chapters 1–12 (save the story of Paul's conversion, 9 : 1–30). But it cannot as yet be shown that it was all written unless C. C. Torrey is right in his theory of an Aramaic document for chapters 1–15, about which we shall have more directly.

But we can feel our way backward in Acts by means of persons with whom Luke came into personal contact. Cornelius, if still living, could certainly tell Luke of the work of grace in Cæsarea when Peter came. We know that Luke met James, the brother of Jesus, in Jerusalem (Acts 21 : 18) and the other elders. James was present during the days of the great Pentecostal outpouring (Acts 1 : 14) and could give Luke valuable data for this epochal event. It is not known that Luke met Peter in Jerusalem or in Rome, though both are possible occurrences. In that case, Peter himself would be Luke's main source. But we do know that Luke was with Mark in Rome. Mark, as the disciple of Peter and cousin of Barnabas, could furnish testimony concerning chapters 9 : 31–13 : 13. And there were Philip and his daughters, who dwelt in Cæsarea. We know that Luke made a visit to this home (Acts 21 : 8) on his way to Jerusalem. During the two years in Cæsarea Luke had abundant opportunities to learn from Philip the story of his work in Samaria and Philistia (chapter 8) as well as the appointment of the seven and the career of Stephen (chapters 6 and 7). Besides, Paul was present at the delivery of Stephen's speech and at his stoning (Acts 8 : 1; 26 : 10) and could help Luke materially at this point. In all these instances notes may have been made concerning the various sections, and turned over to Luke, or he may have made notes of his conversations. There is no way to decide.

There remains the period covered by chapters 1–5. It is in this section, in particular, that Luke confronts supernatural phenomena, and where modern writers find most difficulty in crediting his narrative. Carpenter[3] is sure that Luke worked

---

[1] Lake, Hastings's *Dict. of Ap. Church.*   [2] *Ibid.*
[3] *Christianity According to S. Luke*, p. 23.

backward from Paul to Pentecost. He agrees with Doctor Figgis "that it is right to begin history at this end," as, he argues, "Peter and Paul did in their preaching." "The thinker instantly works backward." This is an important point and confronts us squarely as we face Acts 1–5. "Did S. Paul, at his conversion, or before, or after, engage for his own satisfaction in any kind of historical research? And if so, how thoroughly did he (and, we may add, S. Luke) carry through the process?"[1] Paul knows the fundamental facts of the life, death and resurrection of Jesus, whether he obtained them by personal acquaintance with Jesus or from others.[2] Paul stands in the path of the "Christ-Myth theory" and in the way of the idea of Loisy[3] that "Pauline Christianity was simply a mystery-cult, and that Paul cared no more, and perhaps believed no more, about the historicity of Jesus than the Osiris-worshipper cared or believed about the historical existence of Osiris."[4] As to Pentecost, Carpenter[5] feels certain that "the physician as an educated man, with at least something of the historical spirit, would inquire how and when the immanence of the Spirit in the community had begun."

Harnack[6] thinks that nothing clear can be learned concerning the sources of Luke for the early chapters. He looks with suspicion on chapter 1 as a late legend, and sees a doublet in chapters 2 and 3–5, as does Lake. Harnack manifestly has a lower opinion of Acts 1–12 than he has for the worth of 13–28. Ramsay[7] admits the difficulty raised for modern people concerning the miracles and demons in passages like Acts 5:12 and 8:7. "It is matter for a special book to study the authorities whom Luke used for the first part of his history."[8] He argues for patience about psychic phenomena, and pleads that Luke must be credited with special interest in such cases, since he was a physician and a scientist. As a historian he would be careful to weigh the cases that he records. Ramsay[9] thinks that Luke used some official data or acta of the early Christian

[1] Ibid., p. 25.   [2] Christianity According to S. Luke, pp. 28–32.
[3] Hibbert Journal, Oct., 1911.
[4] Carpenter, op. cit., p. 25.   [5] Ibid., p. 21.
[6] Acts of the Apostles, p. 163.
[7] Bearing of Recent Discovery, p. 200.
[8] Bearing of Recent Discovery, p. 205.
[9] Expositor, VII, 7, pp. 172 f., 262 f., 358 f., 450 f.

community in Jerusalem for the record in Acts 1–5 with the full report of Peter's great sermon at Pentecost, "which is in some ways one of the most archaic passages in the New Testament."[1] Ramsay holds that Philip could have reported Peter's speech, though hardly Acts 2:1–13.

The earlier chapters of Acts show plainly enough that Luke was not a participant. There is care for accuracy about the historical origins of Christianity. "The subject in them is handled in a vague way with a less vigorous and nervous grasp."[2] As compared with the Gospel, Luke "had not the advantage of formal historical narratives such as he mentions for the period described in the First Book (the Gospel)."[3] However, one is not entitled to discredit Luke's narrative in Acts 1–5, since he had ready access to numerous converts at the great Pentecost. Prejudice against Luke in these chapters is primarily prejudice against the supernatural demonstration of the power of the Holy Spirit and is on a par with prejudice against the Virgin Birth of Jesus and his Resurrection from the dead, all of which events are recorded in Luke's Gospel after due research and reflection. We shall see whether Luke is a mere recorder of tales, like Herodotus.

5. *The Theory of an Aramaic Document for Chapters* 1–15.— We know that Luke was acquainted with Aramaic, from his use of original sources for Luke 1 and 2 (except 1:1–4). In Acts 1:19 and 9:36 Luke translates Aramaic words. "Knowledge of Aramaic and the ability to translate an easy Aramaic text may well be assumed in a native of Antioch, and one who was for many years a companion of St. Paul."[4] Harnack considers the results of present knowledge "ambiguous": "There are, on the one hand, weighty reasons for the conclusion that St. Luke in the first half of the Acts has translated an Aramaic source, and yet it is impossible to refute the theory that he was only dependent upon oral information."[5] Harnack feels sure that Luke did not follow a single Aramaic source. He is positive[6] that Luke did not follow a written Greek source for

---

[1] Lake, Hastings's *Dict. of Ap. Church.*
[2] Ramsay, *St. Paul the Traveller*, p. 19.　　　　[3] *Ibid.*, p. 20.
[4] Harnack, *Luke the Physician*, p. 119. McLachlan (*St. Luke; the Man and His Work*) devotes chap. II to "Luke the Linguist." He argues that Luke knew something of Latin, Aramaic, and Hebrew, but was not expert in them as in Greek.
[5] *Ibid.*, p. 119.　　　　[6] *Ibid.*, p. 116.

this part of the Acts. Lake,[1] *per contra*, is confident that Luke had a written Greek source for Acts 3 and 4, possibly 5, and probably 8 : 5–40. So the doctors disagree again.

Blass[2] suggests that Mark wrote out the first narrative of the apostolic period in Aramaic, and that Luke employed this Aramaic document for Acts 1–12. "I say that the language of the Acts is markedly different from that of the later chapters: in the former Aramaisms abound, in the latter they are comparatively very scarce; from these facts I argue that the second part is an independent work by Luke, but the former depends on an Aramaic source."[3] Blass thinks it doubtful if Luke knew Aramaic, and thinks it likely that he had an interpreter for Mark's book. Nestle[4] had suggested a Hebrew document for the early part of Acts. Moffatt[5] states his view thus: "Oral tradition of a heterogeneous and even of a legendary character may be held to explain most, if not all, of the data. There is fair ground for conjecturing, however, that Luke used and translated an Aramaic source." But no one has been able to show specific Aramaisms to any considerable extent. The first half of Acts seems as distinctly Lukan as the second.

C. C. Torrey argued in 1912 that "the compiler of the Third Gospel was an accomplished translator of both Hebrew and Aramaic."[6] He returns to the subject in his monograph, "The Composition and Date of Acts" (1916), and attempts to show that Acts 1–15 is translated from an Aramaic document by Luke, the author of the "we" sections and of the Third Gospel. "The whole book, however, shows unmistakable uniformity of vocabulary and phraseology, so that it is obvious (to him who recognizes the Semitic source) that the author of 16–28 was the translator of 1–15." Professor Torrey proceeds to give what he considers numerous "translation Aramaisms," not Hebraisms. "The truth is that the language of all fifteen chapters is translation-Greek through and through, generally preserving even the order of words."[7] It may be admitted at once that, if Torrey proves his case, the question of the sources

---

[1] Hastings's *Dict. of Ap. Church.*

[2] *Philology of the Gospels*, pp. 141, 193 f., 201.

[3] *Ibid.*, p. 194.   [4] *Expositor*, 1895, p. 238.

[5] *Intr. to Lit. of N. T.*, p. 290.

[6] *Studies in the History of Religions, Presented to Crawford H. Toy*, pp. 269–317.

[7] *Op. cit.*, p. 7.

of Acts is greatly simplified. The Aramaic document (Mark?), Luke and Paul would cover the whole story. It must be said, however, that Torrey apparently weakens his argument by what he calls "especially striking cases of mistranslation in Acts 1–15."[1] The Aramaic list is wholly hypothetical. The supposed mistranslation is not very convincing. Burkitt reviews Torrey's pamphlet in the July, 1919, *Journal of Theological Studies*. He says (p. 326): "I venture to submit that Professor Torrey has not produced a compelling demonstration," though he recognizes "an occasional use by St. Luke of Aramaic sources, written or oral" (p. 329). This is precisely my own feeling in the matter. Besides, Torrey (pp. 14 ff.) presses entirely too far the use of "his name" in Acts 3 : 16 as "a bit of popular superstition," "a certain quasi-magical power in the Name of Jesus." The trouble with this view is that in the Septuagint and in the papyri "name" occurs in the sense of "person" with no necessary "magical" sense.[2] Torrey claims too much and tries to prove too much. He puts all his eggs in one basket. But, as the case now stands, it must be admitted that an Aramaic document (or documents) is possible as one of the sources for the early chapters of Acts. I cannot yet agree that Luke confined himself to one document for the early chapters of Acts when he had access to so many persons who knew various parts of the story.

Torrey's argument for an Aramaic source for Acts 1–15 has started discussion on an extensive scale. Foakes-Jackson in the *Harvard Theological Review* for October, 1917, feels convinced by Torrey's arguments that there were Aramaic sources for the first part of Acts. "That nothing but Aramaic sources were used is, I consider, not proven. That there was only one document appears to me extremely doubtful" (p. 360). He does think, however, that we must agree that Acts was completed by A. D. 64, and hence that Luke made no use of Josephus, and that the Acts is in no sense a *Tendenz* writing (p. 352). In the January, 1918, issue of the same journal W. J. Wilson says of Torrey's work (p. 74): "By his demonstration of a

---

[1] *Op. cit.*, pp. 10–22.

[2] Cf. Deissmann, *Bible Studies*, pp. 146, 197. An inscription of Caria has εἰς τὸ τοῦ θεοῦ ὄνομα, where a purchaser acts as the representative of Zeus. The papyri show ὄνομα in sense of person. Cf. *B. U.* 113. 11 (143 A. D.), ἑκάστῳ ὀνόματι. So Fay, p. 531, ii. 9 f. (111 A. D.), πρὸς ἕκαστον ὄνομα.

document in Aramaic, underlying Acts 1 : 1b–15 : 35 and translated by Luke with painful fidelity into Greek, he has opened up a whole new field for the criticism of the Book of Acts." He then proceeds to make "some observations" on the basis of the Aramaic source. In the *Harvard Theological Review* for July, 1918, W. J. Wilson replies to Foakes-Jackson in defense of Torrey's plea for a single Aramaic document for Acts 1–15. He concludes that "the argument for the new theory appears very strong indeed" (p. 335). Bacon accepted Torrey's theory as a demonstration (*American Journal of Theology*, January, 1918). In the January, 1919, issue of this quarterly Torrey discusses "Fact and Fancy in Theories Concerning Acts" and answers the criticisms of his critics. As has already been noted, Burkitt replies to Torrey in the July, 1919, *Journal of Theological Studies.* So the matter rests for the present.[1] However it may be decided, the whole discussion has strengthened the argument for the early date and historical worth of the Acts, particularly the early chapters which were mainly under attack.

[1] McLachlan (*St. Luke,* p. 67) thinks that the Aramaic source is established.

CHAPTER VII

THE USE OF MEDICAL TERMS BY LUKE

"Luke the Beloved Physician" (Col. 4 : 14)
"Physician, Heal Thyself" (Luke 4 : 23)

Can it be shown that Luke deserves to be called a man of science?

1. *The Point at Issue.*—In Chapter I. 4 it was shown that the companion of Paul who wrote the Gospel and Acts was a physician. The only known friend and companion of Paul who was a physician is Luke. The proof seems complete, but it is now argued by Lake and by Cadbury that Hobart and Harnack make too much of the medical terms in the Lukan writings. Lake[1] sums up his view thus: "That Luke was a physician is argued by Harnack—following up and greatly improving on the methods of Hobart—on the ground of his use of medical language. The argument is, of course, cumulative, and cannot be epitomized. It is beyond doubt that Luke frequently employs language which can be illustrated from Galen and other medical writers. The weak point is that no sufficient account has been taken of the fact that much of this language can probably be shown from the pages of Lucian, Dion of Prusa, etc., to have been part of the vocabulary of any educated Greek."

It should be admitted at once that the proof that Luke wrote the Gospel and Acts is complete without the linguistic argument concerning medical terms. That argument simply adds to the general effect. We know from Paul that Luke was a physician, and we are naturally interested in a physician's use of medical language. Other people employ medical terms. We find such language in the Gospels of Mark, Matthew and John. Lake and Cadbury rather miss the mark in their reply to Hobart and Harnack. It is not the mere tabulation of medical words that have entered the general vocabulary that is pertinent. "When a physician writes an historical work it does not necessarily follow that his profession shows itself in

[1] Hastings's *Dict. of Ap. Church.*

90

his writing; yet it is only natural for one to look for traces of the author's medical profession in such a work."[1] Harnack notes six ways in which a physician will be likely to betray his profession. Medical points may determine the narrative (disease and its treatment), preference may be shown for stories of healing, the language may be colored by technical medical terms, traces of medical diagnosis may occur, medical phraseology may appear apart from cases of healing, and where the writer is an eye-witness medical traits are particularly noticeable. Harnack holds that in all these ways Luke reveals his medical side. Hobart divides his book, *The Medical Language of St. Luke*, into two parts ("Medical Language Employed in the Account of Miracles of Healing" and that "Used Outside of Medical Subjects"). He gives numerous details from Greek medical writers.

Cadbury[2] argues that the medical bias in Luke's vocabulary must be more considerable than in that of non-medical writers like Lucian to be of value as an argument. The reply is that it is not merely a matter of vocabulary, but of medical interest, that crops out in incidental ways. Jerome (*Comm.* on Isaiah 43:6) says that ancient writers assert that Luke "was very learned in the medical art."[3] Naylor[4] finds Luke the "trained physician and a Greek—probably the only one in the Christian Church in his time." He concludes that Luke differed widely from "the spirit and teaching of Greek medicine from Hippocrates down to his own day" because he reports cases of demoniacal possession and cure. But Homan observes that "he nowhere claims for himself the possession of miraculous powers or intimates their exercise by him." Homan[5] adds that Luke's report of miracles was "a possible compromise between the science of the physician and the faith of the disciple." But Homan[6] attempts to show "that Luke must be ranked as one of the choicest medical minds known to any age." "In short, it is felt that the time has come when physicians should take

---

[1] Harnack, *Luke the Physician*, p. 175.
[2] *Style and Literary Method of Luke*, p. 50.
[3] *Medicinæ artis fuisse scientissimum.*
[4] "Luke the Physician and Ancient Medicine" (*Hibbert Journal*, October, 1909, p. 40).
[5] *Luke the Greek Physician*, p. 7.
[6] *Luke the Greek Physician*, p. 13.

steps to reclaim Luke as one of their own in the name of that profession of which he was one of the greatest ornaments."

If it be said that it is merely the wild assumption of a modern apologist to say that Luke was in any true sense a scientist, it is refreshing to note some remarks by the late Sir William Osler, M.D., F.R.S., Regius Professor of Medicine in the University of Oxford, in a recent (May 16, 1919) presidential address before the Classical Association on *The Old Humanities and the New Science*, in which he says: "And the glories of Greek science should be opened in a sympathetic way to 'Greats' men" (p. 28). "Few 'Greats' men, I fear, could tell why Hippocrates is a living force to-day, or why a modern scientific physician would feel more at home with Erasistratus and Herophilus at Alexandria, or with Galen at Pergamos, than at any period in our story up to, say, Harvey" (p. 19). "In biology Aristotle speaks for the first time the language of modern science, and indeed he seems to have been first and foremost a biologist, and his natural history studies influenced profoundly his sociology, his psychology, and his philosophy in general" (p. 20). Sir William Osler laments modern ignorance of the Greek scientists and physicians. "And yet the methods of. these men exorcised vagaries and superstitions from the human mind, and pointed to a clear knowledge of the laws of nature" (p. 20). "To observation and seasoned thought the Greek added experiment, but never fully used it in biology, an instrument which has made science productive, and to which the modern world owes its civilization" (p. 24). Luke lived in the atmosphere of Greek science. But Luke cannot be taken from Christ, even in the name of science. He brought his science and laid it at the feet of Jesus, the Great Physician. He preached the Gospel and practised the science of medicine, as many a man has done since Luke's day. But now let us see the illustrations of Luke's medical knowledge in his writings.

2. *Changes from Mark's Account.*—Harnack[1] has grouped the examples from Hobart with great skill. The point to observe here is whether Luke made any changes that a physician would be likely to desire. We have seen already (Chapter I. 4) that in Luke 8 : 43 Mark's caustic comment that the poor woman "had spent all that she had, and was nothing

[1] *Luke the Physician*, pp. 182-8.

bettered, but rather grew worse" (Mark 5 : 26), has been soft-
ened to "she was not able to be healed by any" (a chronic case
for which physicians were not to blame). But this striking
case does not stand alone.

In the account of the demoniac in the synagogue (Mark 1 : 26
= Luke 4 : 35) Luke adds "having done him no hurt," showing
the physician's interest in the details of the case. Luke also
noted the fall of the man, "threw him down in the midst."
One can observe all through the Gospel Luke's pleasure in pic-
turing Christ as the physician.

The healing of Simon's mother-in-law (Mark 1 : 30 f. =
Luke 4 : 38 f. = Matt. 8 : 14 f.) has some striking touches.
Luke alone notes that she "was holden with a great fever."[1]
Precisely this medical phrase of "great fever" occurs in Galen
and Hippocrates. Galen says that Greek physicians divided
fevers into "great"[2] and "small."[3] Luke, like a doctor, adds
also two items concerning Christ's method of treatment. "And
he stood over her,"[4] as if in careful contemplation of the symptoms of the patient by way of diagnosis. One thinks of the
famous picture "The Doctor," wherein the physician sits
with his head in his hand and watches the rapid breathing of
the sick child on the bed. Luke adds "and rebuked the
fever," showing that Jesus spoke words of authority and cheer
like the wise physician. Jesus spoke not for mere psychological effect on the patient, but also to show his instant mastery
of the disease. So Luke observes that the fever left her "immediately."[5] It is not a matter of vocabulary here, but we
note the physician's interest and insight that give these touches
to the story not present in Mark and Matthew.

The "leper" (Mark 1 : 40 = Luke 5 : 12 = Matt. 8 : 2) is
described by Luke as "a man full of leprosy,"[6] a very bad
case. "This particular is given only by the beloved physician. His face and his hands would be covered by ulcers and
sores, so that every one could see that the hideous disease
was at a very advanced stage."[7] In such a severe case,
strange to say, the law allowed the leper to have freedom to
come and go (cf. Lev. 13 : 12 f.). Once again the physician
describes the case as Mark and Matthew do not.

---

[1] συνεχομένη πυρετῷ μεγάλῳ.
[2] μέγας.   [3] μικρός.   [4] ἐπιστὰς ἐπάνω αὐτῆς.
[5] παραχρῆμα.   [6] ἀνὴρ πλήρης λέπρας.   [7] Plummer, in loco.

In Luke 5:18 (= Mark 2:3 = Matt. 9:2) we have the phrase "a man that was palsied"[1] rather than the popular term "paralytic"[2] of Mark and Matthew. "St. Luke's use is in strict agreement with that of medical writers."[3] Luke never employs the popular term for this disease, but always the medical phrase.

In the story of the man with the withered hand (Luke 6:6 = Mark 3:1 = Matt. 12:10), Luke, with a physician's eye for details of diagnosis, notes that it was his "right hand." So in Luke 22:50 (= Mark 14:47 = Matt. 26:51) Luke first notes it is the "right ear" of the servant of the high priest that is cut off. He was followed later in this item by John (18:10), who also gives the name Malchus. But in the case of Malchus Luke alone adds "And he touched his ear, and healed him" (Luke 22:51), a miracle of surgery that evidently interested him.

In the account of the Gadarene demoniac (Luke 8:27 = Mark 5:2 = Matt. 8:28), Luke alone observes that "for a long time he had worn no clothes" (the physician's care again). Both Mark (5:15) and Luke (8:35) note that, when cured, he is "clothed and in his right mind."

In the story of the raising of Jairus's daughter (Luke 8:55 = Mark 5:41 f. = Matt. 9:25), Luke alone gives the detail that Jesus "commanded that something be given her to eat." Once more the physician's interest in the child's welfare appears (cf. Acts 9:18).

In the case of the epileptic boy (Luke 9:38 f. = Mark 9:17 f. = Matt. 17:15), each Gospel describes the symptoms differently. It was a hard case, that baffled the disciples. Luke represents the father as beseeching Jesus "to look upon my son,"[4] as if for a fresh diagnosis of the case after the failure of the disciples. Alas, how many of us know what it is to see the consulting physician called in! Luke adds the pathetic plea, "for he is mine only child." Hobart adds also: "It is worthy of note that Aretæus, a physician about Luke's time, admits the possibility of this disease being produced by diabolical agency."

---

[1] ἦν παραλελυμένος.   [2] παραλυτικός.
[3] Hobart, *Medical Language of St. Luke*, p. 6.
[4] ἐπιβλέψαι. Hobart cites this word and μόγις ἀποχωρεῖ as medical terms here.

Once more Luke (18 : 25 = Mark 10 : 25 = Matt. 19 : 24) employs a different word for "needle,"[1] the surgeon's needle, not the ordinary needle,[2] as in Mark and Matthew. Luke employs the word that Galen uses for the surgeon's needle, a distinct trace of medical authorship.

The point about these changes lies in the professional interest of the physician, not in the linguistic improvements of an educated man. Luke did make many such changes because of his literary taste, but another explanation clearly holds here. The argument stands, but it does not stand alone, strong as it is.

3. *Items Peculiar to Luke's Gospel.*—Luke reveals a professional interest in medical matters in the portions of the Gospel which he alone has. Hayes[3] has made an admirable summary of this argument. Luke was a medical evangelist and had a vital interest in both forms of the work of Christ (teaching and healing). "And he sent them forth to preach the Kingdom of God, and to heal the sick" (Luke 9 : 2). So Christ commanded the Twelve as he sent them on the tour of Galilee, as Matthew (10 : 8) also gives: "Heal the sick, raise the dead, cleanse the lepers, cast out demons." But Luke alone gives the following. To the seventy Jesus said: "And heal the sick that are therein, and say unto them, The Kingdom of God is come nigh unto you" (Luke 10 : 9). When the seventy returned from their tour of Judea, they say to Jesus: "Lord, even the demons are subject unto us in thy name" (Luke 10 : 17).

In Christ's Messianic sermon at Nazareth he had quoted Isaiah 40 : 1 f., and applied to himself the mission "to preach good tidings to the poor" and "recovery of sight to the blind." Luke makes a specialty of the double mission of Jesus to heal both soul and body. In harmony with this conception it must be noted that Luke alone gives Christ's proverb, "Physician, heal thyself" (Luke 4 : 23). Galen speaks of a physician who should have cured himself before practising on his patients. The saying was evidently common with physicians and Christ's use of it interested Luke. We to-day say that a doctor ought to take his own medicine. The Chinese do not pay physicians

---

[1] βελόνη. A magic papyrus (*P.* Lond., 121, 442, 3 A. D.) has the more general use of the word.

[2] ῥαφίς.   [3] *Synoptic Gospels and Acts*, pp. 224 f.

if the patient gets sick, but only when he is well. The Christian doctor to-day in China has an open door to the souls of the people.

Luke uses a number of general expressions, as do the other Gospels, that picture the vast extent of Christ's work of healing (cf. Luke 4:40 f.; 5:15 f.; 6:17–19; 7:21; 13:32). He has six miracles not in the other Gospels, and all but one (the draft of fishes, 5:1–11) are miracles of healing (the son of the widow of Nain, 7:11–17; the woman with the spirit of infirmity, 13:10–17; the man with the dropsy, 14:1–6; the cleansing of the ten lepers, 17:11–19; the restoration of Malchus's ear, 22:51).

In each instance we see signs of the physician's love of details about the case and the cure. The son of the widow of Nain "sat up" in the bier like a patient in bed, to the consternation of the pall-bearers (Luke 7:15 f.). The word for "sat up"[1] is used by medical writers in the intransitive sense for sitting up in bed.[2]

In the case of the woman with the spirit of infirmity Luke gives an exact description of her disease (curvature of the spine) and of the cure in technical language: "She was bowed together,[3] and could in no wise lift herself up."[4] "And immediately she was made straight."[5] This verb is common in the Septuagint, but medical writers employ it for "to straighten, to put into natural position, abnormal or dislocated parts of the body."[6]

The "dropsical man"[7] (Luke 14:2) is described by a word that does not occur elsewhere in the New Testament, though this adjective as a substantive, as in Luke, "is the usual way in medical language of denoting a person suffering from dropsy."[8] Hobart cites examples from Hippocrates, Dioscorides, Galen.

[1] ἀνεκάθισεν. In a Christian letter of 4 c. A. D. we have ἀνακαθεσθεῖσα used of a convalescent woman who is still sickly. *P. Oxy.*, VI, 939, 25.

[2] Hobart, *Medical Language of St. Luke*, pp. 11 f. So Hippocrates (*Prænot.* 37) has ἀνακαθίζειν βούλεσθαι τὸν νοσέοντα τῆς νόσου ἀκμαζούσης.

[3] συνκύπτουσα.

[4] ἀνακύψαι. Note same root. For εἰς τὸ παντελές, see Heb. 7:25. There is a play on the words ἀνακύψαι and συνκύπτουσα. In Luke 21:28 Jesus employs ἀνακύψατε with ἐπάρατε. See *P. Par.*, 47, 23 ff. for similar use, "a very grandiloquent, but ill-spelt letter" (Moulton and Milligan, *Vocabulary of the Greek N. T.*, p. 35).

[5] ἀνωρθώθη. [6] Hobart, *op. cit.*, p. 22. [7] ὑδρωπικός.

[8] Hobart, *op. cit.*, p. 24.

In the healing of the lepers (Luke 17 : 11–19) Luke uses the ordinary term "leper,"[1] not "full of leprosy," as in 5 : 12. Hobart[2] thinks that Luke, by the use of these two ways of describing the disease that had three forms,[3] according to Hippocrates, means to draw a distinction in accord with the Hippocratic diagnosis. The ten lepers had the milder form of the disease.

It has already been stated that Luke first mentions the healing of Malchus's ear (Luke 22 : 51). Jesus "touched the ear, not the place where the ear had been" (Plummer, *in loco*), and thus Luke means to record the "solitary miracle of surgery" in the New Testament, again with the physician's interest in such a case. It was necessary for Jesus to undo the result of Peter's rash act to show that he was not the leader of dangerous persons.

Luke alone records the parable of the Good Samaritan (Luke 10 : 30–37) with its account of the care of the wounded traveller. Modern hospitals carry out the point of this story which caught Luke's heart, and largely because of what Jesus said. Hobart[4] quotes Galen as saying "that it was not unusual for persons when seized with illness on a journey to take refuge in inns. Galen, too, uses the word 'half-dead'[5] in describing their case." This word occurs here only in the New Testament (see 4 Macc. 4 : 11). But Wellhausen sets aside the medical details in the story by saying: "Into a wound one pours oil, but not oil and wine." But Wellhausen is set at naught by Hippocrates, who recommended for wounds "anointing with oil and wine."[6] Hobart[7] observes that "wine and oil were usual remedies for sores, wounds, etc., and also used as internal medicine." The words[8] for binding up, wounds, pouring, are all common as medical terms.

In the story of the Rich Man and Lazarus (Luke 16 : 19–31) a number of medical terms appear. Lazarus was "full of sores."[9] The word is peculiar to Luke in the New Testament,

---

[1] λεπρός.   [2] *Op. cit.*, p. 5.   [3] ἀλφός, λεύκη, μέλας.
[4] *Op. cit.*, p. 27.   [5] ἡμιθανής.
[6] Mosh. Mul. 656, ἀλείψας ἐλαίῳ καὶ οἴνῳ. See P. Petr., II, 25 (a)[13] for use of χρίσιν for "the lotion for a sick horse" (Moulton and Milligan, *Vocabulary*), in opposition to the view that ἀλείφω was used for profane anointing and χρίω for sacred uses only.
[7] *Op. cit.*, p. 28.   [8] καταδέω, τραῦμα, ἐπιχέω.   [9] εἱλκωμένος.

and is "the regular medical term for to be ulcerated."[1] Hippocrates has a treatise on "ulcers."[2] "The physician thinks
of the absence of medical help: the dogs licked his sores."[3]
The dogs gave "the only attention, and, so to speak, medical
dressing, which his sores received" (St. Cyril). The words
for "cool"[4] and being "in anguish"[5] are common in medical
writers, the latter for pain and the former for alleviation.

It is now evident that Luke has betrayed in his Gospel the
habits of mind of a physician. There is no straining after
effect in this argument. It is cumulative and overpowering.

4. *Medical Matters in Acts.*—How is it in the Acts? Does
Luke reveal his professional interest to the same extent here?
To this question we now turn. As in the Gospel, so in the
Acts, Luke has general statements concerning the great number of cures wrought by the Apostles in Jerusalem (Acts 5 : 16)
and by Paul in Ephesus (Acts 19 : 11). Harnack[6] thinks that
"this invariable disposition to see in the miracles of healing
the chief function of the mighty forces of the new religion,
and at the same time on each occasion to distinguish with
anxious care between ordinary sick folk and the 'possessed,'
points to a physician as the author." Ramsay[7] criticises Harnack for being "too purely verbal," and for having "too little
hold upon realities and facts" in his treatment of Luke. There
is something in this indictment, but Harnack sees clearly the
weight of Hobart's proof that a physician wrote the Gospel
and the Acts. Ramsay[8] is right, also, in seeing that Hobart's
proof stands in spite of his overstatements here and there.
"The valuelessness of one detail, the lightness of one stone,
does not take away from the strength and the weight of the
other details, though it may annoy and mislead the hasty
reader who judges by a sample, and by chance or design takes
the poorest." In cumulative evidence one feels the force of
the whole. In this argument we have simply selected a few of
the most striking examples given by Hobart. These hold true,
whatever is true of the rest. And these prove the point. ·

---

[1] Hobart, *op. cit.*, p. 31.   [2] ἕλκη (Luke 16 : 21).

[3] Harnack, *Luke the Physician*, p. 191.

[4] καταψύχω. Luke has four of these compounds which "were very much
used in medical language" (Hobart).

[5] ὀδυνῶμαι.   [6] *Luke the Physician*, p. 196.

[7] *Luke the Physician*, p. 59.   [8] *Ibid.*, p. 225.

When we come to details in Acts the story of the Gospel is repeated. In Acts 1:3 Luke alone in the New Testament has the word "proof"[1] which "was technically employed in medical language."[2] In fact, Dioscorides uses the word in his Proem to his work *De Materia Medica*. In familiar language "proof" and "sign"[3] were synonymous (*Wisd.* 5:11), yet Aristotle (*Rhet.* 1:2) makes the technical distinction which "was strictly maintained by medical men, although Luke may no doubt have met the word elsewhere."[4] One need not press this point nor the use of "wait for"[5] in 1:4, used only by Luke in the New Testament, and common in medical writings for awaiting the result of medicine or other medical treatment.[6] In Acts 1:18 the word for "headlong"[7] is peculiar to Luke and is common to medical writers in a technical sense. The word occurs in classical writers.

In Acts 3:7 f., Luke has a remarkable description of the sudden healing of the lame man. Note "ankle-bones"[8] which is found here alone in the New Testament and is the technical language of a medical man.[9] Besides, the word for "feet"[10] is unusual in this sense outside of medical works. The word for "received strength"[11] is common enough, but medical writers use it. Luke's word for "immediately"[12] is frequent in both Gospel and Acts, and in the great majority of instances he uses it concerning cases of healing or of death as it appears in medical writers.[13] Notice also Luke's interest in the proof of the sudden cure (leaping, standing, beginning to walk).

In Acts 5:5 and 10 Luke says that both Ananias and Sapphira "gave up the ghost."[14] He uses it also of the death of Herod Agrippa I (Acts 12:23). It occurs in Ezek. 21:7, but "seems to be almost confined to the medical writers, and very seldom used by them."[15] So in Acts 5:6 Luke has "wrapped him round"[16] or "shrouded him." This verb occurs only once in classical Greek in this sense of "shroud," but "in medical

---

[1] τεκμήριον.   [2] Hobart, *op. cit.*, p. 184.   [3] σημεῖον.
[4] Knowling, *Acts, in loco.*   [5] περιμένειν.
[6] Hobart, *op. cit.*, p. 184.   [7] πρηνής.
[8] σφυδρά.
[9] Hobart, *op. cit.*, pp. 34 f.; Knowling, *Acts, in loco.*
[10] βάσεις.   [11] ἐστερεώθησαν.
[12] παραχρῆμα.   Mark uses εὐθύς.
[13] Hobart, *op. cit.*, pp. 97 f.   [14] ἐξέψυξεν.
[15] Hobart, *op. cit.*, p. 37.   [16] συνέστειλαν.

language the word is very, frequent and its sense varied,"[1] for bandaging, binding, etc.

In the account of Saul's conversion Luke says (Acts 9:18) that "scales"[2] "fell"[3] from his eyes. Both words are peculiar to Luke in the New Testament, but are common in medical writers and in conjunction for the falling off of scales from the cuticle or any diseased part of the body.[4]

In the case of Æneas (Acts 9:33) Luke employs the same technical word for "sick of the palsy" that he has in the Gospel (5:18), but he also gives "a medical note of the length of time the disease had lasted"[5] (eight years), as he does in other cases: "The woman with a spirit of infirmity was eighteen years ill; the woman with an issue of blood twelve years; the lame man at the gate of the temple was forty years old, and his disease congenital."[6] Luke has four words[7] for "sick-bed," and this fact itself is remarkable. One for couch or bed, and two diminutives (peculiar to Luke in N. T.) from that and one for the pallet of the poorer classes. Æneas was lying on the pallet. In Acts 5:15 Luke notes that the sick were laid "on beds and pallets."[8] In Acts 10:10; 11:5; 22:17 Luke employs a word for "trance" (our "ecstasy"), common enough for "wonder," but Luke alone in the New Testament has it for vision or trance. It is frequent in medical works in this sense.

Hobart[9] notes that the "mist"[10] and darkness that fell on Elymas (Acts 13:11) was a distinct eye-disease. Galen uses the word for one of the diseases of the eye, and Dioscorides applies it to the cataract. It is not in the Septuagint, and Luke alone has it in the New Testament.

In the case of the lame man at Lystra (Acts 14:8) who was "impotent in his feet,"[11] Luke employs a word common enough in the sense of "impossible," but only here in the New Testa-

---

[1] Hobart, *op. cit.*, p. 38.			[2] λεπίδες.
[3] ἀπέπεσαν. In *P. Par.*, 47, 27 (B. C. 153) we have ἀποπίπτω in the sense of "collapse."
[4] Hobart, *op. cit.*, p. 39.			[5] Hobart, *op. cit.*, p. 40.
[6] *Ibid.*
[7] κλίνη, κλινάριον, κλινίδιον, κράββατος (pallet).
[8] ἐπὶ κλιναρίων καὶ κραβάττων.
[9] *Op. cit.*			[10] ἀχλύς.
[11] ἀδύνατος τοῖς ποσίν. In *P. Lond.*, 971, 4 (iii–iv A. D.) we have ἀδύνατος used of a woman who was not strong, διὰ ἀσθένειαν τῆς φύσεως.

ment in the sense of "impotent." Medical writers use it freely as Luke has it here.[1] One thinks of "foot-drop," "falling arch" and many other weaknesses of the foot.

In Acts 20 : 9–12 Luke twice observes that the lad was borne down by sleep, once by "deep sleep," like Galen and Hippocrates and other medical writers. Luke mentions also that there were "many lights" in the room. Hobart[2] thinks that the heat and oily smells helped to make the lad sleepy and not alone Paul's long sermon. He notes also that he fell from the third story and naturally was taken up dead. "They brought the lad alive." Luke was in the company and doubtless was one of the first to pick up the boy. He saw Paul heal the lad and was deeply impressed by the incident.

In Acts 21 : 1–10 several interesting items call for notice. Luke, like the barbarians, was interested in the fact that Paul did not fall down dead suddenly when bitten by the "viper" or "constrictor," which Ramsay[3] urges as the translation. Constrictors have no poison-fangs and do not technically bite, but they cling or "fasten on"[4] as this snake did to Paul's hand. The word ("fastened on") is peculiar to Luke in the New Testament, and is common in medical writers. "Dioscorides uses it of poisonous matter introduced into the body."[5] Ramsay insists that the constrictor, not the viper in the technical sense, alone occurs in Malta, and Luke uses a general term[6] once, and the word for viper[7] is not always strictly used. In any case Luke is in no trouble. The word for swelling[8] is also a medical term:[9] it is the usual word for inflammation. Besides, Luke's word for "expected"[10] is used eleven times by Luke and only five in all the rest of the New Testament. It is common in medical writers. And then Luke notes that the father of Publius had "fevers"[11] as well as dysentery. The word in the plural for one person is peculiar to Luke in the New Testament, but it is strictly medical, as in Hippocrates, who uses it in connection with dysentery, as Luke does here.[12] Luke alone uses this medical word also in the New Testament. It has

---

[1] Hobart, *op. cit.*, p. 46.
[2] *Ibid.*, p. 48.
[3] *Luke the Physician*, p. 63.
[4] καθῆψεν.
[5] Hobart, *op. cit.*, p. 288.
[6] θηρίον.
[7] ἔχιδνα.
[8] πίμπρασθαι.
[9] Hobart, *op. cit.*, p. 50.
[10] προσδοκώντων.
[11] πυρετοῖς.
[12] Hobart, *op. cit.*, p. 52.

been already observed that Luke employs one verb[1] for the miraculous cure of Publius by Paul and another[2] for the general practice of medicine in which he engaged. The rest came and received medical treatment at Luke's hands.

It is impossible in the light of the foregoing facts not to agree with Harnack[3] that the evidence is of "overwhelming force." The author of both the Gospel and the Acts was a physician. Even if Paul had not told us that Luke was a physician, we could now see it to be true. It is good to be able to see the facts. It is not claimed that Luke knew modern scientific theories, but that he had the spirit and method of the man of science of his day.

[1] ἰάσατο. [2] ἐθεραπεύοντο.
[3] *Luke the Physician*, p. 198.

CHAPTER VIII

A PHYSICIAN'S ACCOUNT OF THE BIRTH OF JESUS[1]

"The Holy Spirit shall come upon thee, and the power of the Most High shall overshadow thee" (Luke 1 : 35).

It is hard to overestimate the world's debt to Luke. But for Luke we should not have the Christmas story. How poor we should be without it.

1. *A Vital Element in Luke's History.*—It is manifest that the more we have stressed the general culture of Luke, his scientific training as a physician and his painstaking research as a historian, the more difficult it is to say that Luke just dumped in the story of Christ's birth because he picked it up and because he wished to have a fuller report than Mark had given. If "Luke is a historian of the first rank,"[2] he must be credited with a serious purpose in giving the account of the Virgin Birth of Jesus. "We can argue, then, with perfect confidence that Luke did not take the narrative of the birth and childhood of Christ from mere current talk and general belief."[3] To say that he was credulous and told legends about Zacharias and Elizabeth, Joseph and Mary, John and Jesus, is to fly in the face of Luke 1 : 1–4 and to brand Luke either as a hypocrite or an incompetent. Every man is a child of his time save Jesus, who is that and also the child of all time. In this discussion no claim is made that Luke is infallible or even inspired. It is only asked that all the facts involved be honestly faced.

One may pass by occasional bias, personal prejudice, or a slip now and then in a historian without throwing him to the discard, if one sees proof of these things. An occasional fly in the ointment can be discounted. But in a crucial matter like the birth of Jesus in Luke 1 and 2 one cannot overlook carelessness or credulity. "If a historian is convicted in a vital error on such a vital point, he ceases to be trustworthy

---

[1] See *Sunday School Times*, May 29, 1920.
[2] Ramsay, *Bearing of Recent Discovery*, p. 222.
[3] Ramsay, *Was Christ Born at Bethlehem ?*, p. 80.

on his own account."[1]   We cannot deny the fact that Luke, great historian and great physician as he was, soberly recorded the superhuman birth of Jesus.[2]   Luke reports that Jesus had a human mother, but not a human father.   This is the core of the problem but not all of it.   Luke likewise narrates the visits or visions of the angel Gabriel to Zacharias and to Mary.   He also tells the message of the angel of the Lord to the shepherds near Bethlehem and the song of the heavenly host and the visit of the shepherds to Mary and the child.   And then he records the prophetic insight of Simeon and Anna, besides the noble hymns of Elizabeth, Mary and Zacharias.   He has written these narratives with consummate care and skill.   One has only to turn to the silly legends about the birth of Jesus in the Nativity of Mary, the Pseudo-Matthew, the Arabic Gospel of the Infancy, the Protevangelium of James, the Gospel of Thomas, to see the restraint and simple dignity of Luke's narrative.   "The frigid miracle-mongering of the so-called Gospels of the Infancy, when compared with the transparent honesty and delicate reserve of our Evangelists, offers one of the most instructive contrasts in all literature."[3]

It is impossible to separate Luke the physician and Luke the historian.   It is the cultured Greek physician, the man of science, who contributes the story of the miraculous birth of Jesus.   It is easy enough to some to dismiss the whole story as due to heathen myth or Jewish legend, with the desire to satisfy devout demands for the deification of Jesus.   The Roman emperors were worshipped.   Why not attribute deity to Jesus?   But heathenism had no influence on Christianity thus early, and it was repellent to Judaism to worship Jesus.   Harnack[4] holds that one "must cherish serious doubts as to whether the idea of the Virgin Birth would have ever made its appearance

[1] Ramsay, ibid., p. 6.

[2] Some modern writers profess to see in Luke 1: 31–33 natural paternity and in 1: 34–35 supernatural causality, claiming that the original document gave only the first, while Luke added the second.   So Weiss in his ed. of Meyer, p. 303.   But that is purely hypothetical.   See Bruce, Expositor's Greek Testament, p. 465.   There is no doubt at all as to the genuineness of Luke 1: 34–35, since all the documents give it.   Here we have the view of Luke whatever was in the source (oral or written).   He attributes the origin of the birth of Jesus to the Holy Spirit, and calls the child the Son of God.

[3] J. Armitage Robinson, Some Thoughts on the Incarnation, p. 38.

[4] Date of the Acts and the Synoptic Gospels, p. 145.

on Jewish soil if it had not been for Isaiah 7 : 14." He thinks[1] that orthodox Jews may have brooded over the idea that the Mother of the Messiah was to be a virgin. At any rate Harnack is sure that Luke "could not have himself invented a fiction like this."[2] But "fiction" he takes it to be. Matthew Arnold[3] bluntly- asserts: "I do not believe in the Virgin Birth of Christ because it involves a miracle, and miracles do not happen." Thus science and history are turned against Luke's narrative. But scientists to-day are not so dogmatic against the possibility of miracle. The eminent scientist Professor Sir George Stokes says in the Gifford Lectures for 1891, p. 23: "If we think of the laws of Nature as self-existent and self-caused, then we cannot admit any deviation from them. But if we think of them as designed by a Supreme Will, then we must allow the possibility of their being on some particular occasion suspended." Miracle is difficult of definition. The English word is from the Latin *miraculum*, meaning a wonderful thing. But in the New Testament the word for wonder (*teras*) never occurs alone, but in connection with the words for mighty works (*dunameis*) and for signs (*semeia*). The New Testament conception of miracle is thus that it is something out of the ordinary, wrought by the special interposition of the Divine Will, for a high moral purpose. Sir Oliver Lodge (*Life and Matter*, p. 198) holds that life transcends and yet also combines and controls the physical forces of the world.

The point is not made here that one "must" believe in the Virgin Birth of Jesus or be damned. It is doubtful if the Twelve Apostles knew the facts about Christ's birth at first. Indeed, it cannot be positively proven that any of them ever became familiar with the facts about the Virgin Birth, unless the Apostle Matthew is the author of our Greek Gospel bearing his name and the Apostle John wrote the Fourth Gospel. Certainly they would not preach them during the lifetime of Mary out of regard for her. In the nature of the. case the subject

[1] *Ibid.*, p. 148.
[2] *Ibid.*, p. 155. Carpenter (*Christianity According to S. Luke*, p. 156) observes that "the Jews had no particular reverence for virginity. Isaiah's words were never regarded by the Jews as a prediction of Messiah's birth of a virgin." See also Box, *The Virgin Birth of Jesus*, p. 220. Philo's teaching is too vague and at most implies divine generation for the Messiah, not Virgin Birth.
[3] Preface to *Literature and Dogma*.

was not, and is not, one for public discourse. Jesus made no reference to the matter so far as we know. Soltau[1] is rather fierce in his protest: "Whoever makes the further demand that an evangelical Christian shall believe in the words 'conceived by the Holy Ghost, born of the Virgin Mary,' wittingly constitutes himself a sharer in a sin against the Holy Spirit of the true Gospel as transmitted to us by the apostles and their school." But surely Soltau is a bit excited in these words. The simple truth is that the only record in the Gospels gives the Virgin Birth. Mark begins with the public ministry and, of course, has nothing at all on the subject. John writes after Matthew and Luke and seems to refer to the Virgin Birth in John 1 : 14. The reference is certainly to the Incarnation and it is not inconsistent with the Virgin Birth. If it be asked why John makes no explicit mention of the Virgin Birth, it may be replied that he was content with what Matthew and Luke tell and saw no occasion to add to what they narrate. There are those who interpret John 1 : 14 as a denial of the Virgin Birth, but that surely is a misinterpretation of John's language. Both Matthew and Luke narrate the birth of Jesus as superhuman without a human father. They give independent narratives, but they agree on this crucial point.

We are concerned with Luke the physician. "Some day we may know how a Greek physician came to write the story of Bethlehem."[2] Luke as a physician had written his birth reports (and death reports), but never one like this. He knew the silly legends about the Cæsars and the Greek gods and goddesses. He has reverence for childhood and for motherhood. He has the soul of the saint and the insight of the scientist. He is perfectly conscious of the importance of this part of his story, but he is not posing. There are no stage theatricals as at the birth of Louis XIV at St. Germain. With matchless art he pictures the Babe in the manger at Bethlehem. We may be sure that this story came out of the Christian circle, out of the inner circle.

2. *Did Luke Believe His Narrative ?*—The question is quite pertinent. We are bound to say that he did. Harnack[3] has no doubt of Luke's sincerity. He clearly thinks that he is narrating facts, not pious legends. Harnack suggests that

---

[1] *The Virgin Birth*, p. 65.   [2] Naylor, *The Expositor*, 1909.
[3] *Date of the Acts and the Synoptic Gospels*, pp. 154 f.

Luke may have been an adherent of John the Baptist before he became a Christian, because of his knowledge of the birth of the Baptist. That is quite unlikely, and Luke's two years in Palestine, with headquarters at Cæsarea, offer abundant opportunity for obtaining such information. Luke tells the Christmas story with utter sincerity, sheer simplicity and transcendent beauty. Christianity thus owes Luke a tremendous debt. The influence of the first two chapters of Luke's Gospel on the race has been incalculable. So far from being a mere teller of old wives' fables in chapters 1 and 2, Ramsay[1] holds that "Luke attached the highest importance to this part of his narrative." "The elaboration and detail of the first two chapters of the Gospel form a sufficient proof that Luke recognized the importance of the central incident in them." We may argue, therefore, that as a historian of the first rank Luke took particular pains with the birth of Jesus. His reputation as a man of science was involved, as was his character as an honest historian. Whether he translated Aramaic documents or oral traditions or rewrote the whole in his own language, Luke makes himself responsible for the narrative.

It is inconceivable that he put in these stories without due reflection. He saw what was at stake and wrote them out deliberately. He would not have done so if he had considered them merely idle tales. He believed in the supernatural birth of Jesus. Was he incompetent? Was he superstitious? Was he credulous? Was he gullible? We may ask these questions if we will. But we are not at liberty to question Luke's intellectual honesty. He may have been mistaken. That is a matter of opinion. But, at least, he is entitled to be heard concerning the Virgin Birth of Jesus on the assumption of his own belief in that event with whatever weight his proved worth as an accurate historian and his opinion as a medical expert of his time may carry. Luke himself says "that he had investigated from their origin the facts which he is going to narrate."[2] "St. Luke has been proved to be a writer of great historical accuracy, and we may be certain that he admitted nothing within his record of which he had not thoroughly tested the truth."[3] The presumption, then, is in favor of the truthful-

[1] *Was Christ Born at Bethlehem ?*, p. 73.
[2] Ramsay, *Was Christ Born at Bethlehem ?*, p. 78.
Grierson, Hastings's *One Vol. B. D.*

ness of the Birth narrative so far as Luke's character as a
man and writer goes, unless, forsooth, the matter in question
is inherently impossible in itself. That condition we pass by
for the present, but it must be considered before we reach a
conclusion. For the moment Luke predisposes one to believe
his narrative.

3. *Where Did Luke Get His Information?*—In Chapter III,
The Sources of the Gospel, it was shown that Luke probably
obtained the facts about the birth of Jesus from Mary herself,
either directly or indirectly. It is quite possible that Mary
herself was still living in Palestine during the years 57 and 58,
when Luke was there.[1] If not, Luke could easily have talked
with some one who knew Mary's heart on this subject. Ramsay thinks that the directness of the whole story implies oral
origin rather than formal autobiography. "There is a womanly
spirit in the whole narrative, which seems inconsistent with
the transmission from man to man, and which, moreover, is
an indication of Luke's character: he had marked sympathy
with women."[2] It is impossible to think that Luke deliberately
attempted to create the false impression by literary skill that
Mary was the source of his knowledge.[3] There were only two
persons who knew the facts concerning the supernatural birth
of Jesus. These were Mary and Joseph.

At first Mary alone knew. But Joseph had to know if he
was to be the protector of his espoused wife. Matthew's report
is from the standpoint of Joseph, and it is plain that Joseph
was disposed to put Mary away privily instead of making her a
public example according to law and custom (Matt. 1:19).
It is not stated in Matthew whether Joseph simply became
suspicious or whether he disbelieved the story of Mary, though
it is implied that she did not tell for a while. Note "she was
found with child of the Holy Ghost" (Matt. 1:19). Certainly Mary's predicament was awkward and embarrassing in
the extreme. The appearance of the angel of the Lord to
Joseph was necessary to clear her in Joseph's eyes (Matt.
1:20-25). Then Joseph was willing to bear the obloquy of
public reproach with Mary and to shield her as his wife. It
is plain from both Matthew and Luke that, outside of Mary's
confidence to Elizabeth, they kept their secret to themselves.

---

[1] Ramsay, *Was Christ Born at Bethlehem?*, p. 88.   [2] *Ibid.*
[3] *Ibid.*, p. 78.

It is undoubted that the neighbors in Nazareth regarded Jesus as the son of Joseph and Mary. Talk would die down in the course of time. Joseph planned to go back to Bethlehem on his return from Egypt, possibly to avoid the gossip of Nazareth. But because of the change in Herod's will he came back to Nazareth, for Antipas was to be preferred to Archelaus (Matt. 11:22). Mary could carry her head erect, for she knew the facts and kept them hid in her heart (Luke 2:19, 51). It was enough that Joseph understood and trusted her. The effort of Herod to kill the Babe would close Mary's mouth all the tighter. Fortunately Mary would not hear all the talk which reappears even in the Talmud. Any claim on her part that her son was to be the Messiah would have made matters worse.

But was Mary to remain silent always? Did she not owe it to herself and to Joseph and to Jesus to tell the facts before she died? Both Mary and Joseph might die. Joseph apparently did die before the ministry of Jesus, but not before telling his story to some one, or drafting it so that Matthew ultimately got hold of it. Jesus was now dead. Elizabeth had long since died. Mary alone was left. She had a sacred responsibility to clear her own honor.[1] Clearly, then, sooner or later, Mary told some one, either her intimate friend Joanna, or Luke, the sympathetic physician who would understand her inmost heart. We can be grateful that she revealed the secrets of her soul. "In these chapters, in short, we seem looking through a glass into Mary's very heart. Her purity of soul, her delicate reserve, her inspired exaltation, her patient committing of herself into God's hands to vindicate her honor, her deep, brooding, thoughtful spirit—how truth-like and worthy of the fact is the whole picture."[2]

It is not hard to imagine the intense interest with which Luke first listened to this story from Mary or read her narrative of her unexampled experience. He satisfied himself of its truthfulness by all the tests that were open to him. His Greek science and Christian theology offered objections and raised difficulties, we may be sure. After accepting Mary's report of her experiences Luke was naturally anxious to do justice to Mary and to Jesus. Doctor Len G. Broughton, of Knoxville,

[1] Orr, *The Virgin Birth of Christ*, p. 86.
[2] *Ibid.*, p. 84.

himself long a physician of skill, remarked[1] to me that Luke
naturally gives Mary's version of the event because that is the
practice of the physician. He talks to the mother before he
makes his birth-report.

4. *But Why Did Luke Tell It At All ?*—Why not keep silent
on the subject as the Apostles did in their preaching and as
Mark did in his Gospel? It is customary to say that Luke
wished to write a complete life of Jesus and not a mere sketch
of his ministry and death, as Mark has done. It is more
complete but it is not a full life of Christ. Luke adds the
Birth narrative and gives only one glimpse of Jesus thereafter,
the visit to Jerusalem of the twelve-year-old boy, till his appearance by the Jordan. The crux of the matter is the supernatural birth of Jesus. He evidently felt that this must be told
whatever else was left out. And he naturally tells it first of
all.

It is usually said that the *Logia* of Jesus (Q) did not contain
an account of the birth of Jesus. This is probably true,
though it cannot be affirmed positively. Matthew and Luke
do, indeed, give different versions of the birth of Jesus, but it
does not follow that Luke was not acquainted with that of
Matthew. Q may very well have included matter that is
represented by either Matthew or Luke and not used by
both Gospels. Q was chiefly discourses. But both Matthew
and Luke, apart from Q, may have known the story from
Joseph's standpoint as Matthew tells it. It is wholly possible
that Luke knew the Gospel of Matthew. "It is now most
probable that Luke had heard the story which Matthew gives,
and it would have been easy to fit this into his own narrative
without disturbing either account. But they do not rest on
equal authority; and Luke would not mix the two."[2] If
Joseph's story was already known among the disciples and
written down in Q or in Matthew, all the more Luke would feel
called upon to give Mary's side of the story which had never
been written in a Gospel and which was not generally known
from the very nature of the case. He would do this with no
thought of reflection on or correction of the Joseph version.
Ramsay[3] thinks that he prefers Mary's version because he

---

[1] At Northfield, August, 1919.

[2] Ramsay, *Was Christ Born at Bethlehem ?*, p. 79.

[3] *Ibid.*

had it on the highest authority, from Mary herself. The confidence of Mary to Luke, if given personally, he took as a sacred trust.

It is plain that Luke's purpose is different from that of Matthew whether he had Matthew's story or not. Matthew writes to convince the Jews that Jesus is the Jewish Messiah. He gives the legal genealogy of Jesus through Joseph, his legal father, though it is made plain that Joseph is not the actual father of Jesus. Even the Sinaitic Syriac, which says in Matt. 1:16 that Joseph begat Jesus, contradicts that statement in 1:18-20 by retaining the conception of Jesus by the Holy Ghost and the refusal of Joseph to keep his troth with Mary till reassured by the angel of the Lord. It is evident that some scribe, probably Ebionite or Cerinthina Gnostic, changed the text in 1:16 to get rid of the superhuman birth and deity of Jesus, but failed to alter 1:18-20. The lineage of Joseph, given by Matthew, was the only way for Jesus to have a legal genealogy from the Jewish standpoint. But Luke is not writing to convince Jews that Jesus is the Jewish Messiah. He is writing for the Gentile world, to prove to all men everywhere that Jesus of Nazareth is the Saviour of the world. All that Matthew has about the birth of Jesus may be true, but it is beside the mark for Luke's purpose. Luke dedicates his Gospel to Theophilus, but he has his eye on the Græco-Roman world. Hence he gives the actual genealogy of Jesus through his mother Mary. He does not even combine her story with that of Joseph, but gives hers alone. The two accounts supplement each other in a way not possible if both are romances. "No two imaginary portraits ever agreed unless one copied the other—which is evidently not the case here."[1] Luke had lived in Macedonia, where women had more freedom than in most places at that time. Luke shows himself the friend of women both in the Gospel and in the Acts. So Luke has every reason for giving the story of the Nativity as he got it from Mary. His narrative comes from a woman who is Hebrew and who is saturated with Hebrew thought, spirit and imagery.[2]

It is sometimes objected that the Birth narratives in Luke and Matthew are legendary because they do not appear in

[1] Sweet, art. "Mary" in *Int. St. Bible Encycl.*
[2] Ramsay, *Luke the Physician*, p. 13.

Mark and John.   The objection about Mark is quite beside the point, since he begins with the Baptist's ministry.   His work is a torso.   As to John, the case is different.   John evidently was familiar with the accounts of both Matthew and Luke. "But John, in particular, assumes that his readers know the facts recorded in the Synoptic Gospels, and his work is an unintelligible phenomenon in literature unless this is recognized."[1]   It is a gross misunderstanding of John 1:14, "the Word became flesh,"[2] to say that John here ignores or denies the Virgin Birth of Jesus.   Indeed, his language only becomes intelligible when we see that he has that fact in mind.   John in his Prologue has given a philosophical statement of the Incarnation of Christ under the term Logos.   He has taken the *Mēmra* of the Hebrew, the Logos of the Stoics and Philo, the Virgin Birth of Jesus in Matthew and Luke, and has put them together in one grand conception on a par with the Jewish idea of Messiah.[3]   The Logos is personal and pre-existent and divine (John 1:1) before his Incarnation (1:14).   Thus he becomes "God only begotten" (1:18) and is in the bosom of the Father, the true Interpretation (Exegesis[4]) of the Father, the Son of God in the flesh.   Jesus is the Son of God (1:34, 49). Here John says nothing, it is true, about Mary, or Joseph, or the angel Gabriel, or the Holy Ghost.   He gives the picture of the eternal Son of God becoming flesh, not entering into flesh from the outside and not seeming to be flesh as the Docetics taught, but actual union of God and man.   Every word that John employs is in perfect harmony with the records in Matthew and Luke.   Indeed, by implication John denies that Jesus is the actual son of Joseph.

We do not know whether Paul was acquainted with the birth narrative in Luke's Gospel.   There is no reason for it

[1] Ramsay, *Was Christ Born at Bethlehem ?*, p. 98.

[2] ὁ λόγος σὰρξ ἐγένετο.

[3] If it be objected that John's failure to speak of the Holy Spirit shows that he did not believe that the Incarnation was due to the Holy Spirit, the answer is that by the same reasoning his failure to mention Mary here might show disbelief in her as the Mother of Jesus, but for later mention as his Mother.   What can be truthfully said is that the historical details of the birth of Jesus are not considered by John germane to his argument covering the Incarnation [of the Logos, a philosophical concept stated in broad general terms.

[4] ἐξηγήσατο.

not to be so if the Gospel was written in Cæsarea. He may or may not have heard of the Virgin Birth of Jesus before that time. In Gal. 4:4 Paul speaks of Christ as "born of woman," which, of course, is true of all men. But his language allows the Virgin Birth. In Romans 1:3 f. Paul presents the human nature of Christ, "who was born of the seed of David according to the flesh," and the divine nature also, "who was declared to be the Son of God with power," language certainly in harmony with the Virgin Birth. It cannot be complained that Paul gives no details on this subject. Why should he do so? The language of Paul is not decisive either way. It may well be that he knew nothing at all about the Virgin Birth though he says nothing that is inconsistent with it. If he was familiar with the narratives in Matthew or Luke or with the fact itself, there was no necessity for his use of the fact in connection with the Resurrection or with the doctrine of the Atonement. The real humanity and the real deity of Christ are the pertinent facts for Paul's argument. He was not giving infancy narratives, as Matthew and Luke did.

5. *Is the Virgin Birth Credible To-day?*—Can a modern man accept the story of the birth of Jesus? Each age is sure of itself and credulous of others. Our own is characterized by a species of cocksureness in its own wisdom that has no foundation in matter of fact. This question of the Virgin Birth of Jesus, attested by both Matthew and Luke in two independent narratives, has been attacked from every standpoint.

On scientific grounds it is argued that it is impossible. At least that argument was once made. Modern science is familiar with *parthenogenesis* or "virgin birth" in the lower forms of life.[1] Hence science cannot set aside the Virgin Birth of Jesus. However, Luke does not present the birth of Jesus as in accord with nature. He distinctly asserts that it was due to the overshadowing of Mary by the Holy Ghost, like the Shekinah or Presence of God. It is miracle that we have, not nature, but miracle cannot be ruled out unless it is ruled out everywhere. To do that rules out God and leaves

---

[1] See interesting article on "Parthenogenesis" in the *New International Encyclopædia*, where a fairly full discussion of the subject appears. The aphis (plant-louse), gall-gnats and other lower forms of animal life show examples of parthenogenesis. Loeb has succeeded in developing sea-urchins in unfertilized eggs by artificial stimulation.

us with materialism, the biggest miracle of all. Besides, men of science to-day do believe in the Virgin Birth of Jesus, just as Luke did before them. And he was also a man of science.

It is objected that Luke has simply followed blindly the heathen myths which tell of gods becoming men. Some have found analogues in Babylonian mythology, some in Greek mythology, some in Jewish theology. But none of them gives us a real Virgin Birth. They each contradict the other. No real connection · with Christianity is shown. "The Jewish theories confute the Gentile; the Gentile the Jewish; the new Babylonian theory destroys both and itself perishes with them."[1] Harnack,[2] who counts the story as legend, yet knocks the "myth" theories in the head: "Nothing that is mythological in the sense of Greek or Oriental myth is to be found in these accounts; all here is in the spirit of the Old Testament, and most of it reads like a passage from the historical books of that ancient volume."

It is objected that the very beauty and charm of Luke's narrative proves that it is all a legend. "That, as an *a priori* statement, I deny. S. Luke may be artistic, but so is God."[3] The point is that the persons and the poems in Luke 1 and 2 suit the actual events even better than they suit Luke's story. The steps of God have a rhythm that puts to shame our noblest measures. If God is at work in the birth of Jesus, everything else is simple enough. The supreme art of Luke lies in telling the story as it was. Ramsay[4] has biting sarcasm for critics that cannot be satisfied: "Luke has already been proved in the process of discovery to be correct in almost every detail of his statement" (in Luke 2:1-3). "The story is now established, and the plea now is that Luke's story is a legend because it is true to facts." We do not have to say that Luke had the same concepts that Mary had at each point. "That there was a more anthropomorphic picture of the messenger in Luke's mind than there was in Mary's I feel no doubt. Yet I believe that Luke was translating as exactly as he could into Greek that which he had heard. He expresses and thinks as a Greek that which was thought and expressed by a Hebrew."[5] I

[1] Orr, *The Virgin Birth of Jesus*, p. 181.
[2] *Date of the Acts and Synoptic Gospels*, p. 156.
[3] Carpenter, *Christianity According to S. Luke*, p. 166.
  Bearing of Recent Discovery, p. 226.
[5] Ramsay, *Luke the Physician*, p. 13. Cf. p. 255.

heartily agree with Carpenter[1] when he says of these events: "I believe that they were beyond the power of either Luke or Mary to invent, though their meaning was not beyond the power of Mary to apprehend. That experience, described so briefly, so simply, so plainly, yet without a single word that could offend the most delicate purity, I take to be the Conception of the Holy Child."

It is even objected that the silence of Jesus concerning his divine birth discredits the narrative in Matthew and Luke. That is an utterly absurd demand. From the nature of the case Jesus could not say anything on that subject. But when only twelve years old he does reveal a consciousness that God is his Father in a peculiar sense (Luke 2:49). He often insisted on this point (John 5:18; 8:19; 10:25) in a way to enrage his enemies, who finally accused him of blasphemy for this very thing (Matt. 26:63 f.).

It is not claimed that all the difficulty concerning the Virgin Birth of Jesus has been removed. We live in a world that has recovered the sense of wonder. The greatness of God overshadows all. The discovery of radium has made men of science humble. Astronomy has enlarged our ideas of God. Einstein has modified Galileo and Newton. Scientists gaze into the heavens with fresh awe. And even men to-day can fly in the air. Loeb claims that by artificial stimulus he has made fertile infertile eggs of some forms of sea-life (the sea-urchin). If Loeb can do this, cannot God? "God laid his hand on the deepest spring of man's being when His Son came to us 'conceived by the Holy Ghost, born of the Virgin Mary.'"[2] All things considered, it seems to me that the Virgin Birth of Jesus is overwhelmingly attested. We have seen the strength of the witness of Luke and the independent testimony of Matthew. John's Gospel really supports them. There is nothing contrary to this view in the New Testament save the erroneous reading of the Sinaitic Syriac for Matt. 1:16, which is itself contradicted by its own text for Matt. 1:18-20.

But the question goes deeper than the witness of documents or the interpretation of Luke. Carpenter[3] puts it fairly: "Matters of this sort, involving belief or disbelief in the doc-

[1] *Op. cit.*, p. 168.
[2] Father Paul Bull, *God and Our Soldiers*, p. 244.
[3] *Op. cit.*, p. 158.

trine of the Virgin Birth, are not determined, and cannot be determined, by sheer literary and historical criticism."

We are confronted by the fact of Christ, the most tremendous fact in human history. All efforts to prove that Jesus never lived, but is a myth, have failed signally. All efforts to separate "Jesus" and "Christ" have likewise failed from the days of Cerinthus with his "Æon Christ" coming upon "Jesus" at his baptism to the recent "Jesus or Christ" controversy.[1] The historic Jesus and the Christ of faith confront us in Mark and in Q (the Logia of Jesus), our earliest known documents concerning Jesus. Besides, Christianity is the vital force for human uplift in the world. Christ to-day is the hope of the race.

Thinking men have to account for the fact and the force of Christ. We have the view of Luke. It does account for the phenomenon of Jesus. If we reject it, we must have an alternative view. There are those who think that the natural birth of Jesus meets all the demands of a real Incarnation and who are disposed to reject the reports in Matthew and Luke as legends or myths. Every one must speak what he sees on this subject. For myself, apart from setting aside these two narratives and the consequent slur on Mary, who was not yet married, the philosophical difficulty is measurably enhanced by denial of the Virgin Birth. That view gives us the picture of a God-possessed man, but not quite the essential union of God and man. The Cerinthian Gnostic held that the divine Christ came upon the man Jesus at his baptism and left him on the Cross.

Carpenter[2] has no doubt that the "Incarnation principle is more clearly exhibited in the doctrine of a Virgin Birth than in any other." For myself I cannot conceive of a real Incarnation of God in any other way. Some men think that they can conceive of an Incarnation of God in Jesus even if Joseph was his actual father. They are certainly honest in their view, but it does not satisfy one. It greatly increases the difficulties for me. Sir W. F. Barrett[3] quotes F. C. S. Schiller as saying: "A mind unwilling to believe, or even undesirous to believe, our weightiest evidence must ever fail to impress. It will insist on taking the evidence in bits and rejecting item by item.

[1] Cf. *Hibbert Journal Supplement for 1909.*   [2] *Op. cit.*, p. 159.
[3] Preface to *On the Threshold of the Unseen.*

The man who announces his intention of waiting until a single bit of absolutely conclusive evidence turns up, is really a man *not* open to conviction, and if he be a logician, he *knows* it."

The testimony of Luke concerning the Virgin Birth of Jesus is part of the larger problem of Jesus as the Son of God in human flesh. That question raises the greatest of all issues, the fact and the nature of God, of man, of sin, of redemption,[1] of law, of miracle, of life, of matter, of spirit. The angel Gabriel said to Mary: "Wherefore also that which is to be born shall be called holy" (Luke 1:35). Peter says that "he did no sin" (I Peter 2:22). John asserts that "in him was no sin" (I John 3:5). Paul declares that "he knew no sin" (II Cor. 5:21). The author of Hebrews (4:15) says that Jesus was "without sin." Jesus himself claimed sinlessness (John 8:46). "This problem of an absolutely Holy One in our sinful humanity: How did it come about? Can nature explain it?"[2] Bruce[3] has the answer: "A sinless man is as much a miracle in the moral world as a Virgin Birth is a miracle in the physical world." It remains true that the best explanation of the whole truth about Jesus lies in the interpretation given by Luke in the opening chapters of his Gospel.

[1] The sinlessness of Jesus is not without moral value if he is God as well as man. He fought temptation, as we know, and kept himself free from sin. He had a clean start, and because of his sinlessness did not have to make atonement for sin of his own.

[2] Orr, *The Virgin Birth of Christ*, p. 191.

[3] *Apologetics*, p. 410.

CHAPTER IX

THE ROMANCE OF THE CENSUS IN LUKE'S GOSPEL [1]

"This was the first enrolment made when Quirinius was governor of Syria. And all went to enrol themselves, every one to his own city. And Joseph also went up from Galilee, out of the city of Nazareth, into Judea, to the city of David, which is called Bethlehem, because he was of the house and family of David; to enrol himself with Mary, who was betrothed to him, being great with child" (Luke 2 : 2-5).

Was Luke born in Bethlehem? Did the Romans have a periodical census? Was Quirinius twice governor of Syria? Is Luke a credible historian?

1. *A Crucial Passage.*—Luke 2 : 1-7 has been furiously assailed by the critics as a bundle of blunders, if not worse. "Wilcken speaks of the passage Luke 2 : 1-3 as 'the Lukan legend' (das Lukas-legende)." [2] The theological critics were more severe than historians like Mommsen and Gardthausen. It is only fair to say that we owe the clearing up of the complicated issues in this passage to Ramsay just as we can thank Hawkins and Harnack for strengthening the case for Luke's use of Mark and the Logia and Hobart for the light on the medical language of Luke. Ramsay [3] tells how a German critic sharply challenged his championship of Luke in *St. Paul the Traveller* by asking this query: "If Luke is a great historian, what would the author of this book make of Luke 2 : 1-3?" Ramsay adds that "nothing more was needed. This brief question was sufficient. It was at that time admitted on all hands that the statements in that passage are entirely unhistorical. Not only did theological critics brush them aside as incredible, every one that had any acquaintance with Roman imperial history regarded them as false and due either to blundering or to pure invention." [4] The issue was put up squarely to Ramsay, who had ranked Luke as a historian of the first rank. "A number of the German critics,

---

[1] The *Biblical Review*, October, 1920.
[2] Ramsay, *Bearing of Recent Discovery*, p. 225.
[3] *Bearing of Recent Discovery*, p. 223.   [4] *Ibid.*

followed by many outside of Germany, used until recently to say without hesitation that Augustus never issued any decree ordering a census, that there never was under the empire any regular system of census, that where any casual census was held the presence of the wife was not required but only of the husband, and that his presence was never required at his original home."[1] Luke said all these things which the modern critics flatly deny.

Who is right, Luke or the critics? The unfair attitude toward Luke has been the assumption that he was bound to be wrong because he stood unsupported by other ancient authorities. It is not so much that they contradict Luke as that they do not give the items that he records. It is coolly assumed that Luke is of no value as a historian when he stands alone. As a matter of fact, it is precisely when the historian stands alone that his real worth as a writer is put to the test. We see then whether he is a mere traditionalist or has made original investigation for the facts. "Their hostility to Luke arose out of their refusal to admit the superhuman element in the government of the world."[2] This prejudice led Baur and the Tübingen school to deny that Luke wrote the Gospel and the Acts and to claim that the books were late party pamphlets of the second century.

Even now the same distrust of Luke as a reliable writer survives on the part of some who accept the Lukan authorship and the early date of both Gospel and Acts. There is a distinct "return to tradition" on both these points, a movement led by Harnack and followed by men like Kirsopp Lake and C. C. Torrey. "The real significance of the 'return to tradition' in literary criticism consists in the support that it affords to those who have not decided to reject the supernaturalistic view of Christian origins."[3] The great majority of radical critics have refused to follow Harnack in his conclusions about Luke's writings. Those who do follow him refuse to admit the reality of the miraculous element. But it has become difficult to discredit Luke on that ground if he wrote within twenty years of the events.

[1] *Ibid.*, p. 225.

[2] *Bearing of Recent Discovery*, p. 225.

[3] Machen, "Recent Criticism of the Book of Acts" (*Princeton Review*, October, 1919, p. 592).

But did Luke make a bad bungle of the facts in the Gospel 2 : 1–7? To the testimony let us turn.

2. *The Two Bethlehems.*—It is actually charged that Luke has confused the Bethlehem in Galilee (Zebulon) about seven miles northeast of Nazareth with Bethlehem of Judea. Usener makes this charge[1] and urges also that the author of the Fourth Gospel (7 : 41 f.) was ignorant of the fact that Jesus was born in Bethlehem of Judea. This is surely a curious argument when the people in John 7 : 42 quote the passage in Micah 5 : 2 with the prophecy that the Messiah was to be born there. There are two Bethlehems,[2] to be sure, but it does not follow that Luke is wrong. He is supported by Matt. 2 : 6. The two distinct traditions (from Joseph and from Mary) locate the birth of Jesus at Bethlehem in Judea. It is true that Mark is silent as he is about the fact of the birth itself. We have seen that John[3] assumes a knowledge of Matthew and Luke. But for Matthew and Luke one might suppose (cf. Luke 2 : 39) that Jesus was born at Nazareth. But Luke is held to be discredited on this point because of his alleged blunders concerning the census and Quirinius, but without any real basis in fact.

3. *"The Whole World."*—Luke is charged with historical looseness in saying that "all the world"[4] was to be enrolled. He might at least be allowed the use of a harmless hyperbole in the popular language of the time. Surely, no one would accuse Luke of meaning that Augustus meant his decree to apply to India and China or even to Parthia and western Germany, where Rome did not rule. The civilized world at that time was the Roman world, the Mediterranean world. Luke reports the Jewish rabbis in Thessalonica as accusing Paul and his company of having "turned the world upside down" (Acts 17 : 63), meaning, of course, the Roman Empire. Demetrius in Ephesus called a meeting of the workmen and roused them to fury by saying that Paul brought into disrepute the worship of Diana, "whom all Asia and the world worshippeth" (Acts 19 : 27). It is pettifogging criticism to pick at Luke's language in the Gospel (2 : 1) on this point.

[1] *Encycl. Biblica.*
[2] Cf. Sanday, *Sacred Sites of the Gospels*, p. 25.
[3] Ramsay, *Was Christ Born at Bethlehem ?*, p. 98.
[4] πᾶσαν τὴν οἰκουμένην.

4. *Herod's Kingdom.*—Ramsay[1] makes a sober argument to prove from Strabo and Appian that the subject or vassal kingdoms were as really under the Roman rule as the provinces (imperial and senatorial). It is perfectly plain that the kingdom of Herod in Palestine was required to pay tribute to Rome, but critics deny that the decree of Augustus applied to Syria, and if it did, not to Palestine. Herod was in high favor with Augustus, but he came near losing his crown and his head when he sent Nicolaus of Damascus to Augustus, to defend him against the charge of treason against Rome made by Syllæus in the matter of the Arabian uprising.[2] Herod was, after all, only a vassal king. Herod knew after that beyond question that his was a dependent kingdom, as were all kingdoms in the Roman Empire. But if the order of Augustus for a general census came shortly after his estrangement, Herod would naturally be a bit reluctant to respond readily. It was a bitter pill, no doubt, for Herod and for the Jews to swallow, for it was a public and general acknowledgment of subjection to Rome.

5. *The Census.*—In particular it has been objected that Augustus never ordered a general census of the empire. Ramsay[3] is careful to note precisely what Luke does say. He does not represent Augustus as ordering "that a single census should be held of the whole Roman world," but "there went out a decree from Cæsar Augustus that all the world should be enrolled."[4] Ramsay properly insists on the present tense of "should be enrolled." Malalas[5] wrongly uses the aorist tense in referring to what Luke says. "It is not stated or implied by Luke that the system was actually put into force universally. The principle of universal enrolments for the empire was laid down by Augustus; but universal application of the principle is not mentioned. That point was a matter of indifference to Luke."[6] But, while this is true, the natural inference from Luke's words is that the principle was applied and that there was a regular system of periodic censuses not only

---

[1] *Was Christ Born at Bethlehem ?*, pp. 118–124.
[2] Cf. Josephus, *Ant.* XV, x.
[3] *Was Christ Born at Bethlehem ?*, p. 123.
[4] ἐξῆλθεν δόγμα παρὰ καίσαρος Αὐγούστου ἀπογράφεσθαι πᾶσαν τὴν οἰκουμένην.
[5] Quoted by Ramsay, *ibid.*, p. 124.   ἀπογραφῆναι.
[6] Ramsay, *Was Christ Born at Bethlehem ?*, p. 125.

for Syria and Palestine, but for the whole of the empire. Besides, we now know, what Ramsay did not in 1898, that Augustus's bold governmental plan for a census was successful. We have evidence for its operation in both West and East, though most for the East.[1]

But twenty years ago we had no knowledge of such a periodical census system in the Roman Empire. "The idea that such a system could have existed in the East, without leaving any perceptible signs of its existence in recorded history, would have been treated with ridicule, as the dream of a fanatical devotee, who could believe anything and invent anything in the support of the testimony of Luke."[2] But epigraphic and archæological research has proven this very thing, and Luke stands vindicated before all the world against a generation of infallible critics who applied the argument from silence against him with deadly effect. Was there such a periodical enrolment in the Syrian province? Was Christ born at Bethlehem at the time of the first of the series? Ramsay[3] frankly admits that Luke's "credit as a historian is staked on this issue." Luke not only speaks of "the first enrolment"[4] in Luke 2:2, but in Acts 5:37 he speaks of "the days of the enrolment."[5] In Acts 5:37 Luke means by "the census" the great census, "the epoch-making census taken about A. D. 7, when Judea had just been incorporated in the Roman Empire as part of the province of Syria."[6] Luke is clearly committed to the idea of a distinction between the first census in Luke 2:2 and the great census in Acts 5:37. Is he correct?

The proof is at hand. Ramsay[7] shows that already Clement of Alexandria "knew of some system of enrolment, either in the empire as a whole, or at least in the province of Syria. His

---

[1] Ramsay, *Bearing of Recent Discovery*, p. 246.

[2] Ramsay, *Was Christ Born at Bethlehem?*, p. 126.

[3] *Ibid.*, p. 127.

[4] ἀπογραφὴ πρώτη. A very large number of the papyri are census papers. The oldest certainly dated is probably A. D. 34, but *P. Oxy.*, II, 254 "probably belongs to A. D. 20" (Moulton and Milligan, *Vocabulary*, p. 60). Grenfell and Hunt think that *P. Oxy.*, II., 256 may even belong to A. D. 6. A very early instance of the annual household enrolment, κατ' οἰκίαν ἀπογραφή, is seen in *P. Petr.*, III, 59 (d), of the Ptolemaic period.

[5] ταῖς ἡμέραις τῆς ἀπογραφῆς

[6] Ramsay, *Was Christ Born at Bethlehem?*, p. 127.

[7] *Ibid.*, p. 128. Clement's words (*Strom*, I, 21, 147) mean this: ὅτε πρῶτον ἐκέλευσαν ἀπογραφὰς γενέσθαι.

use of the plural and the word 'first' force this inference upon us." Clement of Alexandria lived, of course, in Egypt and knew conditions there. Did he have any other information than that which Luke gives us? He makes the definite statement that the system of enrolments in Syria began with the one at which the birth of Jesus took place.[1]

It had been suggested that the "Indictional Periods" of fifteen years, known in the fourth century (see Rainer Papyri), began with the first census of Quirinius.[2] If so, the first census would come B. C. 3. But three scholars,[3] one after the other, made the discovery that fourteen years was the cycle for the enrolments in Egypt in the early Roman empire. The same Greek word occurs in the papyri that Luke employs for "enrolment."[4] The actual census papers have been found for these enrolments in Egypt. "It is proved that enrolments were made for the years ending in the summer of A. D. 90, 104, 118, 132 and so on till 230."[5] No papyrus as yet shows a census for A. D. 76 under Vespasian, but it is obvious that one was held.

"Actual census papers have been found of the periodic year 62 (and also 34) after Christ. Indirect references occur to the census of A. D. 20 and 48. Grenfell and Hunt rightly argue that Augustus must have originated this cycle. Beyond this there is no certainty, and we must await the discovery of fresh material."[6] The next census would be A. D. 6, the one that Luke mentions in Acts 5:37. The first census (Luke 2:2) would then come B. C. 8. An enrolment paper has been found in Egypt with the same officials that belong to the sixth year of Tiberius. "Hence the paper belongs to the census of A. D. 20 and proves conclusively my theory as to the origin of the Periodic Enrolments from Augustus."[7] Surely, after the overwhelming evidence of the papyri on the periodical enrolments in Egypt, one hardly has the hardihood to accuse Luke of error in mentioning the first two, for which as yet we have

[1] Ramsay, *Was Christ Born at Bethlehem ?*, p. 129.
[2] *Ibid.*, p. 130.
[3] Kenyon, *Classical Review*, March, 1893, p. 110; Wilcken, *Hermes*, 1893, pp. 203 ff.; Viereck, *Philologus*, 1893, pp. 219 ff.
[4] ἀπογραφή.
[5] Ramsay, *Was Christ Born at Bethlehem ?*, p. 132.
[6] Ramsay, *Bearing of Recent Discovery*, p. 256.
[7] Ramsay, *Was Christ Born at Bethlehem ?*, p. x.

no papyri data. The inference is now wholly on Luke's side and in his favor. The Augustan census system[1] has been established by irrefragable evidence.

It is true that B. C. 8 comes too soon for the other evidence for the birth of Jesus, which points to B. C. 6–5 as the probable time. But it has to be remembered that in Egypt and Asia Minor the year began, not January 1, as in Rome, "but on some day in the late summer and autumn."[2] We have seen that Herod sat uneasily on his throne in Judea. He had to please both Augustus and the Jews. The Jews hated the Roman yoke and Roman customs and held tenaciously to their own traditions. The second census after the deposition of Archelaus in A. D. 6 caused incipient insurrection against Rome, as Josephus tells us (*Ant.* XVIII, 1 : 1). Hence it is more than probable that the census was slow in moving off in Palestine. Herod would postpone it as long as he could and until brought to time by Augustus. The first census, besides, would be harder to execute on time. Ramsay[3] tells us that "the first enrolment in Syria was made in the year 8–7 B. C., but a consideration of the situation in Syria and Palestine about that time will show that the enrolment in Herod's Kingdom was probably delayed for some time later." Besides, Herod was probably a year or more in putting it through after it was started in Palestine. There is, therefore, no real difficulty as to the date. The new discoveries concerning the cycle of the Augustan census will allow a date around 6–5 B. C., and that is in accord with what we know otherwise concerning the date of Christ's birth. Turner in his article on "Chronology of the New Testament" (Hastings's *Dictionary of the Bible*) concludes by five converging lines of evidence that 7–6 B. C. is the probable date of the birth of Jesus. Luke has met a triumphant vindication in the fact of the census cycle under Augustus and Christ's birth at the time of the first. But the critics are not yet done with this famous passage in Luke 2 : 1–7.

6. *The Enrolment by Households.*—Luke says (2 : 3): "And all went to enroll themselves, every one to his own city." It is charged that, even if there was a Roman census by Augustus,

---

[1] Ramsay devotes Chap. XX to this subject (*Bearing of Recent Discovery*, pp. 255–274).

[2] Ramsay, *Bearing of Recent Discovery*, p. 255.

[3] *Was Christ Born at Bethlehem?*, p. 174.

the people would not have to go to their homes for the enrolment to be made. And even if Joseph went, he did not have to take Mary, "to enrol himself with Mary who was betrothed to him" (2:5). So the critics made merry with Luke's pious fiction and legend to make it appear that Jesus was born at Bethlehem in Judea instead of in Nazareth.[1] Plummer in his great *Commentary on Luke* in 1896 stands by Luke's veracity, though he is not able to show that it is true (p. 46): "How Bethlehem came to be the Birthplace of Jesus Christ, although Nazareth was the Home of His Parents. This explanation has exposed Luke to an immense amount of criticism, which has been expressed and sifted in a manner that has produced a voluminous literature."

But once again Luke is vindicated in his view that it was a household enrolment. The periodic enrolment shown in Egypt[2] was by households. The Romans had the annual enrolments for property valuations as we do, but every fourteen years the enrolment by households took place, like our ten-year census, in which one "gave a complete enumeration of all individuals who lived in the house, children, relatives, etc. In one case twenty-seven persons are enumerated in one paper by a householder."[3]

But why did Joseph and Mary and all the rest go to their homes? We take our census in the homes as the Romans did. Well, for one thing, it was done in Egypt. In Deissmann's *Light from the Ancient East* (1910, tr., pp. 268 ff.) the proof is found "that this was no mere figment of St. Luke or his authority, but that similar things took place in his age." Deissmann adds: "Perhaps the most remarkable discovery of this kind in the new texts is a parallel found some time ago to the statement in Luke 2:3, which has been so much questioned on the strength of mere book learning." It is an edict of G. Vibius Maximus, governor of Egypt, 104 A.D.: "The enrolment by household being at hand, it is necessary to notify all who for any cause are outside their homes to return to their domestic hearths, that they may also accomplish the customary dispensation of enrolment and continue steadfastly in the husbandry

---

[1] So Loisy, *Les Évangiles synoptiques*, I, p. 169, calls it "un anachronisme" "pour faire naître le Christ dans la patrie de David."

[2] The title is always ἀπογραφὴ κατ' οἰκίαν.

[3] Ramsay, *Was Christ Born at Bethlehem ?*, p. 146.

that belongeth to them." This is certainly a most amazing vindication of the record in Luke. Deissmann (p. 269) comments on the "cultural parallelism between Egypt and the birthplace of Christianity."

It is really not necessary to give further proof of Luke's accuracy on this score. But Ramsay makes a sharp distinction between the enrolment in Luke 2:1-7 and that in Acts 5:37. The latter was a census and a valuation of property because Palestine was now in A. D. 6 made a Roman province. "But the census of Herod was tribal and Hebraic, not antinational. It was wholly and utterly unconnected with any scheme of Roman taxation."[1] The "Roman census would be made according to the existing political and social facts, and would not require that persons be enrolled according to their place of birth or origin."[2] We have only to think that Herod agreed to the first census on condition that it be a tribal census of the various families, a thing that the Jews were used to and would not resent so much. "And Joseph also went up from Galilee, out of the city of Nazareth, into Judea, to the city of David, which is called Bethlehem, because he was of the house and family of David" (Luke 2:4). If that system of household enrolment with the "return to their domestic hearths" was allowed in Egypt, it would surely not be refused in Palestine. The proof, once more, is complete. Luke has not made up his facts to suit a theory. He has told the facts as they occurred and has given the precise reason for the journey of Joseph from Nazareth to Bethlehem, "because he was of the house and family of David." The enrolment in Palestine is both by household (the Roman method) and by tribes (the Jewish).

But it is still objected that Mary need not have gone along with Joseph. "It remains difficult to understand why Mary should have accompanied Joseph, especially if it be a fact that she was at that time only 'betrothed' to him."[3] Luke does not plainly say that Mary was enrolled with Joseph, though that is the natural way to take his language "to enroll himself with Mary."[4] The Sinaitic Syriac manuscript does say,

---

[1] Ramsay, *Was Christ Born at Bethlehem?*, p. 108.   [2] *Ibid.*, p. 106.

[3] Carpenter, *Christianity According to S. Luke*, p. 153.

[4] ἀπογράψασθαι σὺν Μαριάμ. Plummer (*Comm.*, p. 52) says that σὺν Μαριάμ must be taken with ἀνέβη, three lines away. But that is wholly unnatural.

"because they were both of the house of David." That I believe to be the fact. I think also that Luke gives the genealogy of Mary, while Matthew gives that of Joseph. At any rate Mary "would be anxious at all risks not to be separated from Joseph," and "after what is related in Matt. 1:19 he would not leave her at this crisis."[1] It is pertinent also to think that both Joseph and Mary would be anxious for the child to be born in Bethlehem, since he was to be the Messiah of promise. Before the birth of Queen Victoria her father made it a point to get the mother back on English soil, so that the possible heir to the British crown should be born in Britain. Ramsay[2] thinks that "the wife, as well as the head of the house, had to go to the proper city (or for some reason felt it her duty to go), so that the household as a whole might be numbered in the tribal and family centre." Certainly, these are reasons enough to justify Mary in her course. But, alas, Wilcken calls the narrative a legend, "because every detail has been demonstrated to be historically correct. There is no way of satisfying those people who have made up their minds."[3]

7. *The Problem of Quirinius.*—This has been the hardest tangle to unravel of all in the tissue of errors woven round Luke 2:1-7. Luke seemed so obviously in error. "This was the first enrolment made when Quirinius was governor of Syria" (Luke 2:2). He himself in Acts 5:37 refers to "the enrolment" when Judas of Galilee rose up and drew away some of the people after him and perished. We know that Quirinius was governor of Syria in A. D. 6, when that census was taken which so angered the Jews (Josephus, *Ant.* XVIII, i, 1). Hence it was argued that Luke simply blundered and dated this census under Quirinius at the time of the birth of Christ, instead of A. D. 6. Lake[4] actually argues that the birth of Jesus occurred A. D. 6, but that view is wholly unlikely to win favor. Plummer[5] says about Quirinius: "We must be content to leave the difficulty unsolved," but he considers it "monstrous" to throw away the whole narrative because of this "mistake as to Cyrenius."

[1] Plummer, *Comm.*, p. 53.
[2] *Was Christ Born at Bethlehem?*, p. 101.
[3] Ramsay, *Bearing of Recent Discovery*, p. 273.
[4] The *Expositor*, Nov., 1912, pp. 462 f.   [5] *Comm.*, p. 50.

It is Ramsay again who has cleared the matter of confusion by a series of inscriptions that bear on the career of Quirinius. "The conclusion of Mommsen, of Borghesi, and of de Rossi, that Quirinius governed Syria twice has been generally accepted by modern scholars."[1] The *"Lapis Tiburtinus"* is accepted as referring to Quirinius,[2] and contains the words *"iterum Syriam,"* "a second time Syria." The Inscriptions of Æmilius Secundus (*Lapis Venetus*)[3] have "*P. Sulpicio Quirinio legatus Augusti Cæsaris*" and "*idem jussu Quirini censum.*" It is not clear to which of the two times when Quirinius was governor in Syria this inscription about the census refers.

But Ramsay[4] gives an inscription from Antioch in Pisidia, examined by himself in 1912 and in 1913 and photographed by Lady Ramsay, which speaks of Gaius Coristanius Fronto as "*prefect of P. Sulpicius Quirinius duumvir.*"[5] This inscription belongs to the date B. C. 10–7. In the village of Hissarardi, close to Antioch, Ramsay found another inscription[6] where the same man is called "*prefect of P. Sulpicius Quirinius duumvir*" and "chief of engineers, tribune of soldiers, prefect of a Bosporan cohort," and also "prefect of M. Servilius." This inscription shows "Quirinius as engaged in the war (the Homonadensian War), and therefore as governor of Syria before 6 B. C." "It is also a crowning step in the proof that the story in Luke 2:1–3 is correct." The proof is complete that Quirinius was twice "governor" in Syria, though not necessarily in the same way each time. Luke does not say that Quirinius was propraetor or procurator in the first census, but only governor.

"Thus Quirinius and Servilius were governing the two adjoining provinces, Syria-Cilicia and Galatia, around the year 8 B. C., when the First Census was made."[7] Surely, it is a remarkable demonstration. "The exact year is a matter of chronological interest; it was in the reign of King Herod. Every circumstance narrated by Luke has been conclusively shown to be natural and probable. The circumstances are those which ordinarily accompanied a Roman census, and

---

[1] Ramsay, *Was Christ Born at Bethlehem?*, p. 109.
[2] Ibid., p. 273.
[3] Ibid., p. 274.
[4] Ramsay, *Bearing of Recent Discovery*, p. 285.
[5] *Præfecto P. Sulpici Quirini duumviri.*
[6] Ibid., p. 291.
[7] Ramsay, *Bearing of Recent Discovery*, p. 300.

Quirinius was in office about that time for several years."[1]
For all these years the record in Luke 2:1-7 has stood all by
itself, the butt of ridicule by historians and theologians. Now
the rubbish-heaps of Egypt and the stones of Asia Minor cry
aloud in support of the narrative. The enemies of Luke are
put to rout.

But it may still be said that Tertullian (*Adv. Marc.*, iv, 19)
states that Jesus was born when Sentius Saterninus was governor of Syria (B. C. 9-6). But Ramsay has a ready solution
for this objection. He admits that Tertullian attempts to
correct Luke because "the first periodic enrolment of Syria
was made under Saterninus in B. C. 8-7. The enrolment of
Palestine was delayed by the census described until the late
summer or autumn of B. C. 6. At that time Varus was con-
trolling the internal affairs of Syria, while Quirinius was con-
trolling its armies and directing its foreign policy." Tertullian
"inferred too hastily" that the enrolment in Palestine was
made under Saterninus. "Luke, more accurately, says that
the enrolment of Palestine was made while Quirinius was act-
ing as leader in Syria." Once it seemed a hopeless task to
clear up all the blunders charged against Luke in these verses.
But it has been done. If Ramsay had done nothing else for
New Testament scholarship, his name would deserve to be
cherished wherever Luke is known and loved. Luke is shown
to be the careful and accurate historian that he professed to
be. There is a veritable romance in the discovery of scraps
of papyri in Egypt that confirm Luke concerning the census
system of Augustus, which is ignored by all the ancient historians except Luke, the greatest of them all.

[1] *Ibid.*, p. 293.

CHAPTER X

A PHYSICIAN'S REPORT OF THE MIRACLES OF JESUS[1]

"And he that was dead sat up, and began to speak. And he gave him to his mother" (Luke 7 : 15).

There is no doubt that the miracles of Jesus greatly attracted Luke. Was he credulous in his report of the wonders wrought by Jesus? They puzzle us and they probably puzzled him. We do not have to think of miracle as a violation of the laws of nature. God is the source of all power and of all the laws of nature. They are all expressions of his will. If a personal God controls the universe, there is no real objection to believing that he can do what he wills to do at any time. The modern theory of evolution is not less, but more, favorable to the belief in miracle (Garvie, Hastings's *One Vol. Dict. of the Bible*). Sanday says: "I fully believe that there were miracles in the age of the Gospels and Acts, in the sense of 'wonderful works' or 'mighty works.' But I do not think that they involve any real breach of the order of nature" (*Divine Overruling*, p. 66). He thinks that miracles can be explained as all in harmony with laws of nature, that were once unknown, except those that have been exaggerated in the telling. It is not necessary for us to be able to explain the miracle in order for it to be true. We must remember that God is greater than the laws of nature and that our knowledge of nature and of God is still very limited. It is doubtless true that some miracles then would not be called miracles by us to-day. The heart of the question is whether God ever interposes at all with his personal will. I believe that he does and that is miracle.

1. *Luke a Man of Science.*—This point has been made before, but it is well to stress it again just here, for the fact has been often overlooked. Luke's witness to the miracles of Jesus has been brushed aside as the credulous ignorance of a non-scientific age. Each age plumes itself upon the scientific progress over the rest. The word science is simply Latin for the Greek *gnosis*, our knowledge. Progress in knowledge has not been

[1] The *Christian Worker's Magazine*, June, 1920.

steady and uninterrupted and uniform.   Reactions and lapses come.   The Renaissance followed the Dark Ages.   The Dark Ages belong to the Christian era and succeeded a period of pagan enlightenment.   We must not forget that Plato and Aristotle lived long before Luke's day.   In the spring and summer semester of 1905 at the University of Oxford over a hundred courses of lectures on Aristotle were offered.   Aristotle is still king in the realm of pure intellect.   The late Doctor W. H. Whitsitt, for long Professor of Church History and then President of the Southern Baptist Theological Seminary, used to talk to his classes of the time when "Plato was king in Zion" and then of the time when "Aristotle was king in Zion." Both Plato and Aristotle have left their mark on Christian thought.

Not simply was Luke a man of general culture, a university man familiar with current literature and literary methods, but he was a man of technical training.   Since Hobart's researches concerning the medical language of Luke, it is no longer possible to treat Luke as a "quack," a charlatan, or an ignorant practitioner.   He was a trained physician like Galen and Hippocrates, and is one of the best products of Greek culture.   So far as we know, he was the first man of science to grapple with the facts and forces of faith and science.   He was superbly equipped for his task.   He had a passion for the truth, for the facts of nature and of grace.   "No other man of his time was so well fitted to judge rightly in questions involving both science and faith; and this ability sprang from the nature of his vivid and varied Greek mentality."[1]   So then we approach Luke's report of the miracles of Jesus with sincere interest.   "His testimony to the miracles is, therefore, the nearest thing possible to the evidence which has often been desired in that of a man of science."[2]

And yet Luke is discounted by some for the very reason that he is a physician.   So Harnack[3] instances the healing of Malchus's ear as a case in point: "This is a flagrant instance of the way in which a story of a miracle has arisen, and of what we expect from Luke.   He certainly is not following a separate source here; but because he thinks it ought to have been so,

[1] Homan, *Luke the Greek Physician*, p. 12.
[2] Wace, *Intr. St. Bible Encycl.* (art. "Miracles").
[3] *Luke the Physician*, p. 187, note 4.

he makes it happen so." That is simply intolerable in Harnack. Luke is here ranked no higher than a peddler of tales or a writer of mediæval miracle-plays, or a dispenser of marvellous cures by a group of "Christian Science" dupes. When Luke has been vindicated by modern research against the whole array of historians and critics who attacked Luke 2:1-7, he is entitled to be heard on his own account before it is assumed that he is incompetent and insincere and even hypocritical. Percy Gardner[1] follows the cue of Harnack and says: "But when we speak of him as a physician, the modern mind is apt to be misled, and to attribute to him a scientific education, and methods of investigation such as are commonly used in the great schools of medicine. From this point of view our author is very far removed." Luke, to be sure, did not know the evolutionary hypothesis or the germ theory of disease, but he did have the Greek physician's love of the study of actual cases and of drawing his theories from the facts. This is the heart of scientific progress and Luke is in the line of succession. Gardner[2] even says, "He loves a good miracle," as if to discredit Luke's testimony on the subject. Carpenter[3] accepts this view of Luke: "Physician though he was, he was uncritical about miracles." Again:[4] "He was undoubtedly what we should call a truthful person, but it cannot be pretended that he had the scientific zeal of the best modern historians. He took pains to ascertain facts, but he was not alive to some of the perils that surround historical inquiry." But I submit that the new discoveries justify precisely this claim concerning Luke.

It is not "pretended" that he had modern views of science and medicine, nor will a true scientist to-day pretend that present-day theories are finalities. The twentieth century has brought a more reverent temper on the part of scientists concerning both God and man. No one claims that he has discovered the ultimate facts concerning nature. The very "atom," once thought to be absolute and indivisible, is now divided into electrons. Modern chemists, like the alchemists of Luke's day, claim to be able to transmute metals by the aid of radium, and to make diamonds to order out of charcoal. He is a bold man to-day who will dare to say what man can or

---

[1] *Cambridge Biblical Essays*, p. 386.   [2] *Ibid.*, p. 390.
[3] *Christianity According to S. Luke*, p. 83.   [4] *Ibid*, p. 82.

cannot do. The Atlantic Ocean has been spanned by the aeroplane in a single flight. One disease after another is conquered by science. Shall we limit the power of God while we enlarge the powers of man? It is easier to believe in mighty works by God because man himself has achieved so much. If there is a God at all, He is greater than any man or than all men. He is greater than the universe about us. We see the influence of spirit upon matter in our own bodies. It is easier to understand how God who is Spirit rules over matter and makes all things subject to His will. There has never been a day when it was easier to believe in miracles than now and harder to tell what is a miracle. We can well believe that some of the miracles wrought by Jesus would not be called miracles by all men to-day. The use of language varies with the growth of ideas. The fundamental question is the fact of Jesus (his birth, his work, his teaching, his character, his resurrection from the dead, his power to-day over the lives of men).

At bottom we face the same problem that Luke faced. In reality we know not one whit more concerning the ultimate reality than Luke did. The new knowledge of our day has filled us with awe in the presence of God. It is no disgrace for us to-day to bow before the fact of God in Christ as Luke did. We must open our minds to learn all we can, but the pride of intellectual arrogance must not blind us to the glory of God in Christ. Luke saw God at work in Christ the Great Physician. No physician to-day can tell precisely how medicine cures disease or what part the mind plays in the cure, or how far the will of God operates in the whole, both in the fight that nature makes and in the special exercise of His will in the individual case. The physician himself often rouses the will of the patient to victory over disease. Can God not do the same?

2. *Luke as an Eye-Witness of Paul's Miracles.*—Carpenter[1] has a curious comment concerning Paul's view of miracles: "It may readily be conceded that S. Paul's attitude toward the miraculous is much truer than S. Luke's." That remark can only mean that Paul is sceptical concerning the miraculous or that Luke is credulous. But Paul claimed that he himself wrought miracles, a thing that Luke never does. "Truly the signs of the apostle were wrought among you with all patience,

[1] *Christianity According to S. Luke*, p. 83.

by signs and wonders and mighty works" (II Cor. 12:12). Paul here employs precisely the three words[1] that Luke reports Peter as using in his address at the great Pentecost (Acts 2:22). So in Romans 15:18 f. Paul speaks of what the Holy Spirit wrought through him among the Gentiles "in the power of signs and wonders." We have Paul's first-hand testimony concerning his own miracles. Besides, Paul testifies to the greatest of all miracles in his own experience, the vision of the Risen Christ (I Cor. 9:1; 15:8; Gal. 1:16). Paul even claims that some of his own converts wrought miracles (I Cor. 12:9 f., 28–30; 14:22; Gal. 3:5). These instances all come from Paul's universally acknowledged Epistles. It is hard to set aside the witness of a man of Paul's intellectual acumen. There were "Counterfeit Miracles" (Warfield) then as there are now, but Paul's miracles do not come in that category.

We have other autoptic witnesses to the miracles. Mark's Gospel reports Peter's description of the miracles of Jesus. If John the Apostle is the author of the Fourth Gospel, we have another eye-witness to the miracles of Jesus. See John 21:24. In John's Gospel we have healings of the sick (4:16 ff.; 5:8; 6:2; 9:6 f.), raising the dead (11:44), the Resurrection of Christ (20 and 21) and miracles over inanimate nature (2:9; 6:11 f., 19; 21:6).

Percy Gardner[2] thinks that Luke "was attracted to the new faith by its power over disease and evil spirits." Even so, we have no right to say that Luke was "taken in" by Paul's "pretense" to work miracles. Luke not only had Paul's word for working miracles, but in the "we" sections of Acts Luke records miracles which he himself witnessed. "It should always be borne in mind that they are recorded by a physician, who was an eye-witness of them."[3] In these cases, therefore, we have a sort of double proof, Paul's general claim that he worked miracles and Luke's testimony to seeing him do them. It is wholly gratuitous to say that Luke's judgment as a historian lapsed when miracles came before him. Let us examine some of the cases in question and see if Luke's treatment of the miracles wrought by Paul disqualifies him for discussing in a credible manner the miracles of Jesus.

[1] σημείοις καὶ τέρασιν καὶ δυνάμεσιν.
[2] *Cambridge Biblical Essays*, p. 386.
[3] Wace, *Intr. St. Bible Encycl.* (art. "Miracles").

The cure of the ventriloquist girl (Acts 16 : 18) is in point. The poor girl had a "*python*."[1] Plutarch says that a ventriloquist was called a *python*. The slave girl may have been diseased in her mind and was the object of superstition and the victim of a group of men who exploited her fortune-telling for gain as men, alas, exploit girls for base gain. The poor girl troubled Paul, Luke and the rest, "the same following after Paul and us" (Acts 16 : 17). Luke reports Paul as charging "the spirit in the name of Jesus Christ to come out of her. And it came out that very hour." The whole subject of demonology is a dark one, but modern scientists are no longer so positive that evil spirits cannot dominate human beings. Luke saw the cure of this girl, sudden and instantaneous.

Luke was a witness also of the earthquake and the release of the prisoners, with the consequent conversion of the jailer (Acts 16 : 26–34). He does not report the earthquake as a miracle, but as a dispensation of providence for Paul and Silas.

Luke saw Paul restore to life the lad who had fallen out of the window at Troas during Paul's long sermon (Acts 20 : 9–12). Luke is careful here in his language. He says the boy was "taken up dead," but he implies that Paul brought him round to life and not by medical means. Luke was evidently greatly impressed.

We have already discussed Luke's description of Paul s shaking off the viper unharmed (Acts 28 : 5), which Ramsay considers a constrictor, a non-poisonous snake. But even so, that explanation cannot apply to the cure of Publius by Paul's prayer (Acts 28 : 8) and to Luke's further practice of medicine in the island (28 : 9 f.). Luke does not create the impression in these narratives that he is credulous and anxious to tell the marvellous. His language is restrained and simple and quite that of a scholar who weighs his words.

3. *Luke's Report of Miracles in Q and Mark.*—In Luke 7 : 20-23 (= Matt. 11 : 4-6) Luke reports the record in Q (possibly by Matthew the publican, himself an eye-witness of the miracles of Jesus) of the words of Jesus concerning his miracles. The two messengers from the Baptist in prison brought his despairing question in his hour of gloom: "Art thou he that cometh or look we for another?" (Luke 7 : 19). But Jesus

---

[1] πύθωνα.

went on with his work, as if not heeding the inquiry. "In that hour he cured many of diseases and plagues and evil spirits; and on many that were blind he bestowed sight" (Luke 7 : 21). Then Jesus turned to the messengers and said: "Go your way, and tell John what things ye have seen and heard; the blind receive their sight, the lame walk, the lepers are cleansed, and the deaf hear, the dead are raised up, the poor have good tidings preached unto them." This was the cure for John's doubt and despair.

We have seen that Q preserves the oldest tradition about Christ that we have. It may even belong to the time when Christ was alive on earth. There is no escape from the fact that Jesus claimed to work miracles and that people believed that he wrought them. Luke had seen Paul work miracles. He would not be prejudiced against the testimony for the miracles of Jesus. But did he not sift the evidence for the miracles of Jesus, as he claims to have done (Luke 1 : 1–4) about everything else? In Luke 7 : 1–10 (= Matt. 8 : 5–13) we certainly have a quite independent record of the same event that Matthew narrates. Luke gives the two embassies from the centurion to Jesus, while Matthew fails to bring out these details.

Mark gives a detailed report of eighteen miracles of Jesus. Of these Luke also reports thirteen. Luke modifies the language in certain instances, but he does not weaken the argument for the real interposition of divine power by Christ. Two of them are nature miracles (the stilling of the storm and the feeding of the five thousand). The rest (counting the drowning of the swine with the cure of the demoniac) are cases of healing.

Few to-day will take the position of Hume that miracles cannot be proven, or even that of Huxley that we can know nothing about the matter at all. Fewer still assert that miracles cannot happen. Goethe said that a voice from heaven would not convince him that water burned or that one rose from the dead. But water can be made to burn by certain chemicals. The more we know about nature and God the more modest we become in our dogmatic statements about God's limitations. Many are now willing to admit that Jesus cured nervous troubles by psychic force, since we have learned that the mind has a great influence on the body. Professor Hyslop even suggests that hospitals be set apart for the curing of certain forms of insanity by casting out demons. And then many cases of insanity are now cured by pulling out diseased teeth. So we learn slowly. But demoniacal possession is no longer scouted by all scientists.

We must remember that nothing is miraculous to God or Christ. With God and Christ nothing is miraculous because all the forces of knowledge and of power are at their command. If we had all knowledge and all power, nothing would be miraculous to us. Christ was not limited to the powers and laws known to us. If God made the universe, all the laws of nature come from him. He still exercises sway over them. Paul says that all things have been created through Christ and unto Christ and all things hold together in Christ (Col. 1:16–17). It is a Christocentric universe. Christ is Lord of all.

If modern science could learn all the secrets of nature, and by the use of the laws of God do the things that Jesus did, surely this would not disprove the cures wrought by Jesus or his claim to divine energy in doing them. "My Father worketh even until now, and I work" (John 5:17). With amazement and with difficulty we unlock a few of the mysteries of nature and pride ourselves on our own attainments. Jesus played with the forces of nature as a master musician. The more we learn of the marvels of nature, the more we marvel at Jesus. There is only one explanation of his person and his claim and his prowess. He was the Son of God.

4. *Five Cases of Healing in Luke Alone.*—Of the thirty-five miracles described in detail in the Gospels Luke gives twenty. Of the twenty-six miracles of healing Luke gives sixteen and five are peculiar to him. For discussion on these, see Chapter VII, "The Medical Language of Luke." These five excited the special interest of Luke. They were all chronic or incurable cases like the old woman with curvature of the spine (Luke 13:10–17), the man with the dropsy (14:1–6), the ten lepers (17:11–19), the case of surgery (22:51), and the restoration to life of the son of the widow of Nain (7:11–17). They were all cured instantaneously by Jesus and were genuine miracles. Not one of these was a case of nervous disorder. These cannot be explained by any theory of modern psychology. Luke was a psychologist, like all true physicians, but he has no hesitation in recording these cases that go beyond all human

power now as then. Luke alone reports the remarkable case of the raising of the son of the widow of Nain. The funeral procession was stopped and the boy given back to his mother. It is one of the tenderest touches in the Gospels. It manifestly touched the heart of Luke. "There is no need to prove that the representation of our Lord given in the Third Gospel is dominated by the conception of Him as the wondrous Healer and Saviour of the sick, as, indeed, the Healer above all healers."[1] But we are not at liberty to distort this fact into meaning that Luke attributed supernatural powers to Christ in order to create that impression. We may, if we will, say that Luke was incompetent to distinguish a miracle from an ordinary case of healing or was a poor judge of evidence, though our opinion makes no change in the facts of the case. Gilbert[2] endeavors to explain away Luke's belief in the miraculous: "We cannot doubt that Luke, who was little interested in the miraculous element . . . was profoundly moved by what he learned of the depth and the universality of the Master's sympathy." But how does Gilbert know that Luke took little interest "in the miraculous element"? Percy Gardner says that Luke loved a good miracle so much that he would lug it in to brighten his narrative. It is hard to satisfy critics of Luke. Luke gives no evidence of being an excitable physician or a poor diagnostician. He writes calm and serious history after prolonged and thorough research. We are bound to give due weight to what he records as true, whether we accept it or not. It is easier to ask questions than to answer them. Who to-day can tell what is the origin of life, or the true nature of life, or what death is and means?

5. *Miracles of Christ Over Nature.*—Luke did not hesitate to record evidences of the power of Christ over animate and inanimate nature outside of man. It is here that some modern scientists take a more positive stand against miracles. Possible explanations have been offered for some of the miracles of healing, so that men of science are less sceptical about the rest. But it must never be overlooked that the fact of the miracles of Jesus by no means depends upon our being able to offer intelligible theories about them. They may thus be rendered easier for some men to believe, but the miracles of Jesus are grounded on the central fact of God's mastery

[1] Harnack, *Luke the Physician*, p. 195.   [2] *Jesus*, pp. 46 f.

over nature. Jesus presents God as personal, and not as an abstract philosophical conception or as misty pantheism. God is like Jesus as Jesus is like God. Personal will rules the universe, the Will of God expressed in his laws, but superior to his laws, the Source of all Energy and Life. This is the view of Jesus and he acts upon it. Luke accepts it and records proofs of Christ's power and claims. It is not unscientific that a real God should be at the heart of the universe. Modern scientists hesitate to say that God cannot or does not guide the universe by his Will. Wonderful powers have been discovered in certain forms of matter, like radium. We must either be materialists or spiritualists (in the proper use of this word). Either matter is eternal and self-sufficient and the source of life and energy, or God is eternal and before matter and the creator of matter and the guide of the universe. No one to-day conceives of a mechanical God who started the universe and then took his hand off of the machine. God is working to-day as much as ever. He works by his laws, by the laws of his own nature, some of which we have discovered. But he works on, whether we are ignorant or whether we know. Nothing is miraculous to God. His Will is the supreme law of the universe. It is thus an ordered world of law, but not a merciless machine that, like a juggernaut, overrides all. Presumption pays the price in such a universe. But we are not hopeless and helpless before the perils of nature red in tooth and claw. Law at bottom is love and God is love. God does not act by whims and caprice, but he is our Father.

So Jesus lets the demons rush into the swine to save the man (Luke 8 : 33 f.). "He gave them leave," Luke says, following Mark's record (5 : 13). Whatever our explanation of the reason that prompted Jesus, Luke puts down what Mark has. The result proves that the people cared more for the hogs than they did for the poor demoniac, for they begged Jesus to leave their shores (Luke 8 : 37). It mattered little that the man was now clothed and in his right mind (8 : 35). This miracle is usually counted as one and the same with that of the Gerasene Demoniac. Huxley had his fun with Gladstone over "the Gadarene Pig Affair," but all the same hogs are subject to mass attacks like sheep and like mobs of men. Huxley's point about Gerasa and Gadara vanishes, for we know that the village of Khersa (Gerasa) by the lake is meant (not

Gerasa thirty miles away), the village tributary to Gadara some six miles distant.

Luke alone gives the draft of fishes (5 : 1–11). Some critics find here another version of the draft of fishes in John 21 : 1–14, but without adequate justification. Peter plays a leading part both times, it is true, but that is not strange. One of the strangest of all theories is that of Schmiedel, who thinks that Luke is giving an allegory of Paul's conflict with the Judaizers about the Gentiles.[1] No wonder Carpenter[2] calls this interpretation "an interesting example of the over-subtlety with which S. Luke can be treated." And that is termed scientific and historical exegesis! The allegorizing is that of Schmiedel, not of Luke. Luke (8 : 22–25) reports the stilling of the storm, following Mark's Gospel (4 : 35–41 = Matt. 8 : 23–27). The mastery of Christ over wind and wave is clearly shown to the marvel of the disciples, who gain a fresh revelation of the person and power of Jesus.

The feeding of the five thousand is given in all the four Gospels, the only one of the miracles wrought by Jesus that is thus attested. Huxley does not ridicule this witness, which is on a par with the Resurrection of Christ in its full testimony. And yet Luke records this amazing incident with much detail (9 : 10–17). Mark's Gospel here preserves the vivid details of Peter's description, the garden-beds and the green grass (Mark 6 : 39 f.), but Luke follows Mark with the orderly arrangement of the crowd and the manifest miraculous multiplication of the loaves and the fishes in the presence of all the multitude. Jesus stood on the hillside and blessed and broke the loaves as the disciples rapidly bore and distributed the baskets. This miracle is a stumbling-block to all who believe in an absentee God or in no God. But we see here Jesus as Lord of nature and of man, with infinite pity and boundless power. He hastened or skipped the usual processes of nature. The miracle created a crisis in the ministry of Jesus and led to his withdrawal from Galilee, because of popular excitement and misunderstanding. It is hard to think that the great crowds were fed by a trick and so purposely misled by Jesus. The picture of Jesus on the eastern slope of the Sea of Galilee near Bethsaida Julias challenged

[1] *Encycl. Bibl.*, pp. 4573–76 (art. "Simon Peter").
[2] *Op. cit.*, p. 84.

the interest of Luke as it compels men to-day to pause. The crowd wanted to take him by force to Jerusalem and crown him political king, as the panacea for earthly ills. If we crown him king of our lives we shall find Jesus to be what Luke took him to be, the Great Physician for soul and body, the Saviour from sin and sickness, the Lord of all nature, the Giver of all grace and good, the Lord of life and of death.

CHAPTER XI

A LITERARY MAN'S RECORD OF THE PARABLES OF JESUS

"And his disciples asked him what this parable might be"
(Luke 8 : 9).

It is not straining after effect to call Luke a man of literary tastes and habits.[1] There is a modern parallel to Luke in Doctor W. T. Grenfell, the Oxford University man who has given himself to work in Labrador as medical missionary, and who writes of life in Labrador with exquisite charm and grace. Luke knew the great literature of his time, one can well believe, and he had, besides, the sure touch of genius in the expression of his ideas. Sir W. Robertson Nicoll says that Mark Rutherford always found the right word in the right place. Luke was not a professional stylist. He did not strive after artificial effects, but he had full knowledge and fine discrimination.

1. *The Beauty of Christ's Parables.*—They made a powerful appeal to Luke. "It is one of the many signs of inferiority in the apocryphal gospels that they contain no parables. While they degrade miracles into mere arbitrary and unspiritual acts of power, they omit all that teaches of the deep relations between the seen and the unseen."[2] But, just as Luke was not credulous in reporting miracles, so he had the insight to see the worth of the parables of Jesus. The true biographer reveals himself in the choice that he makes of the material in his hands and in the skill with which he presents it to create the picture.

There is a literary charm in Luke's report of Christ's parables that marks his Gospel apart from the others. But the beauty of these parables is not due to the genius of Luke. There is a beauty in the Bible facts as well as in the Bible story.[3] Luke is faithful to Christ's words, and yet he gives a

---

[1] McLachlan (*St. Luke*) has his first chapter on "Luke the Man of Letters." "He is a man of literary attainment and scientific culture" (p. 8).

[2] Plummer, Hastings's *D. B.* ("Parable in the N. T.").

[3] Cf. Stalker, *The Beauty of the Bible.*

turn here and there in the setting of the story that one may call literary finish if he will.

The literary perfection of the parables belongs to Jesus and appears in the parables in all the Gospels. Sanday calls the parables of Jesus the finest literary art of the world, combining simplicity, profundity, elemental emotion and spiritual intensity. They were spoken chiefly in the Aramaic, and yet their originality is attested in the Greek translation and even in the English by their freshness, beauty and moral earnestness. They possessed a matchless charm for the people who heard them for the first time as they fell from the lips of the Master Story-teller of the ages. For sheer witchery of words and grip upon the mind and heart, the short stories of Jesus stand alone. Edgar Allan Poe, Hawthorne, Bret Harte, O. Henry and all the rest are on a lower plane.

And yet Jesus did not invent parables. They are common in the Old Testament and in the Talmud. Some of the Jewish rabbis were very fond of using them. Parables are common enough to-day. But Jesus is the master in the use of them. He made the parable preach his gospel—"a picture-gospel" (Plummer). He knew "the book of nature and of human nature" and threw a flash-light on both by means of the parable. The people saw the sins and frailties of the Pharisees in the parables of Jesus, and then their own photographs stamped before their very eyes. The parables of Jesus were so vivid that they were like moving pictures of the soul. Augustine says that Christ's miracles are acted parables and his parables are miracles of beauty and instruction. John Foster says that the miracles of Jesus were like ringing the great bell of the universe for the people to come and listen. The parables caught their attention and drove the lesson home. Christ drew his parables from the life of the people. They are transcripts from the life of the time and so of all time. Those in Luke are the most wonderful and beautiful of all. If Luke loved a good miracle, he was equally fascinated by the parables of Jesus.

2. *Christ's Reasons for Using Parables.*—Scholars have sought to find one reason that covers all the ground. This is not possible, for Jesus himself gives two reasons for the use of so many parables after the blasphemous accusation by the Pharisees, when the atmosphere was electric with hostility.

Jesus had frequently employed parabolic sayings and brief isolated parables before this "Busy Day." But on this occasion "with many such parables spake he the word unto them, as they were able to hear it: and without a parable spake he not unto them: but privately to his disciples he expounded all things" (Mark 4 : 33 f.). There are nine given by the Synoptic Gospels and there were probably more. The very first one, the parable of the sower, puzzled the disciples so that they asked Jesus "what this parable might be" (Luke 8 : 9). Then Jesus explained why he spoke on this occasion in parables. It was a condemnation to the enemies of Christ "that [1] seeing they may not see, and hearing they may not understand" (Luke 8 : 10). And yet the same parable is meant to be a revelation to the disciples: "Unto you it is given to know the mysteries of the Kingdom of God" (Luke 8 : 10 = Mark 4 : 11 = Matt. 13 : 11). One thinks of the "mystery-religions" and their initiations and secrets, like modern Masons and other secret orders. Mark reports Jesus as saying: "But unto them that are without, all things are done in parables." The greatest secret order of the world is the Kingdom of God. Jesus opens the mysteries of grace with no incantations and mocking mummeries, but with the illumination of the Holy Spirit that floods the soul and the life with light. So the parables of Jesus were a pillar of cloud and darkness to the Pharisees, but of fire and light to the disciples when their eyes were opened to see. They were a spiritual smoke-screen to shut off those who were blaspheming Jesus. Thus Jesus keeps from casting pearls before swine (Matt. 7 : 6) and is able to go on with his teaching in an uncongenial atmosphere. Paul later noted that the gospel message was a savor of life unto life or of death unto death (II Cor. 2 : 17 ff.). It is literally true that preaching hardens the heart, the eye, the ear, the mind, or stirs one to a richer life with God. Jesus himself was set for the falling and the rising of many in Israel, as old Simeon saw (Luke 2 : 34).

But there are other reasons why Jesus used parables in his teaching. They served to put truth in crisp form that was easily remembered and that would be afterward understood. The story would stick and would hold the lesson that it carried. The Apostles were not so well educated as the Pharisees.

---

[1] Both Mark (4 : 12) and Luke here have ἵνα, which may express purpose or result (in the Koiné). Matthew (13 : 13) has ὅτι (because).

They had less intellectual training and dialectical acumen, but they could catch the stories of Jesus, for they had less prejudice and fewer predilections. They did see the point of the parables after the private explanation by Jesus (Matt. 13:51).

And then there is power in a good story to win attention and to hold it when interest begins to flag. Jesus had often to say "Listen," as the minds of his hearers began to wander or they were disconcerted. "If any man has ears to hear, let him hear" (Mark 4:23). "Take heed therefore how ye hear" (Luke 8:18), where Mark (4:24) has "what ye hear."

Once more the parables of Jesus stimulated inquiry on the part of the disciples. On this very occasion the disciples twice asked him to explain his parables, that of the sower (Luke 8:9 = Mark 4:10 = Matt. 13:10) and that of the tares (Matt. 13:36).

Jesus thus spoke in parables to the multitudes (Matt. 13:34) what he could not so well have said to a popular assembly already excited by the charges of the Pharisees. But the new style of teaching became a marked characteristic of the ministry of Jesus.

3. *The Meaning of Parables.*—The etymology of the word is simple enough. The Greek word[1] means to place beside for purpose of comparison. The parable[2] is thus a sort of measuring-rod for spiritual and moral truth. Just as the yardstick measures off a yard of silk, so the parable takes a concrete example from life to illustrate the truth in mind. The word illustration is a Latin word and means to throw light upon a subject. This is the purpose, likewise, of parable. The little girl was not far wrong when she said that a parable was an earthly story with a heavenly meaning. The Hebrew word for parable (*māshal*) was used for a discourse that implied comparison. But the Hebrew term had a wide application. It might be similitude, allegory, proverb, paradox, or even riddle. So no one type covers all the uses of parable in the New Testament.

The word is used in various ways in the Gospels. We have a proverb called parable by Jesus in Luke 4:23: "Physician, heal thyself." There is analogy in such a proverb which the

---

[1] παραβολή from παραβάλλω.
[2] John employs παροιμία, a wayside saying, for shorter sayings of an obscure nature (John 16:25, 29) and for longer narratives (John 10:6).

hearer must catch. So Luke terms Christ's proverb about the blind leading the blind a parable (Luke 6 : 39). Hence we can apply the word parable to the proverb of the reed shaken with the wind (Luke 7 : 24) and the green tree and the dry (23 : 31). See also the proverb of the whole and the sick (Luke 5 : 31 f.) and of the bridegroom (5 : 34). Jesus did not always call his parables by the word nor do the Gospels. See Luke 16 : 13 about serving two masters. Sometimes the similitude is drawn by the word "like" or "likened," as in the brief parable of the leaven (Luke 13 : 20 f.). The parable of the fig-tree (Luke 21 : 29–33) is also a good example of formal comparison. See also the foolish rich man in Luke 12 : 16–21, where Jesus draws the lesson clearly.

A parable may be a paradox. W. J. Moulton[1] notes three kinds of paradox in Christ's parabolic teaching. One sort shocks the hearer by its violent contrast, as when Jesus said that it is easier for a camel to enter in through a needle's eye than for a rich man to enter into the Kingdom of God (Luke 18 : 25). Such a parable is meant to provoke reflection, as when Jesus spoke of hating one's father and mother (Luke 14 : 26). The paradox may become clearer in time, as, for instance, Christ's denunciation of the Pharisees as hypocrites (Luke 6 : 42) with "beams" or long sticks of wood in their eyes trying to get a little mote out of the other people's eyes. But the third kind of parabolic paradox retains its inherent difficulty with the lapse of time, as in conquering by the cross and in saving one's life by losing it (Luke 9 : 23 f.; 14 : 27). So as to making friends by the mammon of unrighteousness (16 : 9).

The longer parables have the narrative form, like the sower (Luke 8 : 4–15), the prodigal son (15 : 11–32). In these the formal comparison is not drawn, though it is plainly implied. The great bulk of the longer parables are of this nature.

The parable need not be fact, but it must be truth. The fable is a caricature of animal life, where the animals in a grotesque way act contrary to nature. The parable is always in harmony with nature, whether the lily of the field, the sparrow that falls, the lost sheep in the mountains, the lost coin, or the lost boy. It is not possible to tell whether or when Christ's parables are purely imaginative or have a basis of

[1] Hastings's *Dict. of Christ and the Gospels.*

concrete fact in specific instances. The parable of the pounds (Luke 19 : 11–27) seems to have as its background the deposition of Archelaus in A. D. 6, when Jesus was a boy about twelve years old. But most of Christ's parables are drawn from nature or from human life about him. They are true to form, and picture in lasting colors the life of men then and now.

The allegory is a variety of parable, but scholars do not agree in their use of the term allegory. Plummer[1] puts the matter clearly: "In an allegory figure and fact, or, rather, figure and interpretation, are not mixed, but are parallel, and move simultaneously, as in the allegory of the True Vine or of the Good Shepherd." And Plummer might have added the allegory of the sower and of the prodigal son. The allegory is a narrative parable that is self-explanatory. It means speaking something else.[2] The point of the story is plain as it proceeds for those who have eyes to see, though the disciples did not understand the story of the sower till Jesus explained it. Bunyan's *Pilgrim's Progress* is the great modern allegory. Weinel[3] even says that Jesus never spoke in allegory and Jülicher[4] admits that the Gospels report him as doing so, but misrepresent him in the matter. Jesus did not, it is true, employ the allegorical method of interpretation in the whimsical manner of Philo with his fantastic "spiritualizing" that had such a disastrous influence on the Alexandrian theology of Origen and Clement of Alexandria. All of the parables of Jesus have a point and he uses the parable to point the moral in his teaching. The allegory in the mouth of Jesus follows the line of the parable in being true to nature. The deeper spiritual truth that Jesus expounds lies on the surface for those with spiritual insight. W. J. Moulton[5] regards the allegory with Christ as imperfectly developed, because he does not explain all the details of the story. Compare the sower (Luke 8 : 5–15) and the wicked husbandman (Luke 20 : 9–19). But in all of Christ's parables he holds to the main point with less concern for the setting and the details.

[1] Hastings's *Dict. of the Bible* (art. "Parable in N. T.").
[2] ἀλληγορία. The substantive does not occur in the N. T., but Paul has the participle in Gal. 4 . 24.
[3] *Die Gleichnisse Jesu*, p. 30.   [4] *Die Gleichnisreden Jesu*, I, pp. 61 f.
[5] Hastings's *Dict. of Christ and the Gospels* (art. "Parable").

4. *The Interpretation of Parables.*—The wildest speculation
has appeared in the interpretation of the parables of Jesus.
We must be sure that we understand the language that Jesus
used, as, for instance, "that, when it shall fail, they may
receive you into the eternal tabernacles" (Luke 16:9). The
word "receive" simply means a welcome on the part of those
benefited by the use of one's money, not the purchase of salvation by means of one's money.

The context must be noted to see the precise light in which
the story appears. All three stories in Luke 15 are justifica-
tions by Jesus of his association with publicans and sinners
against the sneer of the Pharisees and the scribes in verses
1 and 2. The lost sheep, the lost coin, the lost son are pictures of the lost (publicans and sinners) whom Jesus came to
save. The elder brother is a picture of the carping Pharisee
who provoked the stories. Again in chapter 16 we have the
parables about the wise and the unwise use of money, and
Luke adds (16:14) that "the Pharisees, who were lovers of
money, heard all these things; and they scoffed at him."

Each parable of Jesus teaches a great truth, and this is the
first thing to find and sometimes the only thing that we need
learn as to the teaching. Certainly in the case of the unjust
steward (Luke 16:1-13) this is true, and nothing can be made
of the fact of the steward's rascality. The same thing is true
of the discovery of the hid treasure and of the story of the
Lord's coming like a thief in the night.

And yet Jesus did sometimes make use of the minor details
as in some of those in the tares and practically all in the sower.
The early commentators went to such excesses that Chrysostom (*Hom. on Matt.*, 64:3) says that the details should be
ignored altogether in the interpretation of the parable.
Broadus (*Comm. on Matt.*, Chap. XIII) thinks that we are safe
where we have the guidance of Christ, but that elsewhere
we should err on the side of restraint rather than license.
Trench[1] has good words in his third chapter. Augustine says
that the parable is not to be used as the basis for argument
unless one has a categorical teaching elsewhere. The three
loaves in Luke 11:5 have been made to teach the doctrine of
the Trinity, and the two shillings in the parable of the good
Samaritan (10:35) to mean baptism and the Lord's supper!

[1] *Notes on the Parables.*

In particular, it should be said that one must be careful about building schemes of theology in the interpretation of the kingdom parables, especially as to the number seven in Matt. 13 or three in Luke 14 and in 15. Luke's kingdom parables deal more with the individual experience rather than with the gradual growth of the kingdom itself. There is an apocalyptic or eschatological element in some of the parables in Luke as in Mark and Matthew, but the parable of the pounds (Luke 19:11-27) was spoken expressly to discourage the wild excitement of the multitude who "supposed that the kingdom of God was immediately to appear" (19:11). And Luke's report of the great eschatological discourse on the Mount of Olives is quite brief (21:5-36). He uses the parable of the fig-tree to warn the disciples about the coming culmination of the kingdom (29-33). But, on the whole, the parables of Jesus in Luke are a stern rebuke to the wild eschatologists who fail to see the spiritual and ethical side of Christ's teaching. The parables show the gradual expansion of the work of the kingdom, and Luke has the pregnant saying of Christ to the Pharisees that the kingdom of heaven is within[1] men, not an external and political organization as the Pharisees expected (17:20 f.). "The truth about Jesus is too great to be seen from any single standpoint. No single category is able to contain him. The truth is more comprehensive than is supposed by either the Mystery school or the thoroughgoing Eschatologists."[2] Jesus "transmuted eschatology" to serve his purpose, but he was not a dupe of eschatological schemes and programmes. Christ is glorified in the Transfiguration, the Resurrection, the Ascension. Pentecost and the Destruction of Jerusalem were forecasts of the end of the world and the coming of Christ in person to judge the world.

5. *Luke's Special Contribution to Our Knowledge of the Parables of Jesus.*—Scholars differ greatly in counting Christ's parables. Bruce[3] gives thirty-three and eight "parable-germs." Koetsweld counts seventy-nine. I have listed some fifty of them in Broadus's *Harmony of the Gospels* (pp. 270 f.). The speech of Christ was full of metaphor and similitude like the lilies of the field and the birds of the air. Of the thirty-five of some length that are usually discussed in the books on the

[1] ἐντός.   [2] Carpenter, *Christianity According to S. Luke*, p. 153.
[3] *The Parabolic Teaching of Christ*, pp. xi f.

parables of Jesus, Luke has twenty-three and eighteen occur in his Gospel alone. Three are also in Matthew and Mark (the sower, the mustard-seed, the wicked husbandman) and two are in Matthew (the leaven, the lost sheep).

The eighteen that occur in Luke alone are beautiful and give a distinct grace and glory to his Gospel. They are the two debtors (Luke 7:40–43), the good Samaritan (10:30–37), the friend at midnight (11:5–8), the rich fool (12:16–21), the waiting servants (12:35–48), the barren fig-tree (13:6–9), the chief seats at feasts (14:7–11), the great supper (14:15–24), the rash builder (14:28–30), the rash king (14:31–33), the lost coin (15:8–10), the lost son (15:11–32), the unrighteous steward (16:1–12), the rich man and Lazarus (16:19–31), the unprofitable servants (17:7–10), the unrighteous judge (18:1–8), the Pharisee and the publican (18:9–14), the pounds (19:11–27). We could ill afford to give up these wonderful parables.

Luke, like Matthew (13, 21, 24 and 25), is fond of bunching the parables, as in 5:36–39; 13:18–21; 14:28–32; chapters 15, 16, 18. It looks as if Jesus at times piled parable upon parable in his teaching, to drive the point home, as in Luke 15 (three) and in Matt. 21 and 22 (three). Sometimes there are pairs of parables in Luke, as in Matthew. Plummer[1] notes how the effect of Christ's parables is intensified by contrasts, as in the heartless clergy and the charitable Samaritan (Luke 10:30), the rich man and Lazarus (16:19), the Pharisee and the publican (18:9).

There is a trace of Luke's own style in some of the parables which he may have translated from the Aramaic into the Greek,[2] but in the main we may feel sure that Luke has preserved the story with the flavor that Jesus gave it. Stanton[3] thinks that the good Samaritan, in particular, has Lukan characteristics.

As a rule parables are drawn from a different realm to illustrate one's point. But Luke gives some that come from the same sphere by way of example, as the good Samaritan, the foolish rich man, the rich man and Lazarus, the Pharisee and the publican, the friend at midnight, the unjust judge. These

[1] Hastings's *B. D.*
[2] Carpenter, *op. cit.*, p. 195.
[3] *Gospels as Historical Documents*, II, p. 300.

are parables of the personal touch. The parallel consists in the application of the story to the life of the hearer. Luke is fond of the personal touch in Christ's stories. "The Lukan parables are not formal expositions of the nature of the kingdom, they are appeals *ad hominem*. And they are drawn, for the most part, not from the processes of nature, but from the facts of human life and character."[1]

Glover[2] thinks that Jesus was fond of telling parables of his home life in Nazareth. He watched his own home life. "It was Mary, we may believe, who put the leaven in the three measures of meal . . . and Jesus sat by and watched it. In after years the sight came back to Him. He remembered the big basin, the heaving, panting mass in it, the bubbles struggling out, swelling and breaking, and the level rising and falling. It came to Him as a picture of the Kingdom of Heaven at work in the individual man and in the community."[3]

It matters little how we classify the parables of Jesus. That is all subjective and more or less artificial. We shall get better results by studying the parables as they come in their own context than by tearing them out by the roots and making them live in our theological pots and pans. They are alive and will bleed if mistreated. They throb with life as Luke has preserved them in his Gospel.

It is doubtless true that Luke's interest in the parables of Jesus was largely that of a literary man who was charmed by these matchless stories of the new life in the kingdom of God. But he had also the interest of a sober theologian[4] to combat the wild eschatological views of the time. Jesus at times used the apocalyptic method and the eschatological motive, but it was always with restraint and reserve. The teaching of Jesus concerning the kingdom of God in Luke's report of the parables discountenances all millennial programmes and set times for the second coming of Christ. The keynote of the parables of Jesus in Luke's Gospel is personal salvation and growth of Christian character. The larger aspect of the kingdom in its social and world relations is present, but it is grounded in the new life of the individual in Christ. The social redemption of

---

[1] Carpenter, *op. cit.*, p. 112.
[2] *The Jesus of History*, p. 30.
[3] Glover, *The Meaning and Purpose of a Christian Society*, p. 18.
[4] McLachlan (*St. Luke*) has a chapter on "Luke the Theologian."

the race is the goal and Luke makes that clear. He has a world outlook and a world sympathy, and Jesus stands forth as the teacher for all the world and for all time with a programme for world reconstruction.

CHAPTER XII

AN HISTORIAN'S IDEA OF THE DEITY OF JESUS [1]

"Thou art my beloved Son; in thee I am well pleased" (Luke 3 : 22)

Luke had to face the problem of the person of Christ when he decided to write his Gospel. The picture of Jesus Christ was already drawn in the Logia of Matthew and in Mark's Gospel, as we know. It was probably clearly presented in his other sources. Luke had heard Paul and others preach that Jesus was the Messiah, the Son of God. There was no escaping this question. Jesus himself had pressed his claim as the Son of Man toward the close of his ministry, so that his enemies and his friends took sides sharply. Luke tells the whole story of the person of Christ as the issue was developed during the life of Jesus and during the period covered by the Acts. He has written an objective narrative, but he did not attempt to conceal his own loyalty to Jesus Christ as Lord and Saviour.

1. *The Jesus or Christ Controversy.*—Luke was not one of the eye-witnesses[2] of Christ, but he was one of the witnesses[3] to the work of Christ. He was a critic of the effect of Christ's personal influence on men who knew him in the flesh and who worshipped him as God and Saviour. Luke had to face squarely the problem of Jesus as the Christ (the Messiah). It was put up to him by the eye-witnesses. Luke, as we have seen, was not a Jew, and so was not expecting a Messiah. He was not prejudiced against Jesus as were the Pharisees, with their theory of a political and eschatological kingdom for the Messiah. But the heathen myths made it more difficult, if anything, for him to accept the facts about the incarnation of Christ, the virgin birth, and Christ's resurrection from the dead. Certainly, the emperor-worship was enough to disgust

---

[1] The *Expositor* (London), 1920.

[2] αὐτόπται. There is a striking example of αὐτόπτης in P. Oxy., VIII, 1154, 8 (late 1 A. D.), αὐτόπτης γάρ εἰμι τῶν τόπων καὶ οὐκ εἰμὶ ξέν[ο]ος τῶν ἐνθάδε, translated by Moulton and Milligan: "For I am personally acquainted with these places, and am not a stranger here."

[3] μάρτυρες.

any intelligent man, as it did most of the men of light of that time. It was not easy for an educated man in Luke's day to accept the deity of Jesus and to worship a man. The cross of Jesus was a stumbling-block to the Jew and foolishness to the Greek. Luke felt the force of both objections.

Luke is the typical man of culture of his time. He does not tell the mental processes by which he came to take Jesus as the Christ. But we may be sure that he would understand the temper of the modern college man or woman who finds difficulty in reconciling the deity of Jesus with modern Darwinism. It was just as hard for Luke to make the person of Christ square with the scientific theories of Galen and Hippocrates. We must try to understand the problems of the college and university life of our day. I wish to recommend McKenna's *The Adventure of Life* as a book admirably adapted to help the really sincere spirits who wish to face the facts of nature and of grace. This English physician and devout Christian wrote his book in his den at the front in France in the midst of death and life. He is a man after Luke's own heart, and looks at all the facts with a calm and clear gaze. He is an evolutionist and gives his conception of the development of the universe up to man. Then he finds a place for Jesus, the Son of God, in the scientific universe of Darwin, and he worships him as his saviour from sin. It is utterly frank and very able and helpful. It is just as gratuitous to accuse Luke of credulity as McKenna. One is bound to believe that Luke had an experience of Christ in his heart and life before he clearly grasped the conception of the person of Christ. Glover in his *Jesus of History* likewise understands Luke and the temper of modern young people of culture with a craving to know Christ. We may be sure that Luke did not write carelessly the tremendous statements concerning the deity of Jesus. He writes in the light of his own extensive researches, after long investigation of the claims and the power of Christ, and out of a full heart. He had himself put Jesus to the test in his own life. He had seen others live for Christ and die for Christ. Luke loved his medical science, but he loved Jesus more. He was a "doctor of the old school," who was able to make the sick-room a sanctuary of God. He was a partner with God and looked to the Great Physician to bless his work.

Luke wrote with the Logia before him. The Logia (Q) had precisely the same elements[1] in its picture of Christ that we find in the Gospel of John.[2]   Mark[3] wrote before Luke, and Mark's picture of Christ agrees with that of the Logia.   Luke was Paul's bosom friend.   Luke knew Paul's idea of Christ. So Luke had to face the Jesus or Christ controversy of modern theologians.[4]   He identified the theological Christ with the historic Jesus.   He did not do so blindly.   From the beginning he found the evidence that convinced him.   It is a modern intellectual impertinence that men of culture do not accept the deity of Jesus.   Gladstone says that out of sixty master minds that he knew, fifty-five of them took Jesus humbly as God and Saviour.

Luke the historian records his idea of the person of Christ. He does not use Pauline terminology.   He follows the language of his primitive sources.   He lets us see that the witness is very old and goes back to the very life of Christ.   It is not a theological dogma of a late date, invented to suit the deification of Jesus.   Luke writes in a true historic spirit, and lets us see how Jesus impressed the men of his time and how Jesus regarded himself.

2. *The Son of God.*—Luke does not write as a theologian. He does not express his own views in theological language, as Paul does in his Epistles.   He makes no theological arguments or definitions.   He keeps his own personality in the background, but he reveals his own views by the nature of the material that he presents.   We may agree or disagree with Luke's picture of Christ, but he has drawn it with absolute clearness and after mature reflection and with manifest conviction.   He comes to the interpretation of Christ without Pharisaic limitations and from the standpoint of a cosmopolitan. Wright[5] thinks that Luke had conversations with John, the author of the Fourth Gospel, since both mention the fact that the sepulchre in which our Lord's body lay was a new one, "where no one had yet lain" (Luke 23 : 53).   He thinks

---

[1] See my article, " The Christ of the Logia," in the *Contemporary Review*, August, 1919.

[2] See my *Divinity of Christ in the Gospel of John* (1916).

[3] See my *Studies in Mark's Gospel* (1919).

[4] Cf. *The Hibbert Journal Supplement for 1909.*

[5] Hastings's *Dict. of Christ and the Gospels.*

that much of John's teaching was "esoteric, intended for advanced disciples only," but there are Johannean patches in
Luke's Gospel, as, for instance, Luke 10:21-24 (cf. Matt.
11:25-30). Be that as it may, it can be shown that Luke
conceived Jesus as the Son of God in the full sense of that
phrase. He has not written his Gospel to prove that thesis
as John has done in his Gospel (20:30 f.), but in numerous
instances he shows clearly what he means his readers to understand about Jesus.

Luke records the angel Gabriel as saying to Mary of the
promised child: "He shall be great, and shall be called the
son of the Most High: and the Lord God shall give unto him
the throne of his father David: and he shall reign over the
house of Jacob forever; and of his kingdom there shall be no
end," (Luke 1:32-33). This is, to be sure, the Old Testament
picture in broad outline of the Messiah, but not the Pharisaic
conception. In II Sam. 7:5-17 Nathan's words to David
from Jehovah are recorded. David's son is to build Jehovah
a house and the throne of his kingdom is to be established
forever. This covenant with David is referred to at length
in Psalm 89, where it is interpreted in Messianic language.
Nearly all of the language of Christ's words to Peter in Matt.
16:18 f. appears in Psalm 89. We need not think that David
or Nathan or the author of Psalm 89 understood the language
about the perpetuity of the Davidic throne in the spiritual
sense as Jesus interprets it in Matt. 16:18 f. Luke clearly
understands the words of Gabriel to Mary in the sense of the
spiritual Israel that Paul teaches in Gal. 3 and Romans 9:11.
The context in Luke's Gospel shows that he means us to understand that by "the son of the Most High" he is describing
the real deity of Jesus.

He is human on the side of his mother Mary, but is begotten of the Holy Spirit. When Mary expressed her wonder
and surprise, Gabriel replies: "The Holy Spirit shall come
upon thee, and shall overshadow thee: wherefore also the
holy thing which is begotten of thee shall be called the Son
of God" (Luke 1:35). The idea of the Shekinah is suggested
here (Ex. 40:38). "The cloud of glory signified the Divine
presence and power."[1] The unborn child is called "holy" as
free from all taint of sin.[2] There is no discounting the fact

---

[1] Plummer, in loco.   [2] Ibid.

that Luke indorses these words of Gabriel as a true forecast of the life of Jesus which he will present in his Gospel. Luke believed the simple story of Mary about the birth of Jesus. Thus he interprets the incarnation of the Son of God. Efforts have been made to empty the words "the Son of God"[1] of their natural content, but with no success. True, Adam is called by Luke the Son of God in 3:38, but the context is utterly different. God created Adam, but begot Jesus by the Holy Spirit. Adam was not an incarnation of God, but God's offspring, as all men are (Acts 17:28).

And then Elizabeth greets Mary as "the mother of my Lord"[2] (Luke 1:43). Here the word "Lord" is not a mere title of rank or even in the sense ascribed in the papyri so often to Cæsar, but it is the Old Testament usage as in Psalm 90:1. Elizabeth means Messiah by Lord. Plummer[3] properly notes that the expression "Mother of God" does not occur in the Bible. Didon[4] wrongly translates the language of Luke 1:43 by "la mère de mon Dieu." But the Greek word for Lord in the Septuagint commonly occurs for the Hebrew Jehovah.

The shepherds hear the angel describe the Babe of Bethlehem as "a Saviour, who is Christ the Lord."[5] It is possible to say that Luke, if translating an Aramaic source, whether oral or written, may have followed the Septuagint in Lam. 4:20, where "the anointed of the Lord" is rendered by "the Anointed Lord."[6] The same peculiar expression occurs in Psalms of Solomon 17:36. "The combination occurs nowhere else in N. T., and the precise meaning is uncertain. Either 'Messiah, Lord,' or 'Anointed Lord,' or 'the Messiah, the Lord,' or 'an anointed one, a Lord.'"[7] But it is, at any rate, plain that the highest dignity is here ascribed to the child Jesus.

In Luke 2:26 we read that Simeon had had a revelation

---

[1] υἱὸς θεοῦ. The use of ὁ υἱὸς τοῦ θεοῦ would have made the point clearer. Luke probably translates from the Aramaic. Deissmann (*Bible Studies*, pf. 131) quotes an inscription of Cos with θεοῦ υἱοῦ Σεβαστοῦ for Augustus and a Fayum papyrus (Pap. Berol. 7006) where καίσαρος θεοῦ υἱοῦ again refers to Augustus.

[2] ἡ μῆτηρ τοῦ κυρίου μου. The use of κύριος as imperial title is very common in the papyri. See *P. Oxy.*, 375 (A. D. 49) τιβερίου κλαυδίου καίσαρος τοῦ κυρίου.

[3] *Comm.*, p. 29.   [4] *Jésus Christ*, p. 111.   [5] σωτὴρ ὅς ἐστιν χριστὸς κύριος.

[6] χριστὸς κύριος.   Cf. Ps. 90:1 and Sirach 51:10.

[7] Plummer, *in loco*.

that he should not die before he had seen "the Lord's Christ"[1] or "the Lord's Anointed" (cf. Lam. 4:20). Here the deity of Jesus is not brought out save as it belongs to the word "Anointed" or Messiah. One may compare Luke 9:20, where Luke has "the Christ (the Anointed) of God" (Mark 8:29, "the Christ," Matt. 16:17, "the Christ, the Son of the living God").

In Luke 2:49 the boy Jesus expresses surprise that Joseph and Mary do not understand that "I must be in my Father's house."[2] This is the correct translation, as the papyri show, not "about my Father's business." But here is the Messianic consciousness in the boy of twelve. God is his Father in a sense not true of other men. The Jews later accused Jesus of blasphemy for calling God "his own Father, and making himself equal with God" (John 5:18).

At the baptism of Jesus "a voice came out of heaven, Thou art my beloved Son;[3] in thee I am well pleased" (Luke 3:22 = Mark 1:11 = Matt. 3:17). It is possible that the voice of the Father suggested Psalm 2:7, which D (Codex Bezae) here follows. But it is beyond question that the Synoptic Gospels here present the deity of Jesus as clearly as does the Gospel of John. It is given, moreover, at the very beginning of Christ's ministry, not merely at the close. It comes not as a new revelation to Jesus, but as confirmation of his peculiar relation to the Father. John the Baptist saw the descent of the Holy Spirit as the sign (John 1:33) and he heard the voice of the Father: "And I have seen and have borne witness that this is the Son of God" (1:34). This is no mere *Bath-Kol* of the rabbis, an echo of God's voice. It is not the Cerinthian Gnostic idea of an emanation upon Jesus, the "Christ" coming upon the man Jesus. Jesus does not here "become" God or the Son of God. As the Son of God, he is recognized by the Father on the formal entrance upon his Messianic mission in the presence and with the sanction of the forerunner. Father, Son, and Holy Spirit unite on this august occasion in setting this seal upon the solemn event.

In the temptations the devil twice (Luke 4:3, 9) challenges Christ's relation to God by the words "If thou art the Son of

---

[1] τὸν χριστὸν κυρίου.

[2] ἐν τοῖς τοῦ πατρός μου δεῖ εἶναί με.

[3] ὁ υἱός μου ὁ ἀγαπητός.

God"[1] or, more exactly, "If thou art Son of God." There is no article with Son in the Greek. There is undoubted allusion to the voice of the Father at the baptism (Luke 3 : 22), but the reference is "to the relationship to God, rather than to the office of Messiah."[2] The condition, being of the first class,[3] assumes the fact of Christ's peculiar relationship to God, though possibly enjoyed by others. The devil does not throw doubt on his own temptation, but seeks to incite doubt in Jesus by urging him to prove that he is in reality God's Son by the exercising of the power of God.

In the discourse in the synagogue at Nazareth (Luke 4 : 16–30) Jesus read from the roll of Isaiah (61 : 1–2; 58 : 6) and definitely claims that this Messianic passage is fulfilled in him (Luke 4 : 21). There is no specific claim to deity here save as that is involved in Christ's conception of the Messiah. "In applying these words to Himself the Christ looks back to His baptism. He is more than a Prophet; He is the Son, the Beloved One, of Jehovah" (3 : 21, 22).[4]

The Pharisees challenged the right of Christ to forgive sins by saying: "Who can forgive sins but God alone?" (Luke 5 : 21). Jesus does not dispute the point raised, but accepts the challenge and heals the man on purpose, "that ye may know that the Son of Man hath authority on earth to forgive sins" (5 : 24). He acts on his own authority in perfect accord with the will of God (John 5 : 19, 21). He allows the Pharisees and the people to draw the conclusion that he claims divine prerogatives.

In Luke 6 : 5 Jesus claims to be "Lord of the Sabbath," with power to change or cancel the day as it suits best his work. This is not a direct claim to equality with God, but is a revolutionary position from the usual Pharisaic theology which made men slaves of the Sabbath.

One does not care to press the point in the language of the demoniac in Luke 8 : 28, who says: "Jesus, thou Son of the Most High God." The word "God" is not certain in the text, and "Most High" is a common name for Jehovah among heathen nations.[5] Perhaps the man was a heathen. The

---

[1] εἰ υἱὸς εἶ τοῦ θεοῦ. Note emphatic position of υἱός. On absence of article, see Robertson, *Grammar*, p. 781.

[2] Plummer, *in loco*.   [3] Cf. Robertson, *Grammar*, p. 1009.

[4] Plummer, *in loco*.   [5] See proof in Plummer's *Comm.*, p. 229.

demoniacs quickly acknowledge the deity of Jesus, a fact that
was turned against Jesus by the rabbis, who used it as a proof
that he was in league with the devil.   But Luke records the
fact and lets his readers draw their own inferences.   Devil
and demons alike acknowledge Jesus as God's Son in Luke's
Gospel.

We have already seen that in Luke 9:20 Peter addresses
Jesus as "the Christ of God," while Matt. 16:16 has "the
Christ, the Son of the living God."   Luke's briefer form in-
volves Matthew's longer report.

On the Mount of Transfiguration Luke (9:35) records that
"a voice came out of the cloud, saying: This is my Son, my
chosen;   hear   ye   him."   Here   many   manuscripts,[1]   like
Matt. 17:5 and Mark 9:7, have "my beloved Son" as in
Luke 3:22.   But the variation in the verbal or participle cuts
no figure in the testimony of the Father to the peculiar sonship[2]
of Jesus.   Luke has points of his own concerning this great
event (Christ's praying, the talk about Christ's decease).

In Luke 10:22 (= Matt. 11:27) Jesus claims equality with
the Father by the use of "the Father," "the Son," as so often
in John's Gospel (cf. 5:19–20).   "And it contains the whole
of the Christology of the Fourth Gospel.   It is like 'an aerolite
from the Johannean heaven';[3] and for that very reason it causes
perplexity to those who deny the solidarity between the Johannean heaven and the Synoptic earth."[4]

When on trial before the Sanhedrin Jesus is finally asked
pointedly by Caiaphas if he is the Christ (Luke 22:67) and
then by all: "Art thou then the Son of God?" (22:70).   To
this he replied, "Ye say that I am," a virtual affirmative.
Luke only gives the ratification after dawn (22:66) of the
illegal condemnation before day given in detail by Matthew
and Mark.   Matthew (26:63) represents Christ as put on
oath by Caiaphas to tell "whether thou be the Christ, the Son
of God," to which Jesus gives an affirmative answer (Matt.
26:64; Mark 14:62).   It is all perfunctory repetition in Luke,
but the same point is clearly made that Jesus before the Sanhedrin solemnly claims to be the Son of God.   On this con-
fession of his the vote was twice taken to convict him of blasphemy.   Clearly, therefore, the Sanhedrin understood Jesus to

---

[1] A C D P R.

[2] ὁ υἱός μου.   Note article.

[3] Hase, *Geschichte Jesu*, p. 527.

[4] Plummer, p. 282.

make divine claims. Jesus had said in so many words: "But from henceforth shall the Son of Man be seated at the right hand of the power of God" (22 : 69). "In the allusion to Daniel 7 : 13 they recognize a claim to Divinity."[1] In simple truth Luke records that the Sanhedrin voted Jesus to be worthy of death because he claimed to be the Son of God, and so equal with God.

Once more Luke represents the risen Christ as claiming that he is the Messiah of Old Testament prophecy, whose sufferings were already foretold (Luke 24 : 26, 46).

The case is made out with abundant clearness that Luke's Gospel gives us a picture of one who claimed to be the Son of God in the full sense of that phrase. Luke presents the real deity of Jesus, not the mere divinity of humanity. In a word, Jesus is the Son of God in the same sense that he appears in the Fourth Gospel, though John's philosophical language in the Prologue is not employed. We see this conception of Christ in Mary's memorials in chapters 1 and 2, in the portions of Luke drawn from Mark and from Q, in the Perean and passion narratives. It is futile to try to make Luke's Christ a mere man, even the best of men. From the virgin birth to the ascension we see the Son of God limned by Luke the painter and the historian.

3. *The Son of Man.*—But Luke is not a Docetic Gnostic any more than a Cerinthian Gnostic. If Jesus is the Son of God in Luke's Gospel, he is none the less the Son of Man. Jesus is a real man and not a make-believe man without genuine humanity. Luke's Gospel is that of "Jesus, our Brother-Man."[2] The Jesus of Luke's Gospel is no pale-faced dreamer out of touch with his environment. As a physician Luke takes special delight in showing the phases and features of his human birth and development side by side with the manifest deity of Jesus Christ.

Jesus is the child of Mary and is from the most humble surroundings, with no comforts for mother or child (Luke 2 : 4–7). Here we see the physician's tender interest in the details of the birth.

Like any other child, Jesus "grew, and waxed strong, filled with wisdom; and the grace of God was upon him" (2 : 40).

[1] Plummer, p. 519.
[2] Hayes, *Synoptic Gospels and Acts*, p. 253.

Luke alone gives the picture of the boy Jesus in the temple and his obedience to Joseph and Mary. "And Jesus advanced in wisdom and stature, and in favor with God and man" (2:52). Luke does not moralize or dogmatize about the wonder of these words. With wondrous skill he helps us to see the human growth of the Son of God, who is also the Son of Man.

The tender sympathy of Jesus is apparent at every turn in Luke's Gospel in his love for sinners and his pity for the sick and the suffering. Luke pictures Jesus as weeping over Jerusalem, that was to reject him (19:41-44). Luke says that in the agony in Gethsemane "his sweat became as it were great drops of blood falling down upon the ground" (22:44). Even after the resurrection of Jesus Luke emphasizes the fact that Jesus was more than a mere ghost by his asking his disciples to handle him and by his eating a piece of broiled fish (24:38-43), difficult as it is to comprehend this transition stage in the body of Christ.

Like the other Gospels, Luke's Gospel reports Jesus as claiming to be the Son of Man, and yet no one of the Evangelists calls Jesus by this term. It is always used by Christ in the more than eighty instances in the Gospels. This agreement is not mere coincidence, and argues strongly for the genuineness of the language. And yet there is great agreement among modern scholars as to the origin and the significance of the expression. Abbott has an exhaustive treatment of every phase of the subject in his notable monograph.[1] It is vain to try to find the Aramaic *barnasha*, a man, any one, in some of the crucial passages in the Gospels, however possible in others. It is plain in Luke, as in the other Gospels, that Christ's enemies understood him to make a Messianic claim by the use of "the Son of Man." That is seen in Luke 22:69 where Jesus calls himself "the Son of Man," who will "be seated at the right hand of the power of God." The Sanhedrin then retort: "Art thou then the Son of God?" The two terms are not interchangeable, but evidently there is a bond of unity. If Jesus had simply claimed to be a man, there would be no meaning in the question. So also in John 12:34 the multitude identify "the Christ" (Messiah) with "Son of Man." In the Book of Enoch the Son of Man has a Messianic

[1] *The Son of Man, or Contributions to the Study of the Thoughts of Jesus.*

connotation, though it is not clear whether all of the book is pre-Christian or not. The word occurs in Ezekiel as his title and it is in Daniel 7 : 13 f. as "one like a Son of Man." The expression emphasizes the humanity of Christ and also his representative position as the ideal and perfect man. But it also presents in popular apprehension the claim to the Messiahship without using the technical word Messiah. Thus Jesus avoided a technical issue with his enemies till his hour had come. But the very phrase that reveals the true humanity of Jesus implies that he is more than a man. The Son of Man is the Son of God, else he could not really be the Son of Man.

So, then, Luke really means that Jesus in his human life, though absolutely genuine, is in a state of voluntary humiliation, as Paul explains in II Cor. 8 : 9 and Phil. 2 : 5–11. He had the limitations of weariness and suffering and sorrow and pain and death. Jesus battled with wrong at every turn. He clashed with the ecclesiastical hypocrites of the time who crucified him for his spiritual reality and hostility to sham. In his very humanity Jesus reveals his deity and is the hope of the race.

4. *The Saviour of Sinners.*—Christ is the great humanitarian of the ages, but he is more. Jesus has drawn the picture of the good Samaritan with his disregard for caste and race and religious prejudice and his sheer pity for a man in trouble. Jesus was the friend of the poor, of the sick, of the suffering. The lepers were not afraid to draw nigh to him. The blind cried out after Jesus when he passed by. Even the dead heard his voice and came back to life. Jesus brought health and healing at every step. He carried light and life with him to all who wished it. Jesus is the true philanthropist. Nowhere is he pictured with such attractive power as he went about doing good as in Luke's Gospel. The very heart of Luke went out to Jesus in his deeds of mercy.

But there is a deeper note than all this blessed work of social amelioration. Jesus is the saviour from sin in Luke's Gospel. He is the friend of publicans and sinners, not to condone their sins or to join in them, but to win them from their sins. Luke's Christ is Mr. H. G. Wells's "Limited God" right down in the midst of sinners, right down in the trenches, struggling and fighting evil in its lair. Jesus not merely has sympathy with

the suffering and the sinful. He has love for the souls of the
lost. He has power to help men. Jesus sees the cross ahead
of him as the way to win the lost. He makes the plain prediction (9 : 43 f.) to Peter (Luke 9 : 20–27) and repeats it. He
knows the cost of redemption from sin and he means to pay
the price with his life. It is no mythical "dying god" of the
autumn who rises, according to the myth, in the spring, as the
mystery religions teach. Jesus sees his baptism of death
(12 : 49–53) before it comes. Jesus is conscious that he is
dying for men (22 : 19 ff.). Substitution is not so hard to
understand now as it was before the Great War. Luke's
account of the death on the cross (23 : 32–54) and of the
resurrection from the dead is all in harmony with the Pauline
gospel of the death of Christ for the salvation of the sinner.
In Luke we have the Son of God and the Son of Man giving
himself as the victim of sin to save the sinner. The Gospel of
Luke has often been called the Gospel of Sacrifice. "The Son
of Man must suffer many things" (Luke 9 : 22). And Jesus
himself will explain to the two disciples on the way to Emmaus:
"Behoved it not the Christ to suffer these things, and to enter
into his glory?" (24 : 26).

5. *The Captain of Our Salvation.*—Luke gives us a Christ
with a world programme. The risen Christ on Olivet (a
wondrous picture) interprets his sufferings, death and resurrection as preliminary to the proclamation of repentance and
remission of sins to the whole world (Luke 24 : 46–49). The
disciples were to tarry in Jerusalem till clothed with power
from on high, and then they were to fare forth to the conquest
of the world. The Gospel closes with this promise of divine
energy (power, *dunamis*, dynamite) to carry out this vast
undertaking. The Acts opens with the same promise of the
Father for which they were to wait, but which was near, and
which did come at the great Pentecost. Jesus did not leave
the disciples in gloom. They were in darkness at his death,
but were full of joy at his ascension (Luke 24 : 52). The
greatest revolution in human history took place in the short
space of fifty days. Defeat was turned into victory. The
cross became the sign of conquest.

Jesus lives as the leader of men with the forward look, who
hope for better days and better men. Luke's Christ is the
risen Jesus, who carries on the work that he began (Acts 1 : 1).

The Acts, like the Gospel, records the words and deeds of Jesus. This is Luke's conception of Christ. He would probably not have written those two books at all if they only recorded ancient history that was over and done. Luke had a profound conviction that he was recording the origin of a movement that was to go to the uttermost part of the earth. The kingdom of Christ was to overturn the kingdom of Satan. Christ was to overcome Cæsar. Luke saw victory in the future. Hence he wrote. He lived to see the proof of the promise. The Acts justifies the Gospel. Paul answered the call of Christ. The Roman Empire would fall at the feet of Jesus. The conflict was to be longer than Luke knew, but he was sure that in the end of the day Jesus would win, for he is the Son of God who is now leading the forces of righteousness on earth from his throne in heaven.

The Holy Spirit is the vicegerent of Christ on earth, not the Pope of Rome. The Holy Spirit is the power of Christ on earth for all men who will let him use them. So the battle goes on. The programme of Christ is not yet completed. He is coming back some day. But that promise and that hope should be an incentive to greater zeal in carrying out Christ's programme, not a sedative to endeavor. Optimism, not pessimism, is the key-note of Luke's Gospel and the Acts. Jesus is risen and reigns. Paul carries the Gospel over the Roman Empire. You and I are to carry the torch to the uttermost part of the earth. We have Luke's Gospel with its wondrous picture of Christ to take with us. We have the Acts with the marvellous story of the power of the Holy Spirit to cheer us. Jesus is king. Let us crown him. That is what Luke means by his Gospel and Acts.

CHAPTER XIII

POINTS OF CHRONOLOGY *IN* THE LUKA*N* WR*I*T*INGS*[1]

"Now, in the fifteenth year of the reign of Tiberius Caesar, Pontius Pilate being governor of Judea, and Herod being tetrarch of Galilee, and his brother Philip tetrarch of the region of Iturea and Trachonitis, and Lysanias tetrarch of Abilene, in the high priesthood of Annas and Caiaphas" (Luke 3 : 1-3).

1. *The Beginning of John's Ministry.*—Ancient historians had great difficulty in giving precise dates for historical events. Chronological data give modern scholars no end of trouble. The ancient writers often made little effort to give the exact time. The years were counted in so many different ways. The commonest way is that pursued by Luke in his Gospel, 3 : 1-3, where by seven synchronisms he dates the beginning of the active ministry of the Baptist. Evidently Luke is taking pains to make plain when John began his work and when Jesus entered upon his ministry. Jesus was "about thirty years old" (Luke 3 : 23). John was six months older than Jesus (1 : 26). John was thus probably about thirty when he began his ministry. If we assume that the crucifixion of Jesus took place at the Passover of A. D. 30 and that there were four Passovers in the ministry of Jesus, "we reach the conclusion that the synchronisms of Luke 3 : 1, 2 are calculated for the summer (say July) of A. D. 26."[2] There is no trouble with any of the seven names given by Luke save those of Tiberius and Lysanias. Luke has been sharply criticised for alleged blunders concerning these two rulers, as he has been for his mention of Quirinius in Luke 2 : 2. We have seen how Luke has been triumphantly vindicated about Quirinius and the census of Augustus. This victory for Luke should at least make us pause before attacking him blindly.

Now Tiberius began to reign in A. D. 14, upon the death of Augustus. The fifteenth year of the reign of Tiberius, however, gives us the year A. D. 28, not A. D. 26, two years

---

[1] The *Methodist Review* (Nashville), Oct., 1920.
[2] Ramsay, *St. Paul the Traveller*, p. 386.

later than the other data call for. Has Luke made a slip here? We know from Suetonius (*Tib.* xxi) that Tiberius was associated with Augustus in the administration of the provinces.[1] Tacitus (*Ann.* I, iii, 3) speaks of Tiberius as "son, colleague in empire, consort in tribunician power."[2] Besides, some coins of Antioch, not accepted as genuine by Eckert, count Tiberius's rule from A. D. 12 instead of A. D. 14. Plummer[3] is doubtful, but is inclined to think that Luke means to count from A. D. 14, not A. D. 12. The argument from silence is always precarious. The Romans counted the beginning of a reign on the death of a previous ruler. But in the case of Titus it was not done. Ramsay[4] argues that thus we get a clew to the date of Acts: "So that Luke, being familiar with that method, applied it in the case of Tiberius. Now that was the case with Titus. His reign began from the association with his father on 1st July, A. D. 71." That is plausible, to be sure, but it is not the only interpretation of the fact about Titus. If it was done with Titus, as we know, it may have been done with Tiberius, though we have no other knowledge of it. If others did it in the case of Titus, Luke could do it in the case of Tiberius, even if he did not know of the Titus case when he wrote. Luke lived in the provinces where Tiberius shared the rule with Augustus. We must remember Quirinius and the census again before we dare to convict Luke of a blunder concerning Tiberius.

The difficulty about Lysanias is more acute. Plummer[5] puts the case clearly: "Not merely Strauss, Gfrörer, B. Baur and Hilgenfeld, but even Keim and Holtzmann, attribute to Luke the gross chronological blunder of supposing that Lysanias, son of Ptolemy, who ruled this region previous to B. C. 36, when he was killed by M. Antony, is still reigning sixty years after his death." That is the charge, put baldly and bluntly. What can be said in reply? Carpenter[6] admits that "it is in any case possible that the reference to Lysanias is a chronological error." It is even suggested that Luke "somewhat carelessly read Josephus" (*Ant.* XX, vii, 1) where he says that Trachonitis and Abila "had been the tetrarchy of Lysanias."

---

[1] *Ut provincias cum Augusto communiter administraret.*
[2] *Filius, collega imperii, consors tribuniciæ potestati adsumitur.*
[3] *Comm.*, p. 82.　　[4] *St. Paul the Traveller*, p. 387.
[5] *Comm.*, p. 84.　　[6] *Christianity According to S. Luke*, p. 229.

Carpenter admits that it is possible that there was a second Lysanias, a tetrarch. Plummer notes the pure assumption that only one Lysanias ruled in those parts. Critics had over-looked the fact that Lysanias, son of Ptolemy, was *king*, not *tetrarch*, as Luke and Josephus say. Besides, an inscription has been known for a century that ought to have taught critics the truth. Plummer notes "that at the time Tiberius was associated with Augustus there was a 'tetrarch Lysanias.'" [1] Moffatt[2] called special attention to the bearing of this inscription, a new and improved copy, found at Suk Wadi Barada, the site of Abila. It is the dedication of a temple and has the words "on behalf of the salvation of the Lords Imperial and their whole household" by "Nymphaios a freedman of Lysanias the tetrarch." Ramsay[3] has seized upon the new copy with avidity and shows that "the Lords Imperial" can only be "Tiberius and Julia" (his mother). Julia Augusta died A. D. 29, and the time of this inscription must come in between A. D. 14 and A. D. 29. Here, then, is an inscription from Abila itself, which says plainly that there was a tetrarch Lysanias in Abilene at the very time to which Luke refers. Plummer had already said that such a mistake on Luke's part was "very improbable." Now we know that it is the subjective critics who were wrong, not Luke. Once more the very stones have leaped up from the ground and have cried out in defense of the historical accuracy of Luke concerning Lysanias the tetrarch.

2. *The Length of Christ's Stay in the Tomb.*—There are various other chronological problems in Luke's Gospel, such as the three journeyings to Jerusalem (Luke 9 : 51; 13 : 22; 17 : 11), interpreted by some as only one, but most likely the three mentioned in John (7 : 2 ff.; 11 : 17 f.; 12 : 1). Lieutenant-Colonel G. Mackinlay[4] seeks to prove that Luke has three parallel narratives. I have endeavored to show[5] that Luke (like Matthew and Mark) really has the death of Christ on the same day as John, and ate the Passover at the regular time. Luke agrees with all the Gospels as to the length of Christ's stay in the tomb, but makes the matter clearer than any of

---

[1] Cf. Boeckh, *Corp. Inscr. Gr.*, 4523, 4521.
[2] *The Expositor*, January, 1913.
[3] *Bearing of Recent Discovery*, p. 298.   [4] *A Difficulty Removed*, 1919.
[5] Broadus's *Harmony of the Gospels*, pp. 253-7.

them. Luke notes (23:54) that the day of the death and burial of Jesus "was the day of the Preparation, and the Sabbath drew on" (or dawned). The word for "Preparation"[1] is to-day the name for Friday in modern Greek. It was the technical name for the day before the Sabbath. The word for "drew on"[2] literally means the coming of light, but it was used not simply of the dawning of the twelve-hour day, but also of the twenty-four-hour day. Matthew (28:1) uses it as Luke does here: "Now late on the Sabbath day, as it began to dawn toward the first day of the week." The first day began at sundown, the Jewish way of reckoning. Luke adds that "on the Sabbath they (the women) rested according to the commandment." Thus we have a part of Friday afternoon (the burial) and all of the Sabbath day. Then Luke adds (24:1): "But on the first day of the week, at early dawn,[3] they came unto the tomb, bringing the spices which they had prepared" (cf. Matt. 28:1 and Mark 16:1). At sunrise (Mark 16:1; John 20:1) Jesus was already risen from the tomb. It is not possible to escape this piece of chronology as Luke has recorded it, unless Luke is in error. There is no evidence that he is incorrect. The use of "after three days" a few times cannot set aside so plain a narrative. Luke represents Christ as saying that he rose on the third day (24:7). Luke has "on the third day" (9:22) where Mark (10:34) has "after three days." Free vernacular in all languages uses the fuller phrase without meaning full seventy-two hours. "On the third day" cannot be understood as meaning "on the fourth day," while "after three days" can be understood to mean "on the third day." So the matter stands against all theories to the contrary.

3. *Theudas.*—The case of Theudas is a test case of one's confidence in Luke. As yet there is no clear solution of the apparent contradiction between Luke and Josephus. In Acts 5:36 f. Luke mentions the revolt of Judas the Galilean as after the revolt of Theudas. Josephus[4] mentions both of them in the same order as Luke (Theudas and Judas), though twenty lines apart, but Josephus explains that the revolt of Judas took place in the time of the great census under Quirinius in A. D. 6, while the revolt under Theudas occurred under the

---

[1] παρασκευή.
[2] ἐπέφωσκεν.
[3] ὄρθρου βαθέως.
[4] *Ant.* XX, v, 1 f.

Emperor Claudius, when Cuspius Fadus was Roman procurator (A. D. 44–46). Luke not only has the chronology reversed, but reports Gamaliel as speaking of the revolt of Theudas that, according to Josephus, took place some thirty years after his speech.

One explanation is that Luke read Josephus and was misled by the mere order there, and failed to see the real dates, and so misrepresented Josephus. But that makes Luke very careless in this use of Josephus, if he did use him. But the differences are so great that scholars like Schuerer,[1] who dates Luke after Josephus, say that Luke either did not read Josephus at all or forgot all that he had read.[2] We have seen already that Luke in all probability wrote the Acts before 70 A. D. So we may dismiss the idea of any use of Josephus.

But the discrepancy remains. It is suggested by some that Luke merely reports Gamaliel, who is responsible for the error, if it is one. But Luke would hardly let it pass in that case with no comment.

At bottom we are called on to choose between the accuracy of Luke and of Josephus, unless both are right. Both can only be right on the hypothesis that there were two men by the name of Theudas who raised a revolt. Rackham[3] thinks that "in all probability both are right. There were similar disturbances throughout this period, as Josephus himself testifies. Theudas is a contracted form, which may stand for a number of names—Theodotus, Theodosius, Theodorus, etc., so it is quite possible that different persons are referred to." Ramsay[4] holds that "there is no real difficulty in believing that more than one impostor may have borne or taken the name Theudas." Nösgen[5] observes that "Josephus describes four men bearing the name Simon within forty years, and three that of Judas within ten years, all of whom were instigators of rebellion."

But, suppose both do refer to the same man and event, who is to be believed? Furneaux[6] says: "There is no reason for doubting the accuracy of Josephus' chronology at this point; and the remarkable accuracy of Luke's historical narrative is

[1] *Lucas und Josephus* (*Zeitschrift. f. Krit. Theol.*, 1876, p. 574).
[2] Cf. Sanday, *Bampton Lectures*, 1893, p. 278.
[3] *Comm.*, p. 74.   [4] *Was Christ Born at Bethlehem ?*, p. 259.
[5] *Apostelgeschichte*, p. 147.   [6] *Comm., in loco.*

no sufficient ground for denying the possibility of inaccuracy in a speech composed, at least to some extent, by himself." We are not assuming in our studies that Luke could not be inaccurate in any particular. We only ask that he be treated as fairly as Josephus. Who has the best reputation as a reliable historian, Luke or Josephus? To-day Luke stands far above Josephus. "In his *Antiquities* Josephus corrects many mistakes which he made in his earlier work on the Jewish War." [1]

But in all candor we must admit that this difficulty has not yet been solved. "We have to leave the difficulty unsolved. We must hope for the discovery of further evidence. Meantime, no one who finds Luke to be a trustworthy historian in the rest of his History will see any difficulty in this passage." Thus Ramsay[2] avows his willingness to trust Luke till he is proven to be wrong. That has not been done as to Acts 5 : 36 f. Luke has won the right to be credited till he is shown to be in error. We can wait here for further light.

4. *Paul's Visits to Jerusalem.*—There are certainly four, probably five, of these visits of Paul to the Jewish metropolis after his conversion (Acts 9 : 26–30; 11 : 29 f. and 12 : 25; 15 : 2–29; probably 18 : 22; 21 : 17–23 : 30). In themselves they offer no difficulty. It is only when we turn to Galatians that trouble arises. In Galatians 1 : 18 and 2 : 1 Paul speaks of two visits to Jerusalem. The visit in Acts 9 : 26 and Gal. 1 : 18 is the same. But where does Gal. 2 : 1 come in? Is it the visit in Acts 11 : 29 or 15 : 2? Galatians was certainly written before the visits in Acts 18 : 22 and 21 : 17. It would not seem to matter much except that in Gal. 2 : 1–10 and Acts 15 : 2–29 the Judaizing controversy is up for discussion. Lake,[3] however, denies this and says "the subject is not the same at all." He holds that in Galatians the subject "is merely whether the mission to the uncircumcised should be continued, while in Acts the circumcision of the Gentiles is the main point." But surely that is a misapprehension of Gal. 2 : 1–10, where Paul so stoutly refused to allow Titus to be circumcised on the demand of the timid brethren to satisfy the Judaizers. Ramsay has urged that Paul means that he was not compelled to

---

[1] Rackham, *Comm.*, note 2, p. 74.
[2] *Was Christ Born at Bethlehem ?*, p. 259.
[3] Hastings's *Dict. of the Ap. Ch.* ("Acts").

circumcise Titus, but did it voluntarily. But that theory makes incomprehensible Paul's vehemence in the matter.

Quite a group of modern scholars obviate the apparent contradiction between the two reports in Gal. 2:1-10 and Acts 15:2-29, by making them accounts of different events. It is argued that in Gal. 2:1-10 Paul really has in mind the visit to Jerusalem in Acts 11:29. It is urged that this view is necessary because Paul in Galatians records all the visits that he made to Jerusalem. But that is not the point in Galatians. There Paul is asserting his independence of the Twelve Apostles and showing that his authority was on a par with theirs. He mentions in Gal. 1:18 f. that he saw only Cephas of the Twelve, and made only a pleasant visit. In Acts 11:29 f. only "the elders" are mentioned. It is possible that the Apostles were absent on this occasion. If so, Paul would not need to refer to this visit. Lightfoot in his *Commentary on Galatians* has made a powerful argument for the identification of Gal. 2:1-10 with Acts 15:2-29. His view is that in Galatians Paul refers to the private conference that took place between the two public gatherings, in which Paul won Peter, James and John to his view of Gentile freedom from Jewish ceremonialism. This is what concerned Paul's argument. In Acts Luke is not interested in that point, but narrates the public gatherings when the programme was carried through. On the whole, this view still seems to be the most plausible explanation of the situation. One has only to keep clearly before him the purpose of Luke in the Acts.

It is not necessary here to discuss what was done at the Jerusalem conference in Acts 15, and whether the text in D is to be followed which omits "things strangled," and adds the golden rule in negative form. This text makes no demands of the Gentiles at all save purely moral issues (fornication, murder, idolatry). On the whole, the other text is most likely genuine.

It is even argued by some that Galatians was written before the conference in Acts 15, and so Gal. 2:1-10 could not refer to the same event. This view is advocated by Round,[1] Emmet,[2] Bartlet,[3] Lake[4] and Ramsay.[5] But M. Jones[6] holds that

---

[1] *The Date of Galatians.*   [2] *Comm. on Galatians.*
[3] *Apostolic Age*, p. 84.   [4] Lake, *Earlier Epistles of St. Paul.*
[5] *Expositor*, viii, 5, pp. 127 f.   [6] *N. T. in Twentieth Century*, p. 248.

such a view utterly discredits Luke. "Acts has, however, an equal claim to be heard on this point, and if the early date of Galatians is adopted it becomes exceedingly difficult to credit the author with any historical accuracy, much less regard him as a historian of first rank." Jones is not able to under-stand how Ramsay, in particular, "the strongest living advocate of the historical value of Acts," is able to reconcile the early date of Galatians "with the repudiation of his (Luke's) clear statement which this date of Galatians involves." Jones[1] feels that "the historical value of the book reaches its climax in the discussion of the story of the Apostolic Council in Jerusalem in Acts 15." The very fact that Ramsay has come round to the early date of Galatians and still takes the view that Luke's history is unsurpassed in respect of its trustworthiness[2] is enough to make one pause. But, on the whole, I sympathize with Jones in his contention that the straightforward narrative of events in Acts calls for a date for Galatians subsequent to the Jerusalem conference. We are not called upon here to settle the Galatian controversy, but only to say that it is gratuitous from the standpoint of Acts to create a difficulty by the early date of Galatians which does not exist on the theory of the late date. The data in Galatians are wholly indecisive in themselves and readily allow the later date between II Corinthians and Romans which Lightfoot proposed. That theory leaves both Paul and Luke intelligible and reliable. It is not scientific and fair to Luke to foist upon Acts a view of Galatians that throws his historical data into a jumble. Once more we can say that Luke's credit as a historian is too great to be upset by a mere speculative theory as to the date of Galatians. I am not willing to say with Jones[3] that, "if the Epistle to the Galatians was written at this period, St. Luke must have entirely misconceived the situation, and he ceases to have any claim to our respect as a serious historian." But I do say that Luke's proved veracity as a historian stops the acceptance of a mere theory, by no means the most probable one, of the date of Galatians. Luke

---

[1] *Ibid.*, p. 242.

[2] *Bearing of Recent Discovery*, p. 81.

[3] *Op. cit.*, p. 249. Jones stands by this position against Plooij, who also adopts the view that Galatians is before the Jerusalem conference in Acts 15 (*Expositor*, June, 1919, pp. 444 f.).

is entitled to that much consideration unless the earlier date
can be proved true beyond controversy.

5. *The Death of Herod Agrippa I and the Famine in Judea.*
In Acts 11:27–30 Luke mentions the prophecy of the famine
by Agabus and the contribution to the poor saints in Jerusalem
by the Gentile (Greek) Church in Antioch which Barnabas and
Saul turned over to the elders.   Luke does not specifically say
that the famine had actually begun when the money was sent,
but Ramsay[1] rejects Lightfoot's view that the money was
brought a year or more before the famine as not "a natural or
a useful procedure."   What was the date of the famine?
Josephus (*Ant.* XX, v) places it in the procuratorship of
Alexander, which ended in A. D. 48 and could not have begun
before 45.   So, then, A. D. 46 is the probable year.   Orosius
(VII, vi), a writer of the fifth century, locates the beginning of
the famine in the fourth year of Claudius, which would be
A. D. 45.   The beginning of the current year of reckoning has
always to be borne in mind, and Ramsay[2] notes a failure
always to do this in Turner's "Chronology of the N. T." in
Hastings's *D. B.*   So, then, the years 45 and 46 can very well
be the years of the famine.

Luke (Acts 12:20–23) gives the death of Herod before mentioning the return of Barnabas and Saul to Antioch (12:25),
though verse 24 suggests an interim of some sort, and verse 25
really belongs to the story of chapter 13.   The precise sequence
of events in chapters 11 and 12 is not clear.   Herod Agrippa
killed James the brother of John (12:2) and put Peter in
prison, who, on his miraculous release, left the city (12:17).
Was this persecution of the Apostles by Herod after the visit
of Barnabas and Saul or before?   The coins[3] say that Herod
Agrippa I reigned nine years, while Josephus asserts that he
died in the seventh year of his reign.   The coins are considered
spurious by some, and others think that Josephus reckons
from A. D. 39, when the tetrarchy of Antipas was added to
the rule of Herod, instead of 37, when he was appointed king
of the tetrarchy of Philip.   In A. D. 41 Judea, Samaria and
Abilene were added, so that till A. D. 44 Herod Agrippa I
ruled over all of Palestine.   Josephus contradicts himself in

---

[1] *St. Paul the Traveller*, p. 69.
[2] *Was Christ Born at Bethlehem?*, p. 222 f.
[3] Madden, *Coins of the Jews*, p. 130.

the *War* and the *Antiquities*. On the whole, A. D. 44 appears as the most likely date for the death of Herod (so Turner).

If this is true, we must think of the events of Acts 12 : 1–23 (up to the death of Herod in A. D. 44) as happening before the famine in Judea of Acts 11 : 27–30 (A. D. 45–46) with the visit of Barnabas and Saul. In that case, the Apostles had left Jerusalem, and Barnabas and Saul performed their mission with the elders (11 : 30) and went back to Antioch with John Mark (12 : 25). The story is intelligible and Luke is consistent. These two dates (A. D. 44 and 45–46) give us a fairly definite point of contact between Luke's narrative and the outside world.

6. *The Expulsion of the Jews from Rome.*—In Acts 18 : 2 Luke says that Aquila and his wife Priscilla had "lately come from Italy," "because Claudius had commanded all the Jews to depart from Rome." Paul found them in Corinth on his arrival there from Athens (18 : 1 f.). Here again Luke gives a point of contact with general history. When were the Jews expelled from Rome? Suetonius[1] mentions the event, but gives no date. Josephus and Tacitus fail to mention the fact. If Suetonius had not done so, this would have been another error charged up to Luke. Orosius (VII, vi, 15) says that it was in the ninth year of Claudius, which would put it about A. D. 50 as he counted the years.[2] This year suits very well Luke's narrative in Acts 18 : 1 f.

7. *Gallio's Proconsulship.*—Luke (Acts 18 : 12 ff.) says that Paul was brought to trial in Corinth "when Gallio was proconsul of Achaia." Turner in his notable article on the "Chronology of the N. T." (Hastings's *D. B.*) had concluded that Gallio entered upon his proconsulship probably not before A. D. 50. But Deissmann in his *St. Paul*[3] has discussed the meaning of an inscription at Delphi, which refers to Gallio as proconsul, with the date the 26th "acclamation" of the Emperor Claudius. A Russian, A. Nikitsky, first published this inscription,[4] but Deissmann has shown[5] that "St. Paul must have come to Corinth in the first month of the year 50, and left Corinth late in the summer of the year 51," unless, for-

---

[1] *Claudius*, 25. *Judœos, impulsore Christo, assidue tumultuantes Roma expulsit.*

[2] Ramsay, *Was Christ Born at Bethlehem ?*, p. 223.   [3] Appendix *I*.

[4] *Epigraphical Studies at Delphi*, 1898.   [5] *Op. cit.*, p. 256.

sooth, the years are 51 and 52 respectively.[1] The date of the
27th acclamation of Claudius is known by an inscription to be
August 1, A. D. 52. So, then, Gallio was proconsul before
that date. We know that "the 22nd, 23rd, and 24th acclamations all came in the 11th tribunician year" of Claudius (Lake),
which was January 25, A. D. 51, to January 24, A. D. 52.
The date of the 25th acclamation has not been found, "so that
really the end of 51 is the earliest probable date for the 26th
acclamation."[2] So, then, the Delphi inscription with the
26th acclamation, while Gallio was proconsul, falls between
the end of A. D. 51 and August 1, A. D. 52. The proconsul
usually entered upon his office July 1. Gallio, then, began his
office either July 1, A. D. 51, or July 1, A. D. 52. The latter
date, though possible, would put less than a month between
the 26th and the 27th acclamations. Paul had been a year
and six months in Corinth before Gallio came (Acts 18:1).
He did not stay long thereafter. Gallio was probably proconsul July 1, A. D. 51, to July 1, A. D. 52. If the Jews brought
Paul before Gallio soon after he came into office, Paul probably
left Corinth in the late summer or early autumn of A. D. 51.
He came to Corinth in the early months of A. D. 50, which
date agrees with the previous date already arrived at in this
chapter. While in Corinth, during A. D. 50–51, Paul wrote the
two Epistles to the Church in Thessalonica.

All things considered, the Delphi inscription gives us the
one certain date in Paul's ministry and in the Book of Acts.
All other dates must now be made to conform to the new light
here turned upon the chronology of the Acts and of Paul's
Epistles. The first mission tour (A. D. 46 and 47, or 47 and
48) follows the famine and visit of Barnabas and Saul to Jerusalem (A. D. 45–46). The Jerusalem conference could come
also in A. D. 48 and the new tour begin in A. D. 48, with the
arrival in Corinth, A. D. 50. All dates in Acts and Paul's
Epistles have to be on a sliding scale. M. Jones[3] has made a
fine survey of *A New Chronology of the Life of St. Paul*, by
Plooij,[4] a Dutch scholar, who has gone over the whole ground
afresh. But we strike *terra firma* in the Delphi inscription.

8. *The Coming of Festus.*—Luke says (Acts 24:27): "But

---

[1] *Ibid.*, p. 255.   [2] Lake, Hastings's *Dict. of Ap. Ch.*
[3] *The Expositor*, May, June and August, 1910.
[4] *De Chronologie van het leven van Paulus.*

when two years were fulfilled, Felix was succeeded by Porcius Festus." Here again we come upon a note of time in touch with the Roman world, but unfortunately the date is peculiarly uncertain. Lightfoot picked out the death of Herod Agrippa I in A. D. 44 (45 for Paul's second visit) and the voyage of Paul and Luke to Rome in A. D. 60 as the foci for fixing Paul's career. "We have thus ascertained two fixed dates in the chronology of St. Paul's life—A. D. 45 for his second journey to Jerusalem and A. D. 60 for his voyage to Rome. The former of these being an isolated event in St. Luke's narrative is of little value comparatively for our purpose; but from the latter the whole of the known chronology of St. Paul's life is determined, by means of the notices in the Acts of the sequence of events and the time occupied by them, together with occasional allusions in the Epistles."[1] But, unfortunately, the date of the coming of Festus is by no means clear. Lightfoot argued that Paul on his arrival at Rome was turned over "to the prefect of the prætorium"[2] according to the reading of some manuscripts for Acts 28:16, and so it was while Burrhus was in office. He died in 62, and 61 would be a good date. But Ramsay[3] shows that this officer was most likely the *Princeps Peregrinorum*, and the argument about Burrhus is beside the point. Eusebius places the coming of Festus in place of Felix in the last year of Claudius, A. D. 54, but if Eusebius is right Luke is wrong, for we cannot add two years in Cæsarea and time for other events from Corinth (A. D. 51) to Antioch, the three years in Ephesus, and the trip to Macedonia and to Corinth and then to Jerusalem, and then two years in Cæsarea under Felix, all by A. D. 54. The thing cannot be done. We have stuck a peg in Corinth when Gallio came in A. D. 51. Who is right here, Eusebius or Luke? Ramsay[4] confesses that his prejudices were all in favor of Eusebius, and he was not willing to admit that he had "committed an inexplicable blunder." But Erbes[5] gave Ramsay[6] the clew to the mistake of Eusebius. Eusebius overlooked

[1] "The Chronology of St. Paul's Life and Epistles" (*Biblical Essays*, pp. 220 f.).
[2] τῷ στρατοπεδάρχῃ.   [3] *St. Paul the Traveller*, p. 347.
[4] "The Pauline Chronology" (*Pauline and Other Studies*, p. 349).
[5] "Todestage Pauli und Petri" (Gebhardt and Harnack's *Texte und Untersuch.*, XIV, 1).
[6] *Pauline and Other Studies*, p. 350.

the *interregnum* between Herod Agrippa I, who died in A. D. 44, and Herod Agrippa II, who began to reign A. D. 50, not A. D. 45. So the tenth ´year of his reign when Festus came was A. D. 59. This comes very close to the date of Lightfoot, who made A. D. 60 as the date of the recall of Felix and the coming of Festus. We may, therefore, accept A. D. 59 as the time when Festus came to Cæsarea. Ramsay[1] even thinks that Acts 20:5 ff. shows that Paul celebrated Passover in Philippi Thursday, April 7, A. D. 57. At any rate, that is in accord with the other dates shown to be probable. Jones[2] agrees that "Felix was relieved by his successor Festus, some time in the summer of 59." The two years of Paul's imprisonment in Cæsarea, therefore, were the summer of A. D. 57 to summer of A. D. 59. Zenos[3] still argues for A. D. 60 for the coming of Festus, but A. D. 59 has the best of it at the present. Luke comes out with flying colors in these various chronological tests in every instance save that of Theudas. In that instance, for the present, we must suspend judgment.

Harnack[4] gives an interesting summary of the chronological data in the Acts, where occur statements of years, months, days, feasts and indefinite dates. They make a considerable list. Harnack notes that nowhere in Acts does Luke give a scientific dating of any event, as in Luke 3:1. That is true, but, as we have seen, he frequently connects his narrative with the stream of history in his time, so that we are now able to draw a reasonably accurate and clear outline for the chronology of the whole of Acts. Ramsay[5] says that "Luke was deficient in the sense for time; and hence his chronology is bad." That is only true so far as making definite dates and keeping the relative proportion of dates. He is far better in this than most of the ancients, who did not have our concern for outstanding dates.

[1] *Pauline Studies*, p. 352.
[2] "A New Chronology of the Life of St. Paul" (*The Expositor*, August, 1919, p. 117).
[3] Article "Dates" in Hastings's *Dict. of Ap. Church.*
[4] *Acts of the Apostles*, pp. 6–30.
[5] *St. Paul the Traveller*, p. 18.

CHAPTER XIV

ARCHÆOLOGICAL AND GEOGRAPHICAL DATA IN THE ACTS

"And the lictors reported these words unto the prætors" (Acts 16 : 38).

1. *The Test of Historical Geography.*—The historian, if he is not a mere rhetorician and word-painter, must call names and titles and places as well as dates. We have seen how Luke fares under the test of modern scholarship in the matter of chronology. It remains to examine his treatment of points of archæological and geographical interest. If Josephus crosses Luke's path in historical details, Strabo in his geography traverses much of the same ground that Luke traces in the Acts. But both Strabo and Xenophon tell much less than Luke does concerning certain parts of Asia Minor through which Paul journeyed. When Ramsay[1] began his researches for the reconstruction of the history and geography of Asia Minor, he was confronted with the fact that "if Luke's narrative was trustworthy, it was for me exceptionally valuable, as giving evidence on a larger scale. There was nothing else like it. No other ancient traveller has left an account of the journeys which he made across Asia Minor; and if the narrative of Paul's travels rests on first-class authority, it placed in my hands a document of unique and exceptional value to guide my investigations."[2] With this idea in mind Ramsay set to work to test Luke's record in Acts from the standpoint of a modern archæological expert. Ramsay had made Asia Minor under Roman rule his peculiar province, and by years of travel and research on the ground had gained a mass of fresh knowledge possessed by no other living scholar. He endeavored to treat Luke as he would Strabo or Xenophon.[3] "This prepossession, that Christian authors lie outside the pale of real literature and that early Christians were not to be estimated as men, has been the enemy for me to attack ever since I began

[1] See his *Historical Geography of Asia Minor.*
[2] *Bearing of Recent Discovery*, p. 81.   [3] *Ibid.*, p. 83.

to look into the Christian authors with unprejudiced eyes." As an instance of how men allow prejudice to shut their eyes to the truth, Ramsay[1] notes that in Acts 21:15 Luke says that "a large party of travellers used horses, a statement inter. preted and confirmed by Chrysostom," though, he adds, "it has seemed almost sacrilegious to some modern scholars to suggest that Paul even made a journey except on foot." Ram. say[2] has found about the New Testament writers that "in becoming Christians those writers did not cease to be men: they only gained that element of thoroughness, of sincerity and enthusiasm, the want of which is so unpleasing in later classical literature."

Luke has stood the test with wonderful success. Moffatt[3] speaks of "Luke's remarkable degree of accuracy in geographical, political, and social data," though he insists that "he must be judged by the canons of his age, and in the light of his opportunities." Lightfoot,[4] Vigoroux[5] and Ramsay[6] have all borne testimony to the value of Luke in these respects. Headlam[7] observes that "a great test of the accuracy of the writer in the last twelve chapters is given by the evidence from archæology." The opportunity for pitfalls is here very great. Harnack[8] devotes a whole chapter to "Lands, Nations, Cities, and Houses" in the Acts. One of Ramsay's most helpful volumes is his *Cities of St. Paul.* The inscriptions have been found of great value in their sidelights on Luke's story. One of the most modern ideas is to note the influence of geography upon the life of a people, as in Palestine, Egypt, Greece and Asia Minor. We see it to-day in America and in Europe. The point of it all is that Luke was in the atmosphere of the first century himself, else he could not have stepped so securely in the mass and maze of shifting political scenes.

• 2. *Roman Provinces.*—Luke wrote of the Roman world and in the Roman world, but "Luke is throughout his work a Greek, never a Roman," and "speaks of things Roman as they

---

[1] *Ibid.*   [2] *Church in the Roman Empire,* p. 176.
[3] *Introduction to the Lit. of N. T.,* p. 304.
[4] Essays on *Supernatural Religion,* pp. 291–305.
[5] *Le nouveau Testament,* 1889, *et les découvertes archæologiques modernes,* 1896.
[6] *Church in the Roman Empire,* chaps. II–VIII.
[7] *Hastings's D. B.* ("Acts").
[8] *The Acts of the Apostles,* chap. II.

appeared to a Greek." [1]   He may have been a Roman citizen,
but his outlook was that of a Greek. "To Luke the great
antithesis—Gentile and Jew—quite obliterated the lesser distinction between Roman citizen and Roman provincial, when
the provincial was a Greek." [2]   Luke "regularly uses the popular phraseology, and not the strictly and technically accurate
terms for Roman things," but all the same "he is never guilty
of the blunders that puzzle the epigraphist in Asian or Galatian inscriptions." All the more surprising, therefore, is the
minute accuracy of Luke in the matter of the Roman provinces. In the Roman Empire there were provinces and vassal
kingdoms. There were constant changes, as can be seen in
Palestine, which was a vassal kingdom under Herod the Great.
On his death, B. C. 4, it was divided into several tetrarchies
(Luke 3 : 1) or petty provinces (Herod Antipas, tetrarch of
Galilee and Samaria; Herod Philip, tetrarch of Iturea and
Trachonitis; and Archelaus, ethnarch of Judea and Samaria,
with hopes of a kingship). But Archelaus lost his rule in
A. D. 6, and a Roman procurator (cf. Pontius Pilate) ruled
over the secondary province of Judea (and Samaria). But
from A. D. 41–44 Herod Agrippa I was king of all Palestine,
when Roman procurators come back, with headquarters in
Cæsarea, like Felix and Festus, termed "the governor" by
Luke (Acts 24 : 1, 27). The temporary reign of Herod
Agrippa I over Judea explains how he was able to compass
the death of James the brother of John (Acts 12 : 1 f.) and to
put Peter in prison (12 : 3 ff.). He clearly deserved the fate
that befell him (12 : 20–23). Judea was rather a sort of client-
state than a full province. It was under the supervision of
the province of Syria and Cilicia and Phœnicia. The imperial
provinces embraced about three-fourths of the empire. The
proprætors held office indefinitely while proconsuls were chosen
annually.

Maclean observes that it is a good test of accuracy in a
writer in the first century A. D. to examine whether he names
the Roman governors rightly. There were two kinds of provinces in the empire: the senatorial and the imperial. The
senatorial provinces were under the control of the senate, and
the governor was called proconsul. [3] The emperor governed

[1] Ramsay, *Was Christ Born at Bethlehem ?*, p. 52.
[2] *Ibid.*, p. 53.   [3] Ἀνθύπατος.

the imperial provinces and the governor was termed prouttor.[1] Luke mentions six senatorial provinces: Achaia (Acts
18:12; 19:21, etc.), Asia (2:9; 19:10, 26, etc.), Crete and
Cyrene (2:10, 11; 27:7, 21, etc.), Cyprus (4:36; 13:4, 8,
etc.), Bithynia and Pontus (2:9; 16:7, etc.), Macedonia
(16:10, 11, etc.). So Luke rightly calls Gallio proconsul in
Acts 18:12. Achaia had been joined to Macedonia and made
imperial in A. D. 15, but in A. D. 44 it was again senatorial.
So Luke is right. It was once claimed that Luke blundered
in calling Sergius Paulus "proconsul" (Acts 13:8, 12) instead
of "proprætor," on the ground that Cyprus was an imperial
province. So it was once, but at this time it was a senatorial
province, though soon afterward imperial again. But General
Cesnola[2] has discovered an inscription on the north coast of
Cyprus which is dated "in the proconsulship of Paulus,"
clearly the Sergius Paulus of Acts 13:8, 12. Ramsay[3] makes
this year A. D. 47. Once more Luke is vindicated by the
rocks.

The six imperial provinces mentioned by Luke are Cappadocia (Acts 2:9), Cilicia and Syria and Phœnicia (Acts 15:41,
etc.), Egypt with title of prefect for governor (2:10), Galatia
on the south Galatian theory (16:6; 18:23), Lycia (27:5),
Pamphylia (2:10; 13:13; 27:5, etc.). There is, besides, the
subordinate province of Judea, with its procurator subject to
the proprætor in Syria.

There was constant interchange of provinces between the
emperor and the senate, but Luke ploughs his way safely
enough.

3. *Ethnographic Terminology.*—The Romans did not destroy
the life of the peoples whom they conquered. They let the
various nations keep up their customs and languages. In a
broad and general way they allowed many religions to be
observed, though all had to be licensed (*religio licita*) and
legalized. The prevalence of the emperor-cult led to severe
persecution of Christianity when it came to be differentiated
from Judaism. But the Roman provinces and kingdoms were
administrative for convenience and efficiency. They were not
drawn upon national and racial lines. But the old lines of

[1] See Mommsen, *The Provinces of the Roman Empire.*
[2] Cf. Hogarth, *Devia Cypria,* p. 114.
[3] *Bearing of Recent Discovery,* p. 157.

race and national cleavage remained. The old languages continued to be spoken along with the current Greek (the *Koinê*) and the official Latin. Thus Paul addressed the people of Lystra in Greek, as usual, but the multitude spoke "in the speech of Lycaonia" (Acts 14 : 11). Ramsay[1] thinks that "the issue of events showed that the Empire had made a mistake in disregarding so completely the existing lines of demarcation between tribes and races in making its new political provinces. For a time it succeeded in establishing them, while the energy of the Empire was still fresh, and its forward movement continuous and steady. But the differences of tribal and national character were too great to be completely set aside; they revived while the energy of the Empire decayed during the second century." But in the first century the Roman system was at its height.

The popular terminology, however, survived all the while. There are abundant evidences of it in Acts, instances where Luke uses popular names for countries rather than official names of provinces. Thus we find Pisidia (Acts 13 : 14), Lycaonia (14 : 6, 11, etc.), Phrygia (16 : 6; 18 : 23) and Galatia (16 : 6; 18 : 23), if north Galatia is meant. Ramsay[2] points out how in southern Galatia (the southern part of the Roman province of Galatia), distinct *Regiones*[3] existed like Phrygia, Pisidia, Lycaonia (as distinct from Lycaonia Antiochiana which was ruled by King Antiochus). Ramsay insists on the accuracy of Luke in the description of these various regions. In any case he preserves the old ethnographic names. Ramsay[4] argues that Iconium was not a part of Lycaonia, like Lystra and Derbe, though in the province of Galatia. We are not yet able to trace every detail in Roman provincial history and administration, but Luke is wholly in accord with all known facts in his use of names for the various divisions of Asia Minor in the first century. He sharply distinguishes Antioch in Pisidia from Antioch in Syria.

4. *Colonies.*—Philippi alone is termed a colony[5] by Luke (Acts 16 : 12), though various other cities are mentioned that were colonies at the time of the events narrated by Luke,[6]

---

[1] *St. Paul the Traveller*, p. 136.
[2] *Ibid.*, p. 104.
[3] χῶραι.
[4] *Cities of St. Paul*, pp. 350 ff.
[5] καλωνία, Latin *colonia*.
[6] Cf. Souter, "Colony," Hastings's *Dict. of Ap. Church*.

such as Corinth (since 27 B. C.), Lystra (since 12 B. C.), Pisidian Antioch (since before 27 B. C.), Ptolemais (since before A. D. 47), Puteoli (since 194 B. C.), Syracuse (since 21 B. C.), Troas (since about 20 B. C.), eight with Philippi. It is possible that Luke mentions the fact that Philippi was a colony because of his long residence there and his natural interest and pride in the city. It used to be said that Luke had blundered badly in applying the word "district"[1] to a division of a province like Macedonia at this time. The Romans had divided the province into four districts B. C. 167. But an ancient Macedonian coin uses the word in this sense.[2] At this time Amphipolis claimed the title of first city of the district in which Philippi was. But Philippi had its own pride in the matter and would not yield the title to its rival city. Lightfoot (*in loco*) suggests that by "first city of the district" Luke merely means geographical location, not importance. But Luke gives the touch of life to his narrative by this detail.

The Roman colonies were small editions of Rome itself. Normally some three hundred Romans went out to establish the colony. These men remained Roman citizens, "a portion of Rome itself planted amidst a community not itself possessed of Roman citizenship" (Souter). These cities were advance-guards of the mother city. They were military outposts to hold in subjection the surrounding country. The various colonies were connected by military roads with each other and with Rome itself. At first the men were citizen-soldiers, but in time of peace the military aspect was not so prominent. "It was an honor for a provincial city to be made into a *colonia*, because this was proof that it was of special importance, specially dear to the Emperor, and worthy to be the residence of Roman citizens, who were the aristocracy of the provincial towns in which they lived" (Souter). The Greeks knew how to colonize with skill. The Romans followed a different plan, but with success. The British have learned how to plant colonies and to give them freedom that stood the strain of the World War.

There were other cities that had special privileges. These free cities, as they were called, had self-government within the Roman province where they were. Luke mentions Athens, Ephesus, Thessalonica and Tarsus. The Romans did not

---

[1] μερίς.   [2] Cf. Ramsay, *Church in the Roman Empire*, p. 158.

give a provincial constitution to a country without a certain amount of civilization. The free cities and the colonies were points of power. Paul went to the colonies and to the free cities as centres of influence. The colonies held themselves above the other cities.

5. *Roman Citizenship.*—One could be a citizen of a free city like Tarsus and not be a Roman citizen. Paul was proud of his native city and had a right to be: "I am a Jew, of Tarsus in Cilicia, a citizen of no mean city" (Acts 21 : 39). Ramsay[1] has shown what it meant to Paul to live as a boy in this great educational centre, this Greek city in the Orient. Those who were not born Roman citizens could acquire it by purchase, as Claudius Lysias did (Acts 22 : 28), sometimes through infamous court favorites. Roman citizenship was sometimes bestowed as a reward for services to the state, as may have been the case with Paul's father or grandfather, according to Maclean's conjecture.[2] Proud as Paul was of being a citizen of Tarsus, he was much more so of his Roman citizenship. With simple dignity he said to Claudius Lysias: "But I am *a Roman* born" (Acts 22 : 28). Luke takes careful note of Paul's pride in and use of his Roman citizenship. Souter[3] observes that the ancient Greeks and Romans had a higher conception of citizenship than we have to-day: "To the ancient member of a *polis* or *civitas* citizenship was life and life was citizenship." When Paul spoke to the Sanhedrin in Acts 23 : 1, "Brethren, I have lived before God in all good conscience until this day," he used the word to live as a citizen.[4] Paul made use of his rights as a Roman citizen to carry on his work of evangelization. "It was no doubt this citizenship which gave Paul such an advantage as the Apostle of the Gentiles, and which inspired him with the great plan of utilizing the civilization of the Roman state to spread the gospel along the lines of communication."[5]

It has been objected that Paul did not take advantage of his citizenship in time to prevent the scourging in Philippi without a fair trial. But it is doubtful if the magistrates allowed Paul to say aught in reply to the claptrap of the master of the girl whom Paul had freed (Acts 16 : 21-23). It looks

[1] *Cities of St. Paul*, part II.
[2] *One Vol. Hastings's D. B.* ("Paul").
[3] Hastings's *Dict. of Ap. Church* ("Citizenship").
[4] πεπολίτευμαι.
[5] Maclean, *ibid.*

as if the mob made such a clamor that Paul had no chance to defend himself. But next morning, when the magistrates sent word for Paul and Silas to be released, Paul had his opportunity: "They have beaten us publicly, uncondemned, men that are Romans, and have cast us into prison; and do they now cast us out privily? Nay verily; but let them come themselves and bring us out" (16:37). His words had the desired effect, for the magistrates "feared when they heard that they were Romans." Silas was evidently a Roman citizen also. In Philippi Roman citizenship was properly appreciated and Paul won his freedom and an apology. The rights of Roman citizenship included exemption from degrading punishment, like scourging and crucifixion, the right to a fair trial, the right of appeal to the Emperor for sentence after trial and in the case of capital offense the right of appeal to Cæsar before trial. Paul was wholly within his rights, therefore, when he grew weary of the insincerity of Festus after the long delays of Felix and said: "I appeal to Cæsar" (25:11). Festus recognized Paul's right in the matter (25:12), though he felt embarrassed by the lack of definite charges against Paul (25:27). There was grim humor in Agrippa's conclusion: "This man might have been set at liberty if he had not appealed unto Cæsar" (26:32). He could have been set at liberty any time for more than two years if Felix and Festus had really wished to do what they knew was right in the case.

Paul was a citizen of heaven as well as of Tarsus and of Rome. He employs the word for the Christian life: "Only let your manner of life[1] be worthy of the gospel of Christ" (Phil. 1:27). In Phil. 3:20[2] Paul says: "For our citizenship is in heaven" (Moffatt has it: "For we are a colony of heaven").

Luke was a Greek and may himself have been a Roman citizen. At any rate, he alone employs the word "citizen"[3] in the Gospel: "He went and joined himself to one of the citizens of that country" (Luke 15:15); "But his citizens hated him" (19:14).

6. *Local Color.*—There are many touches of local color in Luke's writings, particularly the Acts, that are of great interest. In some of these cases difficulties once existed that dis-

---

[1] πολιτεύεσθε. See my book on *The New Citizenship.*

[2] In *P.* Heid. 6 (4 A. D.) we find: τὴν πολιτεία[ν ο]ου ἐνν οὐρανῷ.

[3] πολίτης.

coveries have removed. In Acts 7 : 16 Luke quotes Stephen as saying that Abraham bought the burial-place in Shechem. According to Gen. 23 : 16 Abraham purchased the cave of Machpelah from Ephron the Hittite in Hebron. Jacob bought a field of the sons of Hamor in Shechem (Gen. 33 : 19; Joshua 24 : 32). There were two purchases and Knowling (*in loco*) suggests that, since Shechem was the earliest settlement of Abraham, and he set up an altar there, he probably bought a piece of land there also. But even so Jacob was buried in the cave of Machpelah according to Gen. 1 : 13, while Joseph was buried in Shechem (Joshua 24 : 32). There were two burials, also. Jerome says that the tombs of the Patriarchs were shown at Shechem. It must be admitted that no clear solution of this matter has yet been found. If it is an error, it may belong to Stephen or to Luke. Moffatt[1] observes that Luke was not as much at home in the topography of Palestine as of Asia Minor.

In Pisidian Antioch Luke speaks of "the first men of the city" as a title. These were the *Duumviri* and the "First Ten." Greek cities in the East had a board of magistrates with this title. Luke uses the correct title for these officers, as he does in Acts 28 : 7, where he calls Publius "the First Man" of the island of Malta. A Latin inscription and a Greek inscription both apply the same title to two officers of Malta. Knowling (*in loco*) and Ramsay[2] argue that it is not a mere honorary appellation, but a technical official title in the island.

In Acts 14 : 8-18 Luke gives a vivid picture of heathen superstition in Lystra and of their notion that Barnabas and Paul were Jupiter and Mercury (Zeus and Hermes). Ovid has a story of the visit of these two gods to two Phrygian peasants, Baucis and Philemon. The Greeks looked on strangers as possible gods in human form. A coin of Lystra has a picture of a priest leading two oxen to sacrifice just as they were proceeding to offer them for Paul and Barnabas. The whole story is true to life as we now know it was lived in Lystra. Ramsay[3] says that excavation at Lystra is greatly needed and probably more discoveries will be made here.

In Philippi Luke (Acts 16 : 20) mentions both "prætors"[4]

[1] *Intr. to Lit. of N. T.*, p. 305. [2] *St. Paul the Traveller*, p. 343.
[3] *Cities of St. Paul*, p. 413 [4] στρατηγοί.

and "lictors,"[1] the correct technical titles in a colony and assumed by the magistrates in Philippi.

In Thessalonica, however, Luke (Acts 17 : 6) notes a curious official title found nowhere else. The rulers of the city are called politarchs.[2] No classical author employs this word for the magistrates of any city. Critics once scoffed at Luke for his carelessness and ignorance here. But now seventeen inscriptions have been found that use the title, thirteen of them in Macedonia and five in Thessalonica.[3] One of the inscriptions spans an arch in Thessalonica and has the title politarch with the names of some of Paul's converts there (Sosipater, Gaius, Secundus). There were usually five or six politarchs at a time in Thessalonica.

In Athens Luke not only knows the Areopagus (Acts 17 : 34) but he reproduces the local color with such skill that it is charged that he composed Paul's address in the classical atmosphere of the Parthenon. Stoics and Epicureans and the Athenian curiosity and ennui are drawn to the life.

In Ephesus the worship of the temple of Diana is pictured (Acts 19 : 34) with the graphic portrayal of Demetrius and his labor-union (craftsmen), who are ready to do his bidding when self-interest was aroused. The Asiarchs[4] and the town clerk[5] and the assembly[6] all belong to Ephesus. The Asiarchs superintended the worship of the Emperor in cities where there was a temple of Rome for the emperor-cult. "Their friendliness to St. Paul is a sure sign of an early date, for the book could only have been written while the Imperial policy was still neutral to Christianity"[7] Proconsul in 19 : 38 is the correct title for this senatorial province of Asia. Only one ruled at a time, however.

It is not too much to say that Luke has come out magnificently as the result of archæological research. Ramsay's researches have proven that Luke in Acts reflects the nomenclature and the geography of the first century A. D. The dis-

---

[1] ῥαβδοῦχοι.   [2] πολιτάρχαι.

[3] See Burton, *American Journal of Theology*, July, 1898, pp. 598–632.

[4] 'Ασιάρχαι. See Ramsay's article in Hastings's *D. B.* for copious data and bibliography.

[5] γραμματεύς. See Moulton and Milligan, *Vocabulary of the N. T.*, for numerous quotations from the papyri illustrating this and other uses of γραμματεύς.

[6] ἐκκλησία   [7] Maclean, *One Vol. Hastings's D. B.*

coveries have vindicated him at every turn. Percy Gardner[1] rather condescendingly admits that Luke "shows, it is true, a good deal of local and geographic knowledge, to which Sir W. M. Ramsay has rightly called attention." In a footnote[2] he adds: "Of course, if a writer is at sea in his geographic and local facts, it is a proof of his general untrustworthiness." Quite so. But that is not the case with Luke. It is true that Harnack[3] wrote: "St. Luke is an author whose writings read smoothly, but one has only to look somewhat more closely to discover that there is scarcely another writer in the New Testament who is so careless an historian as he." That is a careless criticism that Harnack has not made good in his books on the Lukan writings. The facts in this chapter favor the view of Ramsay rather than that of Harnack. Ramsay rightly criticises Harnack for too much verbal quibbling over Luke's sources and for not enough knowledge of the actual environment in Asia Minor and in Europe. Ramsay has appealed to the inscriptions from the critics. The rocks in every instance have taken the side of Luke.

[1] *Cambridge Biblical Essays*, p. 391.   [2] *Ibid.*
[3] *Luke the Physician*, p. 112.

CHAPTER XV

LUKE'S KNOWLEDGE OF ROMAN LAW

"An orator, one Tertullus" (Acts 24 : 1)

Christianity had to find its place under Roman law. Luke seems well aware of this problem.[1]

1. *Various Kinds of Law in the Roman Empire.*—Luke was not a lawyer, but he lived under Roman rule, and Roman law shows its hand toward Christianity in the Acts. "The student of Christian origins cannot neglect the influence which the law of the Roman Empire had on the infant Church."[2] Two lawyers are mentioned by name in the New Testament, one a professional Roman pleader and probably a heathen, Tertullus (Acts 24 : 1), the other a Christian worker, "Zenos the lawyer" (Titus 3 : 13). One must not confuse these Roman lawyers with the lawyers (or scribes) and doctors of the law in the Gospels. The Jewish lawyer was also a theologian, a doctor of canon and civil law (LL.D.). They were ecclesiastical lawyers and preachers or teachers.

So in the New Testament we see the reflection of Jewish, Greek and Roman law. And Greek law varied in different cities under local influences. Roman law appears in its provincial aspects as well as in its imperial forms. Roman judicial procedure had a long historical development, and was finally codified (*Justinian's Code*) and lies at the basis of modern jurisprudence. But the Ten Commandments and the Sermon on the Mount have played a powerful part in making modern law more than mere technicalities. English common law is rooted in human rights, and Christ's demand for righteousness dominates the upright judge to-day. But in the

---

[1] Plooij, of Leyden, has argued (*The Expositor*, December, 1914, and February, 1917) that Luke wrote the Acts, specifically as an apology for Paul and for Christianity before the Roman council. Plooij goes so far as to call Luke *juris studiosus*. M. Jones replies to Plooij in *The Expositor* for March, 1915, but Plooij has made a point that deserves consideration.

[2] Maclean, Hastings's *Dict. of Ap. Ch.* ("Roman Law in the N. T.").

first century A. D. one met various kinds of law and Christianity had to square itself with existing institutions. Paul took his stand squarely on the side of law and order and urged "subjection to the higher powers" (Romans 13 : 1) as in theory, at least, the agents of God for the preservation of order and justice. He urged prayer for all rulers, "that we may lead a quiet and tranquil life in all godliness and gravity" (I Tim. 2 : 2).[1]

In the Greek cities of Asia Minor, which in many cases had an excellent system of law already in force, the Romans respected the old law and customs and did not enforce Roman legal procedure, just as they did not interfere with the Greek language, "reserving Latin for state occasions" (Maclean).

So in Heb. 9 : 16 f. the will[2] seems to be of the Roman kind, like ours, which is in effect only on the death of the testator. We get our Old Testament and New Testament from the Latin translation of the Greek word, which also means covenant, as in Gal. 3 ; 15, though here the Greek idea of will is possible. The Greek will, once recorded, was irrevocable.   With us, alas, one never knows when a will is binding, once the lawyers get hold of it.   The best way to-day to give money is to give it before one dies.   A man can be his own administrator, as Andrew Carnegie was.   In Gal. 4 : 2 the father names the date at which the child becomes of age, according to Greek law.   Roman law made the child stay under a tutor[3] (or guardian) till fourteen, and under a curator[4] (or steward) till twenty-five.   Gal. 4 follows Roman law in respect of the tutor and curator but Greek law in the matter of appointing the term of their office.   In Greek and Roman law the master's son by a slave was also slave, but free under Hebrew law. So in Gal. 4 : 21–31 (Isaac and Ishmael) we see Greek and Roman law interpreted in a way to appeal to the Galatians who lived under it.   So Luke writes in a world of complicated legal processes.

[1] See Ball, *St. Paul and the Roman Law* (1901); Buss, *Roman Law and History in the N. T.* (1901); Hicks, *Traces of Greek Philosophy and Roman Law in the N. T.* (1896); Ramsay, *The Church in the Roman Empire* (1893).

[2] διαθήκη.   Same word {for will and covenant.   Moulton and Milligan (*Vocabulary*, p. 1480) say: "In papyri and inscrr. the word means *testament, will*, with absolute unanimity and such frequency that illustration is superfluous."

[3] ἐπιτρόπους (Gal. 4 : 2).   [4] οἰκονόμους (Gal. 4 : 2).

In Gal. 3 : 23-25 the picture of the law (Jewish law) as the child-guardian or pedagogue[1] before the age of faith is after the Greek, not the Roman idea of guardian. Ramsay[2] calls it "that characteristic Greek institution" which the Galatians considered "salutary and good." "Their duty was not to teach any child under their charge, but simply to guard him."[3] The Roman pedagogue was not so highly esteemed, and had no regard to the moral side of the child's life, though he also accompanied the child to school, as did the Greek pedagogue. The Roman failure with the education of the children, Ramsay thinks, led to the disintegration of the moral fibre and of the national life. Luke, like Paul, wrote in a world where the Græco-Roman civilization flourished. He makes his way safely.

2. *Law in the Colonies.*—Here Latin was used in municipal deeds and in trials, though Greek would usually be the language of commerce and every-day life. There was no senate[4] in the colonies, but councils (*decuriones*)[5] and Roman names for the officers as magistrates[6] (*prætores*) in Acts 16 : 20, 22, 35 f., and serjeants[7] (lictors) at Philippi. The business interests of Philippi used Roman legal procedure against Paul. The forms of Roman law are insisted upon by the masters of the poor girl (16 : 21), while Paul pointedly shows the various items in the Roman law that the magistrates or rulers (archons) (16 : 19) had violated (16 : 37). Paul does not mean that it would have been proper to flog them if they had been condemned. That was simply another item in their mistreatment of Roman citizens. Luke has not misunderstood Roman law in his report here. He aptly pictures the fear of the Roman magistrates because of their cowardice before the business men and the mob.

In Antioch of Pisidia, another colony, Paul left before he faced the civil authorities, "the chief men of the city"[8] (Acts 13 : 50), the technical title for the city officials here. The Jews, especially the rabbis, "were filled with jealousy" (13 : 45), and "urged on the devout women of honorable estate" (13 : 50), probably Gentile women of the aristocracy who had become

---

[1] παιδαγωγός.   [2] *St. Paul's Epistle to the Galatians,* p. 382.
[3] *Ibid.,* p. 383.   [4] βουλή.
[5] Ramsay, *Galatians,* pp. 117, 182.
[6] στρατηγοί.   [7] ῥαβδοῦχοι.   [8] τοὺς πρώτους τῆς πόλεως.

attendants at the synagogue, "God-fearers" like Cornelius in Cæsarea (Acts 10:1 f.). These women were open to the influence of the rabbis and were able to reach the city officials. The combination of religious jealousy, social prestige and civil power was too great for Paul and Barnabas. Rackham[1] notes that the word "honorable" is common in the inscriptions at Antioch. The persecution here was effective, apparently without any legal process. The civil authorities were reached by private influence without a public arraignment, but the pressure was too great to resist. Public trial would have come if Paul and Barnabas had remained. The rabbis would have found some charge for the arrest and trial of the preachers, who had become entirely too popular. Roman law did not forbid this recourse to personal spleen. Modern inquisitors have often followed suit as they gained the ear of the men at the helm of city and state.

Lystra was another colony where Paul and Barnabas had trouble at the hands of the set of jealous Jews who had so successfully driven them out of Antioch and out of Iconium. "But there came Jews thither from Antioch and Iconium" (Acts 14:19). Paul and Barnabas had remained a "long time" (14:3) in Iconium (not yet a colony, not till Hadrian's time[2]), till the Jews had stirred the Gentile multitude against them and there came an actual "onset[3] both of the Gentiles and the Jews with their rulers, to treat them shamefully and to stone them" (14:5). Paul and Barnabas fled just in time to escape a lynching at the hands of a mob led by "the rulers" (archons) of the city. But in Lystra the Jews waited till Paul and Barnabas had become the heroes of the hour by reason of healing the crippled man. They had with difficulty dissuaded the populace in Lystra from offering sacrifice to them as Jupiter and Mercury (14:8–18). And now the fickle crowd, like a pack of wolves, led by the same jealous rabbis, turned on Paul and stoned him and dragged him out of the city, supposing that he was dead (14:19). This time they thought that they had put the pestilent preacher out of their way for good and all. Their wrath had grown from Antioch to Iconium and now to Lystra. Here it was a real lynching party and not a near one, as in Iconium. The city officials do not

[1] *Acts*, p. 222.   [2] Ramsay, *Galatians*, pp. 123, 218.
[3] ὁρμή, a "rush" like a modern football team.

here appear in the matter at all. There was no legal process. The Jews made their appeal directly to the mob and trusted to the connivance of the city authorities whom they had reached by private appeal in Antioch and by public demonstration in Iconium. They were apparently safe in their judgment. If one wonders how a lynching like this could have taken place in a Roman colony under Roman law, let him recall recent occurrences in the United States, not alone in the South, where race prejudice has long existed, but in Washington, in Chicago, in Omaha, in East St. Louis, in Springfield, Ohio, and in Springfield, Illinois, the home of Abraham Lincoln. The appeal to the mob is anarchy and Bolshevism. It is always possible, even in enlightened communities, but it never settles anything. It always inflames men's passions and whets the appetite for blood. Paul himself knew only too well what it was to arouse popular prejudice against the followers of Christ. Now a small circle of the faithful, probably Timothy among them, gathered round his dead body, as they thought, when he rose up to their joy (14:20), but he did not tarry long in Lystra. He knew when to leave.

At Corinth, another colony, Paul was arraigned by the jealous rabbis again after Crispus, a ruler of the synagogue, had gone over to Paul's side (18:8). The present ruler of the synagogue, Sosthenes, took advantage of the arrival of a new proconsul, Gallio, to bring Paul into court for violating Roman law: "This man persuades men to worship God contrary to law" (18:13). The Roman law was strict about the introduction of new religions, strict when the Romans cared to be. Judaism was a legalized religion (*religio licita*), hoary with age and allowed by Roman law, though the Romans, like all Gentiles, despised the Jews. Mithraism and Isisism were new religions and were winked at by Roman officials. Christianity had no legal standing before Roman law. Technically it was unlawful (*religio illicita*) save as it passed as a form or sect of Judaism. Paul, as we know, claimed that Christianity was the real Judaism of the prophets (Gal. 3; Romans 9–11): "After the Way which they call a sect, so serve I the God of our fathers" (Acts 24:14). The Jews before Gallio mean for him to understand that Paul has violated Roman law, but their charges made it plain to him that Christianity which Paul preached was really a form of Judaism and so not illegal.

They failed to make a case against Paul in Gallio's interpretation of Roman law. He ruled that the dispute was one between Jews on questions of Jewish theology, and hence not a case in Roman law at all. He would not allow Paul to speak, but threw the case out of court with the famous words: "If indeed it were a matter of wrong or of wicked villainy, O ye Jews, reason would that I should bear with you: but if they are questions about words and names and your own law, look to it yourselves; I am not minded to be a judge of these matters" (18 : 14 f.). The decision was a boomerang. For the moment, and in the province of Achaia, Christianity was given a legal standing before Roman law as a *religio licita* and as a form of Judaism. The rage of the Jews was tremendous. They laid hold on their own leader, Sosthenes, and beat him right before the judgment-seat, but "Gallio cared for none of these things" (18 : 17). He had a blind eye for the poetic justice that came to the jealous Sosthenes. Gallio was a brother of Seneca and was apparently a man of intelligence and with a sense of justice, a Roman official of the higher type, quite other from the kind seen in Palestine in the cases of Pilate, Felix and Festus. There were Roman governors like Gallio. The administration of Roman law depended, after all, upon the character of the officer, as, in truth, is true of all law everywhere.

3. *Law in the Free Cities.*—We have examples in the Acts of legal processes in such free cities as Athens, Ephesus and Thessalonica.

In Thessalonica there was probably a senate and an assembly. Certainly they had politarchs, "rulers of the city" (Acts 17 : 6), as the inscriptions prove. In Thessalonica a great multitude of the devout Greeks or God-fearers, who had been attending the synagogue services, were converted by Paul's preaching as well as a large number of the chief women (17 : 4). Here Paul had a large body of aristocratic women on his side, in contrast with the situation in Antioch in Pisidia, where they were lined up against him. Here the jealous Jewish leaders make their first appeal to the rabble, "certain vile fellows of the rabble"[1] (17 : 5), certain evil men of the crowd

[1] τῶν ἀγοραίων ἄνδρας τινὰς πονηρούς. Lake (*Earlier Epistles of Paul*, p. 69, n. 1) takes ἀγοραίων here to be "agitators" because of Plutarch, *Æmilius Paulus*, 38, ἀνθρώπους ἀγεννεῖς καὶ δεδουλευκότας, ἀγοραίους δὲ καὶ δυναμένους ὄχλον συναγαγεῖν.

in the market-place. The life of a Greek city centred in the agora or market-place. Here the idlers were found very much as professional jurors hang around the court-house in our modern cities. Even some of the Thessalonian converts showed a reluctance to work (II Thess. 3 : 10). So the Jewish rabbis got the ear (probably for pay or by appeal to prejudice) of these "bums," who were ready for any enterprise or excitement. They deliberately undertook to set the city in an uproar. It was a mob made to order that clamored at the door of Jason's house for Paul and Silas. So failing to find them, they dragged Jason before the politarchs and accused him of entertaining Paul and Silas, "these that have turned the world upside down."[1] Certainly this was a tribute to Paul and Silas, though, as a matter of fact, the rabbis and their confederates from the agora had set the city by the ears. Now the Jews appeal to Roman law, as the Sanhedrin posed as friends of Cæsar when Pilate weakened once more (John 19 : 12, 15): "And these all act contrary to the decrees of Cæsar, saying that there is another king, one Jesus" (Acts 17 : 7). The Jews in Thessalonica, as the Jews before Pilate, knew that Paul did not preach Jesus as a political king or emperor[2] in opposition to Cæsar, but they wished the politarchs to think so. The crime of which they accuse Jason and Paul and Silas is high treason, the very charge placed against Jesus (Luke 23 : 2). The charge of treason "cast into a panic both the politarchs and the crowd."[3] So Jason was compelled to give security[4] for good behavior against treason (17 : 9), paying money like a bond or bail. Thus the politarchs saved their face in the presence of this charge of a revolution. It is interesting to note that in writing to the Thessalonians Paul describes the "man of sin," "the son of perdition, he that opposeth and exalteth himself against all that is called God or that is worshipped; so that he sitteth in the temple of God, setting himself forth as God" (II Thess. 2 : 3 f.). "Remember

---

[1] οἱ τὴν οἰκουμένην ἀναστατώσαντες. Used in the papyri for driving one out of hearth and home, B. G. U. 1179, 20 (A. D. 41). So of upsetting one, P. Oxy., 119, 10 (A. D. 2–3).

[2] The word βασιλεύς was applied to the Emperor.

[3] Rackham, in loco.

[4] λαβόντες τὸ ἱκανόν. Cf. Mark 15 : 15. In P. Oxy., 294, 23 (A. D. 22), we have δο[ῦν]αι εἰκανόν for "give security" till the inquiry or trial, a case precisely in point.

ye not, that, when I was yet with you, I told you these things?"
(2 : 5). Evidently, Paul, while in Thessalonica, had been
stirred by the worship of the Roman Emperor and may have
employed language that gave some color to the specious charge
of his enemies. Here in Thessalonica Paul began to face the
inevitable conflict between Christ and Cæsar. The shadow
of Rome was cast upon the Cross. So Paul and Silas were
"immediately" sent away by the brethren to Berœa (Acts
17 : 10). It was a serious moment for Paul. When in Berœa
the same Jews came to attack Paul, "then immediately the
brethren sent forth Paul to go as far as the sea" (17 : 14).
The haste in both instances suggests that Paul's zeal and earnestness against emperor-worship had made it inexpedient
for him to tarry.

In Athens Paul was not put on trial before the court of the
Areopagus. No criminal charge was laid against him at all.
After a round of public discussion with the Stoics and the
Epicureans in the agora at Athens, with ridicule from some
of the people (Acts 17 : 18), others more courteously proposed
that Paul go up unto the Areopagus and in a more formal
address expound his strange teaching (17 : 19 f.). In Athens
there was always a crowd ready to hear some new thing. Paul
was in an embarrassing situation. Like Socrates of old, he
had crossed swords with the sophists of the new time. But
the crowd passed quick judgment on Paul as a mere babbler
or seed-picker[1] (17 : 18), like the birds that hopped about in
the market-place. They little knew that a greater than Socrates was here, one with an infinitely greater philosophy, the
wisdom of God. Socrates was tried and condemned for introducing strange divinities. The same charge is made against
Paul. Three views exist as to what took place on the Areopagus. One is that Paul made a popular philosophical exposi-
tion of Christianity to the crowd that invited him up there.
The conduct of the hearers lends some color to this view
(17 : 32–34). Another view is that a real trial before the
court of the Areopagus took place. Rackham argues ably
that Paul was arraigned before the court for introducing new
divinities as Socrates had been. He suggests that the examination took place before the court of the Areopagus, but in the
Stoa Basilica, and that Paul took advantage of the occasion to

---

[1] σπερμολόγος.

proclaim the gospel. There was one Areopagite (Dionysius) present who was converted. But this view is not convincing. Ramsay[1] is positive that Paul was brought before the council of Areopagus, but not for trial. He thinks that the Stoics wanted him examined by the council to see if he was entitled to a permit to lecture in the university atmosphere. "Certain powers were vested in the council of Areopagus to appoint or invite lecturers at Athens, and to exercise some general control over the lecturers in the interest of public order and morality."[2] It is not certain that the hill of Mars is meant by the Areopagus, which can mean simply the court of Areopagus, whether held on Mars Hill or in the agora. In any case it hardly seems likely that it was a court trial for a crime, but a University court in which Paul made his defense as a teacher. Ramsay[3] shows that the Areopagus is not always topographical. Certainly, this is a plausible view, and on the whole the most likely to be true. At any rate, in Athens Paul is in a Greek atmosphere of freedom, and does not feel the hand of Roman law or the jealousy of Jewish rabbis or the hatred of business interests. The intellectuals of Athens soon lose interest in the wild theories of the new and raw philosopher. They laugh him out of court and out of town.

But in Ephesus we see all the forms and processes of Græco-Roman law (proconsul,[4] town clerk,[5] assembly,[6] courts[7]). Ephesus had thus a Greek constitution besides the Roman proconsul. The popular assembly met every three months and oftener on occasion. The town-clerk was an important official. The proconsul represented the supreme authority of Rome. The Asiarchs (19 : 31), who were friendly to Paul and would not allow him to face the mob in the amphitheatre, were provincial officers who had charge, among other things, of the provincial worship of the Emperor. "A temple and altar to Rome and the emperor were erected in some city, which thereupon was designated Neocoros[8] or Sacristar (literally, *temple-sweeper*), i. e., of the imperial temple."[9] Thessalonica and Berœa were also "temple-sweepers." Ephesus was exceed-

---

[1] *St. Paul the Traveller*, p. 246.
[2] *Ibid.*
[3] *Ibid.*, pp. 244 f.
[4] ἀνθύπατος (19 : 38).
[5] γραμματεύς (19 : 35).
[6] δῆμος (19 : 33), ἐκκλησία (19 : 39).
[7] ἀγοραῖοι (19 : 38).
[8] νεωκόρος (19 : 35).
[9] Rackham, *Acts*, p. 363.

ingly proud of this honor as well as of the title of "temple-sweeper" for the temple of Diana. Inscriptions show that the name "temple-sweeper" was also used in reference to the worship of Diana (Artemis), so that Luke is vindicated on this point. "Great Artemis" was the usual title given this goddess. Inscriptions call her "Great Artemis" and "Most Great Goddess" (cf. "Most High God" in Acts 16 : 17, also in inscriptions). One of the decrees at Ephesus speaks of the decline of the worship of Artemis as Luke does. "Mr. Wood's excavations of this temple and the numerous inscriptions there discovered have given a revelation of this worship which entirely corroborates the lifelike picture in the Acts."[1] It is probable that the Asiarchs induced the town clerk to dismiss the mob. We see here Græco-Roman law invoked in defense of Paul, as Gallio took his side in Corinth. In Antioch in Pisidia the Jewish rabbis got the city officials to act on their side against Paul. In Ephesus Paul had lived three years, and so had won the friendship of the Asiarchs who befriended him. Perhaps, also, Paul in Ephesus was more careful about references to the emperor-worship than he had been in Thessalonica. He seems here to have directed his energy more against the worship of Diana than against the emperor-worship. At any rate the Asiarchs were not charged with the worship of Diana. The town clerk skilfully parried the charge of Demetrius about Diana's proud magnificence and showed that Paul and his friends were not temple-robbers[2] or blasphemers of the goddess Diana (19 : 37). Demetrius had followed the line of the masters in Philippi and had gone a step farther. He had aroused the self-interest of the craftsmen (guild or labor-unions, common enough at that time) by appeals to the peril to the trade and so to their jobs (19 : 24-27). Capitalist and workmen here unite against Paul. In public, however, the cry of peril to Diana was raised (19 : 26 f.), and nothing was said about the business interests hit by Paul's preaching. We see here a close parallel to the modern struggle with the liquor trade. The hatred of vested business interests was turned against Paul and only the quick action of his powerful friends in office saved him and his friends Gaius and Aristarchus. They would have gotten Paul in time had he remained in Ephesus. So he quickly left (Acts 20 : 1).

[1] Rackham, *Acts*, p. 364.   [2] ἱεροσύλους.

4. *The Sanhedrin and Jewish Law.*—We have seen how Luke pictures Paul in touch with Greek and Roman law. It remains to see how he fares with Jewish law. Paul was certainly at home before the Sanhedrin, whose agent he had been in the persecution of Christianity (Acts 8 : 3; 9 : 1 f.; 22 : 4 f.; 26 : 10 f.) and of which he was possibly a member (26 : 10). The powers of the Sanhedrin had been greatly limited since the days of Herod the Great. Rome reserved the right of capital punishment (John 18 : 31) and the Sanhedrin had no jurisdiction in Galilee and Samaria,[1] yet local synagogues were allowed to have a good deal of authority.[2] The stoning of Stephen (Acts 7 : 58) was lynch-law, an illegal murder. Stoning was the old Jewish penalty for blasphemy, but the Sanhedrin no longer had that right. Stephen so enraged this body that they took the law into their own hands, and the Roman procurator seems to have let it pass, if indeed he was in office at this juncture. The persecution of other Christians by the Sanhedrin (Acts 5 : 33; 22 : 4; 26 : 10) was either ignored or winked at by the Roman officials as a matter of slight importance from the standpoint of Roman law and order. The Sanhedrin could arrest persons and imprison them and flog them (Acts 5 : 18, 40; 22 : 4; 26 : 10; II Cor. 11 : 24 f.). The death of James in Acts 12 : 2 was by order of Herod Agrippa I while he was King of Judea. And Peter would have fared the same fate but for the interposition of God and Peter's flight (12 : 3–17).

Stephen stirred up the Pharisees (6 : 11–14) as Peter had aroused the Sadducees (4 : 1 f.; 5 : 17 f.). Paul carried on the persecution of the disciples as a Pharisee, and Gamaliel, his great teacher, no more interposed to stay his hand as he had done once in behalf of the Apostles, to score a point against the Sadducees (5 : 33–42). Paul, on his last visit to Jerusalem, met the hatred of the Jewish mob as he had faced mobs of Jews or Gentiles in Antioch in Pisidia, Iconium, Berœa, Corinth, Ephesus. The rage of the Jerusalem mob is due to charges made by Jews of Asia, probably old enemies in Ephesus, who were angered by Paul's association with Trophimus, a Greek Christian of Ephesus, in Jerusalem (21 : 27–31). The mob mind is very much alike anywhere. The crowd-consciousness of these Jews is outside of the pale of law. It is the same

---

[1] Maclean, Hastings's *Dict. of Ap. Ch.*
[2] Biggs, *St. Peter and Jude*, p. 25.

thirst for blood that Paul had once felt as a persecutor. It is the Roman chief-captain who rescues Paul by the aid of soldiers from death by the mob (21 : 33–36). The position of Paul is now peculiar. He appears to Claudius Lysias as a criminal of some sort. He first suspects him of being the famous Egyptian leader of the band of "assassins" (21 : 38) and is astonished that Paul speaks Greek. On learning that Paul is a Jew of Tarsus he allows him to speak to the mob from the steps of the tower of Antonia, which he does in Aramaic, so that the chief-captain did not understand his address, but saw only the wild confusion at the end (21 : 39–22 : 23). He tried to ferret out the guilt of Paul by scourging only to find that he was dealing with a Roman citizen and was in peril of a crime himself (22 : 24–29): "The chief-captain also was afraid when he knew that he was a Roman, and that he had bound him."

In his perplexity Claudius Lysias called a meeting of the Sanhedrin[1] in order to see if that body could define Paul's guilt to guide his course (22 : 30). Paul was at home before this body of the fathers, but at once lost all chance of a fair inquiry by the claim that he had lived in all good conscience up till now, including his conversion to Christ. The upshot was the claim by Paul that he was still a Pharisee on the subject of the resurrection and this claim was followed by the violent cleavage of the body who were about to tear Paul in pieces in the effort to get at each other. Once more Claudius Lysias rescued Paul from the Jewish court and he was still in the dark about his prisoner (23 : 1–10).

The conspiracy against Paul and the wit of Paul's nephew led the chief-captain to send Paul away from Jerusalem by night under guard of a company of soldiers in order to get him away from the forces of Jewish hate in Jerusalem. His letter puts the best face on the matter for Claudius Lysias, and is not in accord with the facts (23 : 26–30). So Paul has escaped the toils set for him in Jerusalem, but he is still a prisoner in Cæsarea in Herod's palace.[2]

[1] Ramsay ("Trial Scenes in the Acts," *Bearing of Recent Discovery*, p. 90) is sure that this was not a formal meeting of the Sanhedrin, but was a hurried called meeting.

[2] Or prætorium (πραιτώριον). On the meaning of this word and other legal and technical terms, see Ferguson, "The Legal Terms Common to the Macedonian Inscriptions and the New Testament" (*Historical and Linguistic Studies of University of Chicago*, vol. II).

5. *Roman Law in Palestine.*—Paul has escaped the jaws of death from the mob, the Sanhedrin and the conspirators in Jerusalem. He now stands at the bar of the Roman procurator in Cæsarea. Once before Paul had faced the Roman governor, the proconsul Gallio, in Corinth. Then, as now, it was the Jews who made accusations against him. Then he was set free, with the result that Christianity was given a legal standing in Achaia as a *religio licita*, a form of Judaism. That was in a heathen city, where the Jews were disliked as they were everywhere. "Beware of the Jews"[1] Serapim wrote to Heraclides, who was in money difficulties A. D. 41. In Palestine, at least, Christianity is no longer regarded as a form of Judaism by the Jews. Peter and John once worshipped in the temple. Slowly the lines have been drawn. Paul's great Gentile propaganda has stirred many of the Jewish Christians, the Judaizers, against him. But the Roman government has not yet assumed a hostile attitude toward Christianity. The case of Paul really carries with it the future of Christianity in the Roman Empire. It is for this reason that Luke devotes so much space to the details of his imprisonment and trials in Cæsarea. Paul stands at the bar of Roman provincial justice, but he is in Palestine, where the Roman governor feels the full force of Jewish hate and Jewish power, as Pilate did when he surrendered to the demand of the Sanhedrin. Luke told that story with great power in the Gospel. What will Felix now do with the case of Paul? Will he surrender him to the Sanhedrin as Pilate did Jesus?

Felix makes a fair start. He would wait for the accusers to come (23 : 35). Ananias, the high priest, appeared with five elders and a Roman lawyer or pleader (orator), Tertullus, who argued the case against Paul after the accusations of Ananias (24 : 1–9). It ·is a characteristic demagogical harangue with flattery of Felix and denunciation of Paul. Paul pleads his own case (24 : 10–21). He shows the falsity of the charge about profaning the temple, the vagueness of that about causing disturbances and admits that he is a member of the sect of the Nazarenes, which he claims is in accord with the Jewish hope. Luke adds a curious comment about Felix "having more exact knowledge concerning the Way" (24 : 22). More exact than what? The Way is Christianity. Felix is acute

---

[1] *B. G. U.*, 1079, 24 f., καὶ σὺ βλέπε σατὸν ἀπὸ τῶν Ἰουδαίων.

enough to see that in reality Christianity is on trial for its legal
status in Palestine. He probably knew of the decision of
Gallio. At any rate, he knew enough to be unwilling to convict Paul and yet he feared the Jews too much to set him free.
So he put off the case, possibly influenced, also, by the mention of "alms" by Paul, as holding out hope of a bribe. At
any rate, that came to be a definite motive[1] with him (24 : 26)
after he recovered from the shock of Paul's powerful sermon
to him and to Drusilla (24 : 24 f.). But Felix dallied with the
case for two years, and left Paul a prisoner, when recalled, to
please the Jews (24 : 27). Felix makes a sorry spectacle of
Roman justice, but Luke's picture is in keeping with what is
known of him elsewhere.

The coming of Festus revived the hopes of the Jews, who at
once (cf. coming of Gallio to Corinth) undertook to induce
Festus to bring Paul from Cæsarea, plotting again to kill him
on the way (25 : 1-5). But Festus was not so easily caught
and he also began well. He demanded that the accusers come
to Cæsarea, where he held court. So they came again with
the same old charges, which Paul promptly denied. Now
Festus asked Paul if he were not willing to go up to Jerusalem
and be tried there before him (25 : 9) indeed, but probably
according to Jewish law. The procurators sometimes applied
Jewish law in such cases. It was a trap set for Paul for the
purpose of pleasing the Jews. Paul's patience was at last
exhausted. He knew what Jerusalem held in store for him.
He now knew that Festus was no better than Felix, and that
he lacked the courage to stand up against the Jews. He had
waited two years on Felix. There was but one hope left, and
that lay in the right of appeal to Cæsar, which he could make
as a Roman citizen. This he did and at once took the case
out of the hands of Festus (25 : 10-12). Luke has told this
story with great detail and vividness. He was probably present during these arraignments of Paul, though he may not
have remained in Cæsarea all of the two years. Ramsay[2]
thinks that Luke regarded Paul's trials in Cæsarea and the
appeal to Cæsar as a test case for Christianity. Hence he felt

---

[1] Ramsay (*St. Paul the Traveller*, p. 310) thinks that Paul came into his
patrimony about this time and was thus able to bear the expense of his
long lawsuit.

[2] *St. Paul the Traveller*, p. 308.

justified in devoting so much space to it. He evidently com-
pleted Acts when it was clear that Paul would be acquitted,
and hence a new day would dawn for Christianity in the
Roman Empire. Incidentally, this is an argument for dating
Acts before A. D. 64, when all of a sudden Nero turned against
Christianity. There is no hint of this outcome in the Acts.
"The importance of the trial for Luke is intelligible only if
Paul was acquitted,"[1] and, one may add, Luke wrote in igno-
rance of the reversal of Roman policy by Nero in A. D. 64.
Felix and Festus show the Roman governors at their worst.

The so-called trial of Paul before Herod Agrippa II was no
trial at all. The case was no longer in the hands of Festus.
It was really a sort of mock trial or entertainment arranged
by Festus to relieve the ennui of Agrippa and Bernice on their
visit to Festus, as Luke makes plain (25 : 13–27). It is evident
that Paul need not have spoken unless he cared to do so. No
charges were placed against Paul. Agrippa, as a fellow Jew,
was more likely to understand Paul and so he took advantage
of this opportunity to state his case and make an apology for
his whole life (26 : 1–23). The plea of Festus that he had no
charge against Paul to send to Cæsar was doubtless true, nor
did he secure one on this occasion (26 : 24–32). Ramsay[2]
notes how true Luke is to the facts in each case: "Legal pro-
ceedings are taken against Paul and his friends in many places,
and accusations have to be made in each case, according to
the forms of Roman law. The accusation varies in each case;
it is nowhere the same as in any other city; yet it is everywhere
in accordance with Roman forms." Ramsay lucidly shows
how the accusers had to find some crime in Paul's conduct at
Philippi, Thessalonica, Athens, Corinth, Ephesus, Jerusalem
and Cæsarea, and how skilful they were in relating their
grudges to the Roman legal forms, as we have already shown.

The Acts closes with Paul still a prisoner in Rome, but with
a hope of release implied, as in Paul's Epistles to Philippians
and Philemon. But at the close of Acts the future attitude
of Rome to Christianity is problematical. It seems probable
that Paul was set free by Nero without a trial, the case going
by default. But the burning of Rome by Nero in A. D. 64
quickly[3] changed the whole atmosphere. He laid that crime

---

[1] *Ibid.*　　　　　　　　　　　　　　[2] *Bearing of Recent Discovery*, p. 97.
[3] Probably by A. D. 65.

at the door of the Christians and began to treat them as criminals. There are echoes of this attitude in I Peter 4 : 16.

The Romans learned to distinguish between Christians and Jews. The Jews drew the line against Christians. The author of Hebrews (13 : 13) will urge the Christians to follow Christ without the camp. The Christians had already had to choose between Lord Cæsar and Lord Jesus (cf. I Cor. 12 : 1–3). When Trajan writes to Pliny it is unlawful to be a Christian and the natural implication is that it had long been a crime to be a Christian. Paul saw the fight coming between Christ and Cæsar for world conquest. Luke has drawn in Acts the picture of the events that led up[1] to that conflict which lasted for centuries, which in essence still rages. The Christian still has to face the problem of loyalty to Christ or to Cæsar when Cæsar tramples the cross beneath his feet. But at first Roman law did not seriously interfere with the spread of Christianity. Judaism was tolerated and Christianity was treated as a sect of Judaism. "This tolerance of the Jewish religion was of incalculable importance to infant Christianity, which at first professed to be no more than a reformed and expanded Judaism."[2] When the distinction was finally drawn by Roman law, Christianity was too powerful to be suppressed. It was able to fight the mightiest empire of earth.

[1] Harnack, *Acts of the Apostles*, p. 288. Luke "reflects very early conceptions and expresses historical relations which existed at the time of St. Paul."

[2] Angus, *Int. St. B. Encycl.* ("Roman Empire").

CHAPTER XVI

NAUTICAL TERMS IN ACTS 27[1]

"And casting off the anchors, they left them in the sea, at the same time loosing the bands of the rudders; and hoisting the foresail to the wind, they made for the beach" (Acts 27 : 40).

Few chapters in any book have a fascination surpassing that in Acts 27. Here we see Luke the sailor, the man of travel, the man of observation. The habits of diagnosis as a doctor played him in good stead in seeing the points of interest in the voyage and shipwreck. He had quick eyes that saw the salient points at issue. He may have made notes during the storm, or he may have written out his vivid recollections after reaching Rome. He had doubtless made many voyages before and knew the ways of the sea.

1. *The Immense Value of Acts 27.*—Luke makes it plain that Paul made frequent voyages to carry on his work. He sailed from Seleucia to Cyprus (Acts 13 : 4), from Troas to Neapolis (16 : 11), possibly from Berœa to Athens (17 : 14), from Cenchreæ to Ephesus (18 : 18), from Ephesus to Cæsarea (18 : 21 f.), to Macedonia again (20 : 1), from Philippi to Troas (20 : 6), from Assos with various stops to Cæsarea (20 : 13–21 : 14). But it is plain that Luke has not recorded, even in this summary fashion, all the voyages of Paul, for he himself says: "Thrice I suffered shipwreck, a night and a day have I been in the deep" (II Cor. 11 : 25), and he also spoke of "perils in the sea" (II Cor. 11 : 26). These experiences were several years before the famous voyage narrated at length and with such power in Acts 27.

But it is Acts 27 that really shows Luke and Paul at their best in the sea. "The story is told with such a wealth of detail that in all classical literature there is no passage which gives us so much information about the working of an ancient ship."[2] We have other narratives of ancient voyages in merchant vessels. Josephus[3] tells that the ship on which he was

---

[1] The Record of Christian Work, August, 1920.

[2] Rackham, p. 476.

[3] *Vita*, III.

wrecked carried about six hundred persons. Lucian[1] pictures
the voyage of an Alexandrian wheat-ship on its course from
Alexandria to Myra and to Athens. The ship had a tonnage
of twelve hundred tons. Herod the Great had a shipwreck
also on his way to Rome from Alexandria. In stormy weather
he took ship to Pamphylia and was shipwrecked at Rhodes,
with loss of the ship's cargo. There he built a three-decked
ship and set sail with his friends for Brundisium in Italy and
so reached Rome.[2] In the *Periodoi of Barnabas* we have the
description of "a voyage from Seleucia in Syria to Cyprus in
the face of a prevailing steady westerly wind the work of a
person familiar with the circumstances."[3] But these narratives all fall short of the one by Luke in Acts 27. "It is to
Luke that we owe the most vivid as well as the most accurate
account of sea-voyaging that has come down to us from antiquity. Experts in naval science agree that it is without a
parallel."[4] There is no trouble in believing that the second
vessel in Acts 27 carried two hundred and seventy-six souls
(27 : 37), or that the third vessel, the *Castor and Pollux*, carried
these besides its crew and cargo (28 : 11).

The Phœnicians and the Greeks were the sailors of antiquity.
They were those "who go down to the sea in ships and occupy
themselves in great waters." The Book of Revelation
(chap. 18) speaks of Rome as the city whose ships cover the
Mediterranean, whose merchants trade with all the earth.
That is true, for Rome drew the commerce of the world to her
doors. The mariners of all nations, "who work the sea"[5]
(Rev. 18 : 17) set sail for Rome. "Woe, Woe, the great city,
wherein all that had their ships in the sea were made rich by
reason of her costliness" (Rev. 18 : 19). The ancients dreaded
the sea, for they were without chart or compass and at the
mercy of wind and wave with their rowboats and sailing-ves-
sels. One of the joys of heaven will be that "the sea is no
more" (Rev. 21 : 1). "The modern joy and delight in the sea
was a sentiment almost unknown to the peoples of antiquity.
One Greek poet, Æschylus, could write of 'the many-twinkling

---

[1] *The Ship or Wishes* (Πλοῖον ἢ Εὐχαί).
[2] Josephus, *Ant.* XIV, xiv.
[3] Ramsay, *St. Paul the Traveller*, p. 317.
[4] Robinson, Hastings's *Dict. of Ap. Ch.* ("Ship").
[5] ὅσοι τὴν θάλασσαν ἐργάζονται.

smile of ocean,' but to the ancients generally the sea inspired only emotions of dislike and dread. The incommodious ships and the possibilities of long delays owing to contrary winds made the voyage anything but a pleasure."[1] There was lack of knowledge of navigation, and winter closed down the seas on the Mediterranean. Neptune had terrors for the ancients that appear in the allusions in classical literature, terrors enough, one may add, without the modern agent of the devil, the submarine. And yet some of the Greeks loved the sea. Ramsay[2] says that Luke "shows the true Greek feeling for the sea." It is interesting to observe that Nelson had been reading Acts 27 on the morning of the battle of Copenhagen.

2. *The Same Note of Accuracy in Acts 27.*—We have come to have confidence in Luke the historian as we have tested him in so many ways. It was to be expected that Acts 27 would be subjected to the most minute research. Luke uses a great deal of technical detail from the nature of the case. Every statement here has been challenged by experts in naval matters. The literature is now considerable.[3] Far the most valnable is the work of Smith, of Jordanhill, *The Voyage and Shipwreck of St. Paul.* He made a minute study of every aspect of the voyage. There is a discussion of each of the three ships (Cæsarea to Myra, Myra to Malta, Malta to Puteoli) in which Paul and Luke sailed, the size of the ships, the winds, the tonnage, the number of passengers, the direction and speed of the second ship in the storm, the island of Malta and every point that is involved. It is all done with great thoroughness and fairness, with the use of all knowledge that can be obtained about ancient ships and seafaring.

Smith[4] says that Luke possesses two great qualifications for writing this chapter. "The first of these is his perfect acquaintance with nautical matters, and the second is his accuracy. No man who was not in an eminent degree gifted with this quality could have given a narrative capable of being tested as

---

[1] Rackham, *Acts*, p. 475.   [2] *St. Paul the Traveller*, p. 21.

[3] J. Smith, *The Voyage and Shipwreck of St. Paul*, 4th ed., 1880; A. Breusing, *Die Nautik der Alten*, 1886; J. Vars, *L'Art nautique dans l'antiquité et specialement en grèc*, 1887; H. Balmer, *Die Romfahrt des Apostels Paulus*, 1905; C. Torr, *Ancient Ships*, 1894; Everitt, *St. Paul's Journey to Rome*, 1904; cyclopædic article; E. Smith, "Last Voyage and Shipwreck of St. Paul" (*Homiletic Review*, August, 1919).

[4] *Op. cit.*, pp. 25 f.

his has been in the following examination. He must not only have been an accurate observer, but his memory must have been accurate, and his habits of thought and reasoning no less so." This judgment Smith renders after thorough and painstaking examination of every detail. "St. Luke, by his accurate use of nautical terms, gives great precision to his language, and expresses by a single word what would otherwise require several." [1] As one illustration of his accuracy take the distance and direction from Clauda to Malta. Luke has only a few disjointed allusions to these matters in his narrative, and yet they work out like a modern log-book the dead reckoning of the ship's course and speed. The distance was four hundred and seventy-six miles, and this would take a little over thirteen days (on the fourteenth day, 27 : 27), at the rate of drifting of one and one-half miles an hour. The direction, as the result of the Euraquilo or east-northeast wind (27 : 14) and tacking eight points to the north (as close to the wind as was safe), would bring one to the island of Malta.[2] "Hence, according to these calculations, a ship starting late on the evening from Clauda would by midnight on the fourteenth be less than three miles from the entrance of St. Paul's Bay." [3]

And this is not all. The measurements by fathoms, twenty and fifteen (27 : 28), corresponds to the coast there. And there is a bay with a place where two seas meet (27 : 41), and to this day it is called St. Paul's Bay.[4] Surely, then, Luke is entitled to consideration in the details to be examined.

3. *The Personality of Paul Dominant in the Narrative.*—Fascinating as the story is, Luke did not write his narrative just to depict a shipwreck. He is not consciously writing a "purple" passage. He describes the voyage at all only because of his interest in Paul. "The very desperateness of the situation throws into the strongest relief the personality of S. Paul. At the moment of utter despair he rises up in the midst and is found a rock on which all can trust, the inspirer of hope and the master-mind which is able to direct and command as the crisis requires—in a word, their saviour. Nowhere in the Acts is there a finer display of sympathy and strength. Thus the very passages which glorify the apostle—and for that reason suspected by some critics—are those which contain S. Luke's

[1] *Ibid.*, p. 61, note.   [2] Smith, *op. cit.*, pp. 122–6.
[3] *Ibid.*, p. 126.   [4] *Ibid.*, p. 172.

motive for relating the history of the voyage, and the multitude of details supply the necessary background." [1] ⬦

It is true that Paul is a prisoner, but he is ·treated with the utmost consideration[2] by Julius the centurion, who has charge of all the prisoners and the soldiers[3] and is the ranking Roman officer on each of the ships, outranking the captain, who with us would be in complete control of the vessel. Ramsay[4] argues plausibly that Luke and Aristarchus were able to accompany Paul by offering themselves as his slaves for the voyage. Prisoners would not be allowed to have mere friends. In Luke's narrative "Paul admonished them" (27:9 f.) at Fair Havens, where the centurion[5] called a council to determine what to do now that it was so late in the season, for "the Fast was already gone by" (27:9), the Great Day of Atonement, about October 5 in A. D. 59, and it was now necessary either to spend the winter in Fair Havens or to find a better harbor like Phœnix near by in Crete (27:12). Luke does not mention that it was a formal council, but Ramsay[6] feels sure that one was held else Paul would not have dared to offer his advice. Probably Paul, though not Luke, was invited to the council because of his prominence. Those next to the centurion in rank were "the pilot[7] and captain[8] of the ship" (27:11), and not "the master and owner of the ship," as even the Revised Version has it. The captain and sailing-master (pilot) were merely advisers of the centurion in this council. Paul gave his advice with his warning and prophecy along the line of common sense and experience, but he was brushed aside as not a technical expert. Preachers are not credited with business sense, but he laughs best who laughs last. The centurion found the soft south wind proof of his wisdom and set sail (27:13). The sequel justifies Paul up to the hilt, though he remained quiet till neither sun nor stars had shone upon the ship for many days, and all hope of being saved was now taken away and

---

[1] Rackham, *Acts*, 476. [2] φιλανθρώπως (Acts 27:3).
[3] σκεῖρα Σεβαστή (27:1), "the troop of the Emperor," Ramsay calls it (*St. Paul the Traveller*, p. 315), in popular Greek language.
[4] *St. Paul the Traveller*, p. 316. | [5] ἑκατοντάρχης.
[6] *Op. cit.*, p. 323. [7] κυβερνήτης, our "goVernor."
[8] ναύκληρος. Ramsay, *op. cit.* (p. 324), shows by inscriptions that ἔμπορος is the name for "owner" of the ship and ναύκληρος "captain." Knowling, *in loco*, agrees with Ramsay, though Breusing argues for "owner" for ναύκληρος.

they had been long without food (27 : 20). Then he was able to say with telling effect: "I told you so." But he did it courteously and aimed to help the despairing company. He urged courage and confidence in God, who will spare their lives, though the ship will be lost, as an angel of God has shown him. Paul himself is to stand before Cæsar, and God has spared them in answer to his prayers (27 : 21–26). It is a crowning moment for Paul. From henceforth he is the real master of the company. All now look to Paul for light and leading.

Once again Paul stepped to the front to expose the dastardly plot of the sailors to escape in the life-boat and to leave the ship and all on board to the mercy of the storm (27 : 30–32). Now the centurion was quick to hearken to Paul and he had the soldiers "cut away the ropes of the boat, and let her fall off."

Once more as they waited for dawn on the fourteenth day Paul urged that they break their long fast and eat something, appetite or no appetite, so as to have strength for the work of rescue, promising that God would spare all their lives (27 : 33–36). Thus he restored the courage of all. "Then were they all of good cheer, and themselves also took of food."

Paul was never more Luke's hero than on these great occasions. Rackham[1] thinks that Luke also meant to draw a spiritual lesson in the obvious parallel between the experience of Paul to that of Jonah in the Old Testament, with the difference that the New Testament prophet of the Gentiles, unlike Jonah, was obedient to the heavenly vision, and did not bring on the storm, but, rather, was the reason for the rescue of all on board. The glory of the occasion was that Paul so led the crew and passengers to trust God and to be courageous that "they all escaped to the land" (27 : 44). One may think as he will about the parallel to Jonah, but there is no dispute as to the dignity of Paul's bearing throughout the whole voyage. His conduct on the island of Malta was of a piece with that on board the ship. Paul won power with the barbarians as he had gained power on the ship (28 : 1–10).

4. *The Language of a Cultivated Landsman.*—The autoptic character of Luke's narrative is obvious to all. And yet, in the main, he "regularly uses the terms of educated conversa-

[1] *Acts*, p. 477.

tion, not the strict technical names." [1] Lieutenant Edwin Smith notes that "St. Luke fails to make any reference to the condition of the ship (on the arrival at Fair Havens), an omission which a real sailor would not have made." [2] Lieutenant Smith, of Toronto, was in command of a patrol ship that patrolled from Dunkirk to Zeebrugge and assisted in putting up a smoke-screen for the monitors during the bombardment of Zeebrugge. From November, 1918, to March, 1919, he was in the Mediterranean service. He spent some time with his ship in Valetta harbor in the island of Malta, "within ten miles of the very spot where this, the most famous shipwreck in the world's history, took place." [3] Hence his interest in Luke's narrative.

Smith, of Jordanhill,[4] says that "although his descriptions are accurate, they are, as I have already observed, *unprofessional*." Smith explains what he means by "unprofessional": "The seaman in charge of the ship has his attention perpetually on the stretch, watching every change or indication of a change of wind or weather. He is obliged to decide on the instant what measures must be taken to avail himself of favorable changes or to obviate the consequences of unfavorable ones. Hence in describing them he naturally dwells upon cause and effect. He tells us not only what he has done, but why it was done." We do not see this seaman's interest in the technical matters. The landsman notes what the seaman would take for granted and omits scientific details for which he would care most. "Now these are exactly the peculiarities which characterize the style of St. Luke as a voyage-writer." [5] This judgment can be shown to be correct by ample illustrations.

Luke speaks of loosing the bands of the rudders (27:40), but does not tell how it was fastened. He speaks of hoisting the boat on board (27:16) with difficulty, but does not say what the difficulty was. He gives picturesque details that interest the general reader like the frequent allusions to the wind, "because the winds were contrary" (27:4), "the wind not farther suffering us" (27:7), evidently the northwest wind, though he does not say so. He mentions the south wind

[1] Ramsay, *St. Paul the Traveller*, p. 315.
[2] *Homiletic Review*, August, 1919, p. 104.
[3] *Op. cit.*, p. 102.   [4] *Op. cit.*, p. 21.   [5] *Op. cit.*, p. 21.

(27 : 13) and the sudden Euraquilo or E. N. E. wind that "beat down from it (Crete) and caught the ship" (27 : 14 f.). Ramsay[1] quotes a ship-captain who told him his experience in the Cretan waters: "The wind comes down from those mountains fit to blow the ship out of the water." The mountains tower seven thousand feet high and the sudden squall is typhonic[2] in violence. The ship "could not face the wind" (27 : 15), "look the wind in the eye,"[3] as Luke picturesquely puts it. The effect of the wind on the waves appears often, as in 27 : 27, 41. This E. N. E. wind evidently blew steadily for fourteen days on the second ship as the northwest wind had blown on the first ship and the second to Fair Havens. There is some doubt as to what Luke means in 27 : 12 about the harbor at Phœnix, "facing northeast and southeast," or "looking down the southwest wind and down the northwest wind."[4] The harbor faces east, not west. The language is that of sailors on inbound vessels, as they sailed into the harbor. The mention of Syrtis, the quicksands, the rapid measures taken for safety and the drifting before the wind (27 : 15–17) shows that Luke is thinking of the main features of the events.

The use of the term the Sea of Adria (27 : 27) is also popular. The technical use of the name was for the present Adriatic Sea, but ancient writers sometimes applied it, as Luke does, to the lower and wider expanse from Malta to Greece. The fear and treachery of the sailors is a human touch, as is the lightening of the ship of the cargo. It is not clear what Luke meant by "driven to and fro in the Sea of Adria" (27 : 27), probably the tossing of the waves by the wind as the ship neared land. The beaching of the ship where two seas met[5] (27 : 41) probably refers to currents meeting between Falmouth Island and Malta, where "the two seas continue to meet until this day."[6] But the main points of the story stand out in sharp relief and the four stages of the voyage in three ships (Cæsarea to Myra, Myra to Fair Havens, Fair Havens to Malta, Malta to Puteoli).

5. *Technical Terms in the Narrative.*—Luke was not a sailor,

---

[1] *St. Paul the Traveller*, p. 327.   [2] τυφωνικός (27 : 14).

[3] ἀντοφθαλμεῖν τῷ ἀνέμῳ (27 : 15).

[4] βλέποντα κατὰ λίβα καὶ κατὰ χῶρον.

[5] εἰς τόπον διθάλασσον ἐπέκειλαν τὴν ναῦν.

[6] Lieutenant Smith, *Hom. Rev.*, August, 1919, p. 110.

but a landsman. And yet he was not a landlubber. He loved the sea and knew the sea by experience, else he could never have written this chapter. No study of books could have given him the ready and accurate use of technical terms that we see. Lieutenant Smith[1] holds that Luke spent years on the sea as a traveller. He suggests that Luke may have been a surgeon on some of the Mediterranean vessels. Luke knew the language of the sea. "We sailed under the lee of Cyprus" (27:4), "keeping northward with a westerly wind on the beam."[2] So "we sailed under the lee of Crete" (27:7), but "running under the lee[3] of a small island, Clauda" (27:16). "Here they ran before the wind under the lee of Clauda."[4]

The officers (27:11) on the second ship are the pilot or sailing-master or steersman,[5] and the captain. These are both under the control of the centurion. The sailors[6] (27:27, 30) detected the nearness of land by the soundings. The ship is called by the old classic Greek word[7] only once (27:41) and it occurs here alone in the New Testament. The skiff or lifeboat was towed behind.

The word for the gear[8] or sail (27:17) which was lowered in the storm was used of the sheet seen by Peter in his vision at Joppa (10:11). There was another word for the small foresail[9] which was hoisted up to the wind in time of storm (27:40). Roman ships did not usually have a sail at the stern.[10] The large mainsail was fastened to a long yard. It was reefed[11] in time of storm: "We gave way to it and were driven" (27:15). Robinson[12] thinks that Paul may have made sails as well as tents, and may have thus earned his passage in some of his voyages. Some (Blass, Breusing) interpret "gear" (27:17) to mean cables with weights attached to retard the progress of the ship. Luke does not speak of masts, though they are implied. The Romans had three-masted vessels, though most of them, like the corn-ships, had only the mainmast and the foremast.

---

[1] *Op. cit.*, p. 103. [2] Ramsay, *op. cit.*, p. 328. ὑπεπλεύσαμεν.
[3] ὑποδραμόντες. [4] Ramsay, *op. cit.*, p. 328.
[5] Called ὁ εὐθύνων in Jas. 3:4. [6] ναῦται.
[7] ναῦς. Elsewhere πλοῖον for the ship (27:15, 30) and the little boat was termed σκάφη (27:16).
[8] σκεῦος. [9] τὸν ἀρτέμωνα.
[10] J. Smith, *op. cit.*, p. 192. [11] ἐπιδόντες ἐφερόμεθα.
[12] Hastings's *Dict. of Ap. Ch.* ("Ship").

The word "helps"[1] (27 : 17) was applied to cables for under-girding and strengthening the hull of the ship to prevent the ship's timbers from straining too much in a storm. They were used either transversely amidship under the keel or lengthwise from stern to stern. The tackling[2] of the ship (27 : 19) included all the ship's necessary furniture, everything movable lying about or on the deck. The cargo or lading[3] (27 : 10) was wheat[4] (27 : 38) and it was thrown out only toward the last. The ropes[5] (27 : 32) held the little life-boat.

The ship was impelled only by sail and not by rowers, as many of the Greek ships were. The only paddles were the rudders[6] (27 : 40), which were braced up with bands[7] so that the anchors[8] could more easily be lowered at the stern (27 : 29, 40). Four anchors are here mentioned, but others were probably for use both at the prow (27 : 30) and the stern. Anchors, now of iron with hooks or teeth-like extremities for gripping, and no longer mere stones, were needed to keep the vessel from dashing upon the rocks. As soon as they cast off the anchors, the vessel, under the impact of the wind, made for the beach (27 : 40). The anchors from the stern made it unnecessary to turn the vessel in the storm, which was very dangerous. Nelson lowered anchors from the stern at Copenhagen. In Heb. 6 : 19 a beautiful use is made of hope, as the anchor which lays hold of Jesus, the rock of our salvation, out of sight within the veil, but sure and steadfast. This anchor holds in every storm.

Each ship then, as now, had its individual ensign[9] (28 : 11). The third ship in this memorable voyage in which Paul and Luke and Aristarchus embarked for Puteoli from Malta had the sign of Dioscuri[10] (sons of Zeus) or twin brothers. As a rule the sign was painted on the prow.[11] A flag usually floated from the stern[12] and the whole hull was painted. The ancients may not have used camouflage, though ornaments (a swan or a goose head) were painted on the stern-post. Sometimes eyes[13] were painted on the prow of the vessel (27 : 15).

---

[1] βοηθείαις ἐχρῶντο ὑποζωννύντες τὸ πλοῖον.

[2] σκευή.

[3] φορτίον. Cf. Gal. 6 : 5.

[4] σῖτον.

[5] σχοινία.

[6] πηδαλίων

[7] ζευκτηρίας.

[8] ἀγκύρας.

[9] παράσημον.

[10] Διοσκούροις. Castor and Pollux.

[11] ἐκ πρῴρης (27: 30).

[12] ἐκ πρύμνης (27: 29).

[13] So had the wind eye to eye.

The sounding[1] was done by sounding-leads[2] or plumb-lines dropped at intervals. Modern sailors follow the same method for telling the approach of land.

It is a wonderful story that Luke has told in Acts 27. ` He knew the lingo of the sailors and was at home on the sea. He employs fourteen verbs about the progress of a ship, and all but three occur in Luke alone in the New Testament.[3]

Ramsay[4] concludes that the only difficulty that remains in Smith of Jordanhill's identification of St. Paul's Bay in Malta as the scene of the shipwreck is the fact that it is not now a sandy beach. But the waves may have washed away the sand during the centuries. It is a wonderful story and one is content to leave it now as it stands. "We have seen in our examination that every statement as to the movements of the ship from the time when she left Fair Havens until she was beached at Malta, as set forth by St. Luke, has been verified by external and independent evidence of the most exact and satisfying nature."[5] What more has one a right to demand of Luke or of any historian? This chapter alone would rank Luke among the great writers of the world.

[1] βολίσαντες.   [2] βόλις.
[3] J. Smith, op. cit., pp. 27 f.   [4] Op. cit., p. 241.
[5] Lieutenant Smith, Hom. Rev., August, 1919, p. 110.

CHAPTER XVII

THE SPEECHES IN THE ACTS[1]

"Paul, standing on the stairs, beckoned with the hand unto the people; and when there was made a great silence, he spake unto them in the Hebrew language" (Acts 21 : 40).

The decision that Luke wrote the Acts does not necessarily show that the speeches in the book are authentic.[2] This separate question calls for special inquiry.

1. *The Custom of Ancient Historians.*—We have the example of Herodotus, Thucydides, Xenophon, Polybius, Livy, Josephus, Tacitus, Dio Cassius, to go no further. These writers record numerous speeches. Are they *verbatim* reports such as a modern stenographer takes down or like the speeches in the *Congressional Record*, printed even if not delivered? We know that the ancients did have a system of shorthand. Speakers then, as now, would make notes of speeches that were not written out in full. Part of the business of advocates, like Lysias in Athens, was to compose speeches for men to make in self-defense before the Athenian assembly. The speeches of Demosthenes were written by himself, and bear the marks of the most elaborate preparation and finish to the last detail. The same remark applies to the speeches of Cicero, which he himself wrote out. But the funeral oration of Pericles does not stand upon the same level of genuineness. Thucydides composed such an address as was suitable to represent the ideas of Pericles for the occasion. To-day we have modern reporters for addresses of importance that are not in manuscript form. Percy Gardner says: "We know very well that there was no class of reporters of speeches in antiquity. Nor if there had been would they have reported the words of an obscure itinerant Jew."[3] But Luke was not wholly dependent upon official reporters for his knowledge of the various ad-

[1] Homiletic Review, Vol. 80.
[2] M. Jones, *St. Paul the Orator*, p. 9.
[3] "The Speeches of St. Paul in Acts" (*Cambridge Bible Essays*, p. 392).

dresses that he has preserved in Acts. Still, we must not try
to hold ancient historians to the precise methods and aims of
modern writers. Gardner[1] insists that ancient writers cared
more for style and convention, and were more conventional
when they were composing works of art. "When an ancient
historian inserts in his narrative a speech by one of the characters of his history, it is only in quite exceptional cases that
we are to suppose that such a speech was actually delivered,
or that he means to say that it was actually delivered. It
was a regular convention of historical writing that the historian should express his views of a situation by making the
chief actors in that situation utter speeches in which it is explained."[2] That is true, but it does not follow that Luke necessarily did the same thing. At any rate, one must look at
the facts as far as they can be obtained. Gardner[3] refuses to
put the speeches of Paul in Acts on a par with Romans and
Galatians in historical value.

There were three methods employed by ancient writers in
reporting addresses. One plan was to write a sort of prose
drama with free composition of speeches for the characters like
the English and Roman historical plays of Shakespeare. One
sees this method in Herodotus and Tacitus. Another method
was rhetorical rather than dramatic and is seen in Thucydides
and Sallust. Thucydides frankly acknowledged his practice.
These are free compositions of the writer, but they embody
reminiscences of the author and of witnesses of the events who
heard the address. Machiavelli as late as the sixteenth century had the same method. Here the address was a fact and
the report contains a modicum of the real ideas of the speaker
as touched up by the writer. Another method was to give a
condensed report of the address such as we find in the Gospels, where often extracts from Christ's sermons occur rather
than the full discourse. There was freedom in the rendering of
the sense of the sayings of Jesus, though the substance be the
same. One can test Luke's own method here in using Mark,
the Logia and the other sources for his Gospel. Gardner[4]
thinks that each writer had his own custom in the matter.
"And that which at present concerns us is what conventions in
this respect were observed by Luke, who must, as has already

[1] *Ibid.*, p. 392.   [2] *Ibid.*, p. 393.
[3] *Ibid.*, p. 392.   [4] *Ibid.*, p. 393.

been observed, be regarded as a Greek literary man, and one of very great talent." [1]

2. *Luke as a Reporter.*—One class of writers regards the speeches in the Acts as mere rhetorical exercises without any historical worth (Schmiedel, S. Davidson, Bacon). These men [2] argue that the picture of Paul in the speeches in the Acts is contradictory and unlike that in his Epistles. If Luke followed the method of Herodotus and Tacitus, we must not appeal to the speeches in Acts for the ideas of any one but Luke himself.

Gardner [3] holds that "Luke in his use of speeches stands between the ethical and dramatic tendency of Herodotus and Tacitus and the rhetorical tendency of Thucydides and Sallust." That is to say, Gardner ranks Luke above Herodotus, but below Thucydides. "In the Gospel the rhetorical bent is far less clearly to be traced than in the Acts." That is to say, Gardner considers the birth stories in Luke 1 and 2 to be "in a region of myth," "hymns, very beautiful and very Christian, but freely composed for the persons in whose mouths they are put." Gardner [4] offers us this consolation that "if so, we gain a very high view of the extraordinary versatility and literary skill of the Evangelist." He thinks that Luke is more of a compiler than a composer in the sayings of Jesus. In the Acts "the circumstances are different." "It is impossible to deny the possibility or even the probability that the author may have built in some degree upon reports and rumors of speeches made upon striking occasions by the leaders of the Church. But the language is certainly Lukan." [5] Gardner [6] thinks it far more likely that a careless historian like Luke would freely compose the speeches than that he "would search out hearers of these speeches and make precise notes of their recollections." That is plausible, but it is wholly *a priori*, as one can see, and rests upon a theory of Luke's historical worth that has been discredited by the researches of Ramsay. Moffatt [7] holds that "the excellent historical sense of the author" restrained Luke, "who, while following in the main the ordinary methods of ancient historiography in the composition of such speeches, was careful to avoid moulding and

---

[1] *Ibid.*, p. 394.
[2] See Schmiedel, "Acts" in *Encycl. Biblica*.
[3] *Op. cit.*, p. 394.
[4] *Op. cit.*, p. 394.
[5] *Ibid.*
[6] *Ibid.*, p. 395.
[7] *Intr. to Lit. of N. T.*, p. 306.

shaping his materials with a freedom which should obliterate the special cast of their aim and temper. These materials were probably furnished in the main by oral traditions." Certainly, this is a much more likely picture of the facts than that of either Schmiedel or Gardner.

But, after all, with Luke's own account of the sayings of Jesus in the light of Mark and Q, one cannot help wondering why we are forbidden to think that Luke followed the same method in the Acts. If he consulted sources, written and oral, for the addresses of Jesus in the Gospel, as can be proven, it is natural to think that he pursued the same careful research in the Acts. He made selections from the material in the Gospel, as he apparently did in the Acts. His reports in the Acts vary in the degree of completeness, as in the Gospel. We know that Luke heard some of Paul's addresses, which he reports. He had abundant opportunity to consult those who heard others, as we have seen in the study of the sources of the Acts. Luke was in touch personally with James and Paul. Philip and Paul heard Stephen. Mark and Philip and Manaen heard Peter. "The speaker in the earlier part may represent not untrustworthily the primitive Jewish-Christian preaching of the period." [1]

Besides, one can test the speeches of Peter, James, and Paul by their Epistles. No one claims that Luke read those Epistles and aimed to reproduce their style and teaching. It is admitted on all sides that the speeches of the different speakers in the Acts differ and have a striking verisimilitude to the probable facts.[2] If Luke composed them all, he was a remarkable literary genius. It is worth while to examine the facts and see if it is not true that, while Luke's own style appears in various ways in the condensed reports, after all the reports faithfully represent the substance and the essential language of the original addresses.

3. *The Speeches of Peter.*—Fortunately there are a number of these, such as the address to the one hundred and twenty concerning the fate of Judas and the choice of his successor (1 : 15-22), the great address at Pentecost (2 : 14-39), the

---

[1] Moffatt, *ibid.*, p. 305.

[2] Blass, *Acta Apostolorum*, p. 11: "*Quo intentius has orationes inspexeris, eo plura in eis reperies, quæ cum sint temporibus personisque egregie accommodata, ad rhetoricam licentiam scriptoris referri se velint.*"

speech at Solomon's porch (3 : 12-26), three before the Sanhedrin (4 : 8-12, 19; 5 : 29-32), one to Ananias (5 : 3-4) and one
to Sapphira (5 : 9), the address to Cornelius and his household
(10 : 28-29, 34-43, 47), the defense in Jerusalem (11 : 4-17),
the address at the Jerusalem conference (15 : 7-11). Here we
possess data sufficient for a comparison with I Peter and
II Peter, also, if one does not reject it as a basis of comparison.
Bigg[1] in his excellent *Commentary* does not draw any comparison between the language and theology of I Peter and
Peter's speeches in Acts. He thinks it likely that Silvanus
polished up Peter's Greek in this Epistle, and as Luke's own
style appears to some extent in the speeches the comparison is
not easy.

And yet the fundamental ideas in Peter's theology appear
in his speeches. Peter's speeches reflect the new light and the
new courage that came with Pentecost and that shine in his
Epistles. It is probable that Peter delivered all these addresses in Aramaic, as was his later custom, with Mark as
interpreter, except that at Pentecost, where Jews from all over
the world were present, and that at Cæsarea to Cornelius.
These two were probably in Greek. Peter was bilingual, as
was Paul, though he was far less at home in the Greek than
Paul. If Luke made use of Aramaic sources for the Gospel
(chapters 1 and 2), he could do so for Peter's speeches when
necessary. Knowling thinks that Luke had written sources
for Peter's speeches besides the benefit of the recollections of
those who heard them. We know that Peter's addresses are
not reported in full, for "with many other words he testified
and exhorted them" (Acts 2 : 40). It is quite possible that
Peter himself made brief notes of some of his more important
addresses after they were delivered, or others may have done
so at Luke's request. Moffatt[2] quotes Overbeck as saying:
"To the doctrinal discourses of Peter we may in a certain sense
grant that they faithfully represent the primitive preaching of
the Messiah by the Apostles, and that so far they possess a
certain originality." That is a very cautious statement and
far short of the whole truth. The Christology of Peter's
speeches is primitive and is to be compared with that of Mark
and Q. It is primitive in comparison with that of Paul's
Epistles and of Peter's Epistles. "It is clear that these early

[1] P. 6.   [2] *Op. cit.*, p. 305.

chapters give a picture of the primitive community which is quite different from what existed within the experience of the writer, and [which is in itself probable."[1] The speeches of Peter reproduce an early stage of development, just as the birth narratives in Luke 1 and 2 are the most primitive things in the New Testament. There is no doubt whatever about the primitive picture of Christianity in Acts 1–12, where Peter figures. It is natural to think that Luke drew this picture from actual data.

4. *The Speech of Stephen.*—This speech (7 : 2–53, 56, 59) has every mark of genuineness. It will not do to say that Luke could not have gotten a report of this address. Paul himself heard it (Acts 8 : 1; 26 : 10). Philip almost certainly heard it. Either could have reproduced the line of argument for Luke. Stephen himself may have made a full outline of his address in Aramaic, since it was a formal defense or *apologia*. There are Lukan turns of thought in the report, but not more than is natural if Luke translated an Aramaic document. There are in the speech a number of variations from and additions to the Old Testament, some of which appear in Philo. Stephen disputed in Jerusalem in "the synagogue of the Libertines, and of the Cyrenians and of the Alexandrians" (Acts 6 : 9). He was a Hellenistic Jew, like all the seven (6 : 5), and may have been from Alexandria, and probably disputed with Saul in the synagogue of Cilicia (6 : 9). It is not necessary here to survey the points where Stephen and Philo agree. Rackham[2] has presented them fully. They are chiefly extrascriptural details, such as appear also in the Talmud and in Josephus. In the ministry of the angels in the giving of the ten commandments (Acts 7 : 53) Stephen is followed by Paul (Gal. 3 : 19). But the significant thing is that Luke preserves these items, which are so different from the Old Testament and from the rest of the New Testament.

The speech itself fits in perfectly with the picture that Luke has drawn in the Gospel and in the Acts. Jesus himself was arraigned before the Sanhedrin on the charge of blasphemy, because false witnesses were bribed to say that he was going to destroy [the temple, with the pretense that he could build it again in three days. Jesus kept silent and only confessed on oath that he was the Messiah, the Son of God, but they

[1] Headlam, Hastings's *D. B.* ("Acts").   [2] *The Acts*, pp. 99–102.

crucified him. Stephen made a formal apology, and they stoned him in a rage, lynched him like a mob, as they tried to do to Jesus several times, and probably would have done if he had made a defense as Stephen did.

The inner connection of the spirit of Stephen with the history argues for the authenticity of the speech. The Twelve Apostles had trouble from the Sadducees because they proclaimed the resurrection of Jesus, while the Pharisees held aloof. Stephen, himself a Hellenist, was the first to see the wider reach of the mission of Jesus, that not only included Gentiles and Jews, but treated Gentiles as on a par with Jews. Stephen saw that Jesus thought the spiritual nature of worship independent of place or race, as Jesus expounded to the Samaritan woman in John 4. The Hellenistic Jews in the synagogues in Jerusalem saw that Stephen robbed the Jews of their prerogatives and privileges, and bluntly charged him with preaching against Moses and God. Thus quickly Stephen had created a revolution of which he was the victim. He roused the Pharisees, who turned on him as they had on Jesus, but more suddenly and more fiercely. Stephen's passionate speech is the longest in the Acts, as long as any three of Paul's sermons, and is justified, because of the importance and significance of it to Luke's narrative. Stephen's career marks the second stage in the apostolic history. "He, being made perfect in a short time, fulfilled a long time; for his soul pleased the Lord. Therefore it hasted from the midst of wickedness" (Wisdom 4 : 13 f.). \

Stephen is the bridge (Rackham) from Peter to Paul in the interpretation of Christ. Like Peter, Stephen makes Jesus a second Moses, a prophet like unto Moses, but, unlike Peter at this stage, he saw beyond the temple and the law to the freemen in Christ among the Gentiles who would come to Christ without becoming Jews. Peter saw that later at Joppa and Cæsarea (Acts 10). Paul will one day become the great champion of Gentile liberty against the Judaizers (see Galatians). But now his soul raged against the man who had struck at the glory of Moses, as he thought. Some day Paul will find the true Israel in those very Gentiles (Romans 9–11). At Athens Paul will expound eloquently to the cultured Greeks the very gospel that God dwells not in temples made with hands, for which he helped to stone Stephen now. Stephen appealed to the covenant with Abraham before the law, as Paul will do in Gal. 3 : 17. Stephen finally turned on the stiff-necked and uncircumcised Jews who always resisted the Holy Spirit (7 : 51), precisely as Paul will one day turn away from the Jews to the Gentiles at Antioch in Pisidia (13 : 46) and at Corinth (18 : 6). "If Stephen had not prayed, Paul had not preached." Paul finally took up the torch of Stephen and passed it on. Peter will preach the same glorious message, also. Stephen was the man of vision, who saw the full truth ahead of his time and dared to proclaim it.

Luke has given the trial and defense of Stephen a dramatic setting and has shown the historian's insight in the way that he has presented the whole story. The speech bears every mark of a real report. It is full of life and power. It left its mark on Paul. It blazed the way for the future expansion of Christianity. It broke the shackles of Judaism. It defied Pharisaism. It flashed before the Jewish world the heart of Christ's message and mission to the whole wide world.

5. *The Speech of James.*—In Acts 15 : 13-21 Luke has a speech delivered by James, the brother of Jesus, who presided over the conference in Jerusalem. In 15 : 23-29 he gives the circular epistle drawn up apparently by James and adopted by the conference and sent to Antioch by Judas and Silas, along with Paul and Barnabas (15 : 22 f.), and later carried by Paul and Silas to the churches of Galatia (15 : 4). It was common enough to send a formal epistle by messengers or "apostles," as Paul did (cf. II Cor. 8 : 23) and as the churches did. The Second Book of Maccabees begins with a letter about the purification of the temple. It was easy enough for Luke to obtain a copy of this circular epistle, since so many were distributed to the churches. But this epistle embodied the resolution of James in his address, and was almost certainly written by James and read to the conference for their indorsement. In the epistle the order is "Barnabas and Paul" (15 : 25), for in Jerusalem it is still "our beloved brother Barnabas" who has more influence with the Christians then than Paul. In Galatia and Antioch it had already become "Paul and Barnabas."

The style of the epistle and the speech of James is the same. James calls Peter "Symeon," the Aramaic form of Simon, seen also in II Peter 1 : 1. James indorses the speech of Peter and proves by Scripture that Peter is right. James shows the same kind of practical wisdom in his speech[1] which settles the controversy with freedom for the Gentiles and in harmony with the teaching of the Old Testament in a way to satisfy all Jewish Christians save the extreme Judaizers. It was a real *eirenicon*, but no half-way compromise, and is strikingly like the discussion in the Epistle of James (1 : 5; 3 : 10–18). Luke was with James (Acts 21 : 18 f.) and would have no trouble in getting the speech of James and the circular epistle to which James refers (21 : 25), practically claiming to be the author of the letter: "We wrote, giving judgment." James may have delivered his speech in Aramaic, but he knows Greek well, as his Epistle shows. If Luke translated the speech and the circular letter, that would explain any Lukan traits discernible in them.

The Epistle of James shows striking similarities to the speech of James and the circular letter written by James. Mayor[2] says: "I cannot but think it a remarkable coincidence that, out of two hundred and thirty words contained in the speech and the circular, so many should reappear in our Epistle, written on a totally different subject." It is possible that the Epistle of James was written before the conference in Jerusalem.[3] If so, James has written the first Epistle which has come down to us, unless Galatians comes earlier, which I consider quite unlikely. The circular letter, also written by James, would then be the second Epistle preserved for us. The Epistle of James bears a resemblance to the Cynic diatribe,[4] but the Jews were long familiar with this form of literature.[5] Once more the data fit all the known facts, without saying that Luke made up the speech of James and the circular letter.

6. *The Speeches of Paul.*—These addresses are the most important items on this phase of the subject. They are the basis of special treatises by Bethge,[6] Percy Gardner[7] and M. Jones.[8] We may agree at once that these speeches of Paul

---

[1] Rackham, *Acts*, p. 254.   [2] *Comm. on James*, p. iii.

[3] Robertson, *Practical and Social Aspects of Christianity*, p. 35.

[4] Ropes, *Ep. of James*, p. 16.

[5] Cf. letters in II Chron. 21 : 12; 30 : 1; 32 : 17; Jer. 29 : 1, 25.

[6] *Die paulinischen Reden.*

[7] "The Speeches of St. Paul in Acts" (*Cambridge Biblical Essays*, pp. 379–418).

[8] *St. Paul the Orator.*

in Acts must all be examined separately, and that they do not
necessarily stand on the same level in point of proof as to
authenticity. Bethge[1] argues that the speeches of Paul all
show the marks of an eye-witness. We may agree with Gardner[2] that the speech to the elders of Ephesus at Miletus (Acts
20: 18–35) has the best claim of all to be historic. But that
admission does not discredit the others as Gardner thinks.
He holds the speech at Athens (17: 22–31) to be "the least
authentic of the Pauline discourses in Acts." That is precisely the point to be examined. It is plain that the speeches
of Paul in Acts are only a small selection of an immense number of addresses made by Paul.[3] It is true, also, that Luke
has chosen the occasions for the speeches which he does give,
so "as to bring into strong relief the various sides of his ministry and of his doctrine."[4] But it is just as easy to suppose
that Luke, being with Paul in Rome when he wrote the Acts,
drew upon Paul's memory and upon Paul's notes and outlines
of his discourses as to imagine that Luke made a free composition of Paul's addresses for the purpose of representing Paul
properly on various occasions. To me it is far simpler and
more natural to conceive that Luke followed his usual plan of
using all available data for his narrative. It is hard to see
why he should pass Paul by in the matter of his own speeches,
which he would surely wish to win Paul's sanction.

One must not make too much of Paul's reference to the
charge of his enemies in Corinth that "his speech is of no
account" (II Cor. 10: 10), as if Luke had to write out eloquent
addresses for Paul on the set occasions in the Acts. Paul himself did make disclaimers of rhetorical oratory after the order
of the Greek dialectic.[5] He preached the Gospel "not in wisdom of words" (I Cor. 1: 17) and "my speech and my preaching were not in persuasive words of wisdom" (I Cor. 2: 4).
That is, from the standpoint of the false taste of the Corinthians, some of whom later made the very charges against
him. But we have abundant proof of Paul's real power of
speech in his Epistles. There is no lack of passion and of
power in them and, at times, Paul rises to the heights of real

---

[1] *Die paulinischen Reden*, p. 174.
[2] *Cambridge Biblical Essays*, p. 401.
[3] M. Jones, *St. Paul the Orator*, p. 3.
[4] Gardner, *op. cit.*, p. 395.   [5] Jones, *op. cit.*, p. 2.

eloquence (cf. I Cor. 13, 15; Romans 8; Phil. 3). There is variety in the style of Paul's Epistles according to subject-matter and time and mood. It is no surprise, therefore, to find like adaptations in his addresses to time and place and theme. Paul spoke, as he wrote, to the audience before him. He went after the verdict, though he always applied the eternal principles of the Gospel to the topic in hand.

Gardner[1] thinks that two influences helped Luke to make a good report of Paul's speeches: (1) his close relation to Paul and (2) his fine dramatic sense, which would keep him from grossly misrepresenting Paul. On the other hand, he thinks that Luke was handicapped (1) by his sense of the conventions of historic writing, and (2) "looseness and carelessness of statement, which almost obliterates for him the line between fact and rumor, between that which actually occurred and that which ought to have occurred." It is pure hypothesis to shackle Luke with the conventional theories of Thucydides and Josephus, when we can test his critical habit by his use of Mark and Q. The alleged "carelessness" of Luke lies in the imagination of Baur and Schmiedel. The facts of modern discovery have effectually disposed of those wholesale charges as we have already abundantly seen. The thing to do is to test the reports of Paul's speeches by the canons of criticism.

Gardner[2] divides Paul's speeches into two classes: (1) those at Antioch and Athens, which were "free compositions of Luke"; (2) the later speeches, "which would naturally be largely affected by personal memories." Gardner[3] denies that he has taken away the "value" of Paul's speeches, for Luke knew Paul's views so well that "his fine dramatic sense would render him apt at expressing Paul's usual way of proceeding." Chase[4] holds that Luke had actual data for all the speeches, and retained Paul's original ideas, though he may have given them "greater fulness and elaboration, and a more distinctly literary flavor." *Per contra*, one must bear in mind that the reports all bear evidence of great condensation. Hence Jones[5] is right in contending that "while they betray considerable proofs of editing on St. Luke's part, in the way of summarizing and epitomizing, many expressions and phrases being undoubt-

[1] *Op. cit.*, pp. 415 f. [2] *Op. cit.*, p. 396.
[3] *Op. cit.*, p. 396. [4] *The Credibility of the Acts*, pp. 108 f.
[5] *Op. cit.*, p. 17.

edly Lukan, the utterances are, in the main, those of the Apostle, and that through the major portion of their contents we are listening to the voice of St. Paul himself." I feel sure that this is a very moderate statement of the facts. The voice of Paul is heard in these addresses as the voice of Jesus comes to us in Luke's Gospel.

This judgment is reinforced by a consideration of the probable sources of the speeches of Paul. We know that Luke was present at Miletus: "We came to Miletus" (Acts 20:15). So he heard that notable address to the elders, the noblest of all talks to preachers, save the many to the disciples by Jesus in the Gospels. We know also that he was present in Jerusalem (21:17 f.) where Paul spoke to the mob from the steps of the tower of Antonia (22:1-21). There is no reason for thinking that he was not present in Cæsarea, where Paul spoke before Felix, Festus and Herod Agrippa II (24-26). Jones[1] argues that beyond a doubt the report of the address before Agrippa is "the work of an eye-witness, or a copy from an original source." We know that Luke was with Paul in Rome (28:14, 16), and so heard Paul's two addresses to the Jews there (28:17-28). Luke was also with Paul in Philippi (Acts 16), but he was not present in Thessalonica, Berœa, Athens or Corinth. We do not know that he was with Paul in the first campaign in south Galatia. Jones[2] thinks that the extremely vivid narratives and reports of Paul's extended address at Antioch in Pisidia (13:16-41), and the striking speech in Lystra (14:12-17) argue for Luke's presence with Paul. But that is very uncertain. What we do know is that Luke was with Paul and had every opportunity to obtain Paul's recollections or notes of these addresses, which he himself did not hear. "The trustworthiness of the speeches is, therefore, in some measure, guaranteed by the fact, in the case of many of them, that they are reported by one who actually listened to them, and where this is not the case, they are reproduced from materials supplied either by the speaker himself or by his companions."[3]

It is hard to overestimate the value of the Pauline speeches. "The primary Pauline Gospel we owe almost entirely to the speeches, and from this aspect they are invaluable. By means

[1] *Op. cit.*, p. 236.   [2] *Op. cit.*, p. 19.   [3] *Ibid.*, p. 20.

of these we are able to trace the Pauline system of doctrine from its very rudiments."[1]

The genuineness of the speeches alone explains Luke's report of two addresses so much alike as those in Acts 22 and 26, and that cover the conversion of Paul already adequately told in Acts 9. Besides, there are apparent inconsistencies on minor points in these three accounts of Paul's conversion that yield to plausible explanations on close study, but that are unnatural if Luke composed all three reports. The repetition is otherwise needless and the discrepancies superfluous.

Ramsay[2] calls attention to the marvellous adaptation of Paul's speeches to the local atmosphere, a coincidence hardly possible for a writer composing at a distance. He cites the address at Antioch in Pisidia, Lystra and Athens as instances. Local color is reproduced precisely in each case. Ramsay notes a likeness of tone in the speeches in Antioch and Lystra and the Epistle to the Galatians. The speech in Athens is attacked as unlike Paul in language and in spirit. But it is as unlike Luke as it is Paul. The Attic flavor can be proof of Paul's versatility. The appeal to natural theology occurs also in the speech at Lystra and is precisely in harmony with Paul's argument in Romans 1 and 2. It is not true that Paul surrendered his Gospel message in the presence of the Stoic and Epicurean philosophers, for he accented repentance, judgment and the resurrection of Jesus from the dead. He probably meant to stress other great doctrines, if the whimsical Athenians had not cut short his address. Ramsay[3] notes that the address at Lystra was more simple while that at Athens before an educated audience took on a more philosophical turn. But Paul attacked idolatry as courageously in Athens as in Lystra. The sermon at Antioch in Pisidia is remarkable for its Pauline doctrine of justification by faith instead of by works, and for its grasp of the salient points concerning the life and death of Christ. By means of the speeches we see Paul the preacher as we could not otherwise know him.[4]

There is no doubt that Luke has shown consummate skill in reproducing strategic and dramatic staging for Paul's various addresses. That was his task as the historian. But he has not been convicted of merely following the conventional

[1] Jones, ibid., p. 21.   [2] St. Paul the Traveller, pp. 144 ff.
[3] Op. cit., p. 147.   [4] See Rosser, Paul the Preacher.

practice of inventing the discourses for Peter, Stephen, James and Paul which cut so large a figure in his book.

The very diversity exhibited is more readily explained by the use of actual data for the various addresses. The short speech of Tertullus (Acts 24 : 2–28) was made in public, as was that of Festus in 25 : 24–27. The letter of Claudius Lysias in 23 : 27–30 was a public document. It is not so easy to explain how Luke got the data for the conversation between Festus and Agrippa in 25 : 14–22. But Luke may have resources of which we know nothing. It is really amazing, all things considered, how we can follow his tracks for nearly the whole of the many discourses that adorn the Book of Acts. "He chose rather to include the speeches as we possess them, with their many difficulties, their manifest inconsistencies on some points, because they represent the genuine utterances of his master." [1] We may thank Luke for this fidelity as for his other gifts and graces.

[1] Jones, *op. cit.*, p. 291.

CHAPTER XVIII

A BROAD OUTLOOK ON LIFE

"There was a man of Macedonia standing, beseeching him, and saying, Come over into Macedonia and help us" (Acts 16: 9).

This man was probably Luke, as we have seen. At any rate, the sentence properly pictures Luke as a man of his times who was interested in the world problems of his day.

1. *The Versatility of Luke.*—We cannot have come thus far in the discussion of the writings of Luke without seeing that he was a man of great gifts and of fine culture. He had the opportunity of scholastic training. He was accurate without pedantry. Plummer[1] terms him "the most versatile of all the New Testament writers." He was a man of genius who toiled at his task like a plodder. "The humanism of the Hellenistic world pervades him"[2] and yet he is simple in his love and loyalty to Jesus as Lord and Saviour. He is a skilful physician who reverently sees in Christ the Great Physician for both soul and body. He can write literary *Koiné* like Plutarch and yet closely follows his Aramaic sources. He hides himself all the while, and yet his own beautiful style crops out at every turn. He has "the power of merging himself, all but his style, in the persons of those whose story he is telling."[3] He is a Greek and a Christian, a friend of Paul and of Theophilus, a physician and a preacher, a literary man and a friend of the poor, a champion of women and of children, a friend of the good and of sinners, a historian and a poet, a mystic and a musician, a humanitarian and a humanist, a traveller on land and on sea, a student of the Scriptures and a medical missionary, a harmonizer of science and of theology, the interpreter of Peter and of Paul, but most of all the lover and interpreter of Jesus Christ, a man of prayer and of faith. "One cannot help feeling how delightful and lovable as a man he must have been."[4]

[1] *Comm.*, p. xlix.   [2] Gardner, *op. cit.*, p. 387.
[3] *Ibid.*   [4] *Ibid.*

231

I cannot close this volume without some expression of my own admiration for Luke. Even Percy Gardner[1] can say: "All these qualities color the Gospel and the Acts alike, making them exquisite works of literary art and great monuments of refined Christian feeling." It is small wonder that this man so won the heart of Paul that he calls him "the beloved physician." He has won the heart of the whole world. Ramsay[2] has a chapter on "The Charm of Paul." One could easily write on the charm of Luke who charmed Paul. It is impossible to exaggerate the importance of Luke's contribution to Christianity. Luke and John and Paul and the author of Hebrews (Apollos?) represent the acme of culture in early Christianity. The author of Hebrews is the masterful interpreter of Christianity in the light of Judaism and as its successor and superior. John is the rapt and clear-eyed mystic, the eagle soaring above the clouds and the storm. Paul is the mighty and masterful protagonist of Christ, the "Illuminator of Luke," as Tertullian calls him. Luke is the versatile scholar and the humane and gentle scientist who has painted his picture-gallery of Jesus and his followers on broad canvas and in bold and yet delicate lines.

2. *Luke a Cosmopolitan.*—Luke was a citizen of the world like Paul and even more so. Paul was a Jew with a touch of the Greek and of the Roman who became a Christian. Luke was a Greek in a Roman world who became a Christian. He was without the racial and religious prejudices of the Jew, though he came to take a lively interest in all things Jewish in his study of Jesus. He shows great knowledge of the Septuagint. But Luke did not have to overcome the Jew's hostility to the Gentiles. The Greek and the Roman were not taboo to him as they were once to Peter and Paul. "He is a Universalist who would have all men to be saved, and for whom the difference between Jew and Gentile does not present itself with the same rigidity which it has in the mind of Paul."[3] It is Luke who records the parable of the Good Samaritan who does good to a poor wounded Jew by the roadside whom the pious priest and the Levite pass by in dread of contamination.

For this reason Luke has no trouble in doing justice to the Gentiles. He draws a kindly picture of Gallio, the Roman

[1] *Ibid.*   [2] *Pauline Studies*, pp. 25–45.
[3] Gardner, *op. cit.*, p. 387.

proconsul, of Cornelius and Julius, the Roman centurions, of
Gamaliel, the Pharisaic leader and sage, of the kindly curiosity
about Paul in Athens. "He has got the sympathetic insight
which can thoroughly enter the feelings of different parties—
such as Pharisees and Sadducees, Hebraists and Hellenists;
different classes of society—Jews and Greeks, the populace and
better classes, local magistrates, Roman officials, Herodian
princes; different interests—Pharisaic rabbis and Sadducaic
priests, Ephesian silversmiths and Jewish sorcerers, Roman
aristocrats and Greek citizens; differences of culture—Athenian
philosophers and rustic Lycaonians; different professions—soldiers and sailors. Then this appreciativeness is made effective
by a gift of style. By a few vigorous touches he can make a
scene live before us."[1] Carpenter[2] devotes one chapter to
"S. Luke the Universalist." Hayes[3] calls his Gospel "The
Gospel for the Gentiles" because it was written by a Gentile
with Gentiles as well as Jews in mind.

He wrote for the whole Christian world. "Of the three
synoptic Gospels this is by far the most catholic in its sympathies and universalistic in its outlook."[4] Luke traces the
genealogy of Jesus back to Adam. He is fond of the words
grace, Saviour, salvation and evangelize. He makes Simeon
say that Jesus is "a light for revelation to the Gentiles" (2 : 32).
He alone calls three Roman emperors by name (Augustus,
Tiberius, Claudius). Van Oosterzee says that Luke raised
"sacred history from the standpoint of Jewish national nationality to the higher and holier ground of universal humanity."
Hayes[5] puts it thus: "It is the Gospel of the real humanity of
Jesus. It is the Gospel of Jesus as our Brother-Man. It is
the Gospel of the Kinsman-Redeemer of the race." It is the
Pauline Gospel and it is our Gospel, for we are mostly Gentiles,
but it is most of all the Gospel of Jesus the Saviour.

Chesterton[6] says of Jesus: "What nobody can possibly call
Him is a Galilean of the time of Tiberius." He was that, but
he was much more than that. He was the Son of Man as well
as the Jewish Messiah. This Luke saw clearly. Carpenter,[7]

[1] Rackham, *The Acts*, p. xlvi.
[4] *Christianity According to S. Luke*, pp. 212–227.
[3] *Syn. Gospels and Acts*, pp. 205–216.
  Ibid., p. 206.   [5] *Op. cit.*, p. 253.
[6] *Hibbert Journal*, July, 1909, p. 748.   [7] *Op. cit.*, p. 223.

however, adds: "Some of the Jews themselves had formed the habit of speaking of their expected Hero as the Son of Man. Who is this Son of Man? God is His Father, and the holy nation is his mother. And for all his Jewish outlook, His national patriotism, and His Galilean accent, He has over-leaped the bounds of nationality, and transcended the limitations of station, century, and sex. . . . He has created, incidentally, and almost casually, in the course of His redeeming man's soul, the only true democracy that is ever likely to exist." Luke sees and seizes the universal humanity of Jesus and traces with masterful pen the expansion of the kingdom of God from the handful of Galilean Jews to the confines of the Roman Empire with the conquest of the world and of the ages as the legacy of the risen Christ.

3. *Luke's Picture-Gallery.*—But Luke is no abstract dreamer. He is an internationalist, but a patriot first. He is not carried away by ideas to the neglect of personalities. Luke is a lover of his human kind. He draws pictures of persons in the Gospel and in the Acts by a few artistic touches. One can never forget the picture of Zacharias, of Mary, of Elizabeth, of Simeon, of Anna, in the opening chapters of the Gospel, or of Martha and Mary in Luke 10, or of Cleopas and his companion in Luke 24. But in the Gospel these all radiate around Christ. Harnack[1] devotes a chapter to Luke's "Treatment of Persons." In the Acts there are two chief characters, Peter and Paul, but many others of second and third rank rotate around these. Harnack sees nothing of value in the supposed parallelism between Peter and Paul in the Acts, though he thinks that Luke's picture of Paul is much more distinct than that of Peter, probably because Paul was so much better known to Luke and because, also, Paul was a bolder figure.

In the Acts there are mentioned one hundred and ten names, besides groups of persons whose names are not given, "and of these how extraordinarily their individuality is preserved."[2] After all, persons are the most interesting data for the historian. One can easily recall in the Acts Peter and John, Ananias and Sapphira, Annas and Caiaphas and Gamaliel, Stephen and Philip, James the brother of John and James the brother of Jesus, Barnabas and Judas, Simon Magus and Bar-jesus, John Mark and Silas, Ananias and Judas of Damascus,

---

[1] *The Acts*, pp. 117–132. [2] Rackham, *Acts*, p. xlvii.

Saul also called Paul, Sergius Paulus and Gallio, Cornelius and Julius, Dorcas and Lydia, Timothy and Erastus, Aristarchus and Trophimus, Agabus and Apollos, Herod Agrippa I and II, Aquila and Priscilla, Claudius Lysias and Tertullus, Felix and Festus, Drusilla and Bernice, Demetrius and Publius.

Of this number Harnack[1] notes only five personages of secondary rank from Luke's standpoint (Stephen, Philip, Barnabas, James and Apollos). He observes, also, that all of these save James the brother of Christ are Hellenists. Harnack thinks that the emphasis upon Stephen lies in the fact that his message was the bridge from Judaism to the Gentile world, and that this motive dominates Luke in all his use of persons in his story. At any rate, Luke writes his book largely by the use of biographical sketches.

But it is not a haphazard jumble. He has two heroes, Peter and Paul, but Paul is the dominating figure of Acts next to Christ, whose words and deed overshadow all (Acts 1 : 1).

It is interesting to note that Luke reveals his true historical insight by his estimate of Paul, who by no means cut so large a figure with his contemporaries as he does with us. Luke has the love of the disciple for his master in the case of Paul, but he does not mar the history because of this attachment. "Finally, S. Luke has demonstrated his artistic skill by welding this complex variety of persons and places, times and seasons, characters and circumstances, into one whole—a whole in which no tendency or side-issue dominates: and a whole so complete that we entirely forget the variety, we are unconscious of the author and his method."[2] We are swept on with the onward march of Christianity from Jerusalem to Rome. We see the greatest of all revolutions transforming Peter and Paul from Jewish pride of privilege to world evangelization and Christian freedom in Christ.

4. *Sympathy with Sinners.*—We judge the sympathies of Luke by his choice of material. The Christ of Luke is the friend of sinners. A physician is brought into close contact with the outcasts of society, those who are "down and out." In a pre-eminent sense Luke pictures Christ as the friend and saviour of sinners. The matchless parables in Luke 15 (the Lost Sheep, the Lost Coin, the Lost Son) are told by Christ, as Luke explains (15 : 1 f.), because, when "all the publicans and

---

[1] *Acts of the Apostles*, p. 119.   [1] Rackham, *Acts*, p. xlvii.

sinners were drawing near unto him to hear him," "both the
Pharisees and the scribes murmured, saying, This man receiv-
eth sinners, and eateth with them." The charge was true,
gloriously true as we see, as Luke saw, but as the ecclesiastics
of the time did not see. "S. Luke's Gospel is a Gospel of sacrifice and a Gospel for sinners. It contains the word 'sinners'
more often than all the other three put together."[1] In Luke
7:37 the woman that was a notorious sinner anoints our
Lord, but Luke does not identify her with Mary Magdalene
in 8:2 or with Mary of Bethany. That is a gratuitous insult
that mediæval theologians and painters have cast upon these
two noble women. But Jesus did forgive the sinful woman
who showed more love for Christ than his host, the proud
Pharisee (7:47). Luke rejoices in the courage of Jesus, as in
the case of Zacchæus (19:2–10): "The Son of Man came to
seek and to save that which was lost." Luke's Christianity
is for the bad as well as for the good, to cure sin as well as
sickness. Glover[2] quotes the German Jew Börne as saying:
"Christianity is the religion of all poor devils."

5. *Sympathy with the Poor.*—So pronounced is the sympathy
of Luke with the poor that his Gospel has actually been charged
with Ebionitism and with class prejudice, with the modern
"Soviet" conception of class domination, the poor ruling the
rich. That is not true at all. Luke is interested in the rich
(19:2; 23:50), but he champions the poor because they needed
a friend (1:53; 2:7, 8, 24; 4:18; 6:20, 21; 7:22; 14:13, 22;
16:20, 23). Luke reports the special form of communism
among the early disciples in Jerusalem (Acts 4 and 5), but he
would not be a modern syndicalist, certainly not a Marxian
Socialist, or a Bolshevist. The physician sees the need and
hears the cry of the poor. "The physician who works only
for fat fees and who goes only when summoned by the well-
to-do may make his fortune, but he will miss his greatest professional opportunity in the service to the poor."[3] Luke records
Jesus as saying at Nazareth that the spirit of the Lord had
"anointed me to preach good tidings to the poor" (4:18).
Luke has simply "Blessed are ye poor" in 6:20. In the story
of Lazarus and the wicked Rich Man the beggar comes out

[1] Carpenter, *op. cit.*, p. 219.
[2] *Nature and Purpose of a Christian Society*, p. 34.
[3] Hayes, *op. cit.*, p. 237.

ahead in the end (16 : 19–31). No fiercer indictment of a rich fool was ever drawn than in the parable of Jesus recorded by Luke in 12 : 16–21. Luke represents Christ as inviting "the poor and maimed and blind and lame" to the supper in the parable (14 : 21). One of the amazing things about Jesus was his interest in the poor. This great fact was reported to John the Baptist as proof that Jesus was the Messiah (7 : 22).

Certainly, then, Luke believed in the dignity of man. Luke wrote the gospel for the poor that Burns sang. "S. Luke's conception of the Church was that it was a body in which the poor and needy for the first time had a fair and equal chance."[1] We need not ask whether Luke wished to abolish slavery, though he may have once been a slave himself, as we have seen. Professor Gilbert Murray[2] thinks that what made Christianity conquer in the Roman Empire was "its intense feeling of brotherhood within its own bounds, its incessant care for the poor." We see that in I Cor. 1 : 26–31, where Paul glories in the choice of the poor by God to confound the rich and the mighty. Christ calls the men from the bottom up. That is his crown of glory. There is no doubt about Luke being a democrat. He traces the babe in the manger in Bethlehem to the ascension on Olivet. Luke was a democrat who was striving for a spiritual aristocracy, not of money, not of blood, not of privilege, not of power, but of character, the brotherhood of the cross of Christ, that is still the hope of the world, the salt of the earth. Luke does not teach that it is a virtue to be poor, but a poor man is, after all, a man, a man worth saving, a man who may be rich toward God, and who may enrich man by the noblest qualities of manhood and service. "Even when Christianity had risen from the workshop and the cottage to the palace and the schools of learning, it did not desert the workshop and the cottage. The living roots of Christianity remained in their native soil and in the lower ranks of society."[3]

6. *Understanding Women.*—Christ made an appeal to women, who early formed a band to help support him and his disciples (Luke 8 : 1–3). The rabbis in their liturgy thanked God that they were not born women. But Jesus is the eman-

---

[1] Carpenter, *op. cit.*, p. 204.
[2] *Four Stages of Greek Religion*, p. 180.
[3] Deissmann, *Light from the Ancient East*, p. 404.

cipator of women. Luke sees this truth and emphasizes it. One of the traditions[1] about Jesus is that once when asked "When shall the kingdom come?" he replied: "When the two shall be one, and that which is without as that which is within, and the male with the female, neither male nor female." One may think what he will of the logion, but Paul in Gal. 3 : 28 says that in Christ "there is neither male nor female." To the women of Palestine Jesus appeared as their sole champion and hope because he treated them as personalities on a par with men. "Mithraism, the most popular of the heathen religions, was, like Islam, a religion for men only."[2] The humanity of Christ is deeper than sex. Christianity made great headway in the first century, partly because of its powerful appeal to women.

Luke was a physician and was brought into close contact with women and their problems. He also lived in Philippi for some years, where women had unusual privileges and opportunities, Macedonia being in this respect far ahead of Achaia or Asia. Luke knew how both Gentile and Jew looked down on women. He saw the difference in Jesus. So we have sketches of Elizabeth and Mary the mother of Jesus, the prophetess Anna and the widow of Nain, the sinful woman in the house of Simon and the woman with an issue of blood, Mary Magdalene and the others of her band, Mary and Martha of Bethany, the widow with the two mites and the daughters of Jerusalem, the women at the tomb, Dorcas and Mary the mother of John Mark, Sapphira and Priscilla, Drusilla and Bernice, Lydia and Damaris. Luke wrote the gospel of womanhood, full of sympathy and tenderness, full of understanding of their tasks and their service. Dante describes Luke as "the writer of the story of the gentleness of Christ." If women have understood Christ often better than men, it is in part due to Luke's representation of Christ's interest in women. Christ has enfranchised women in the true sense of spiritual privilege and prowess and service. They are entering into their heritage after centuries of indifference and hostility. But the women were last at the cross and first at the tomb. They have been loyal to Christ through the ages.

7. *In Touch with Children.*—The good physician loves children and seeks to save the child from death and from disaster.

---

[1] *Ps. Clem.*, xii.　　　　　[2] Carpenter, *op. cit.*, p. 217.

The hope of the race is in the children. The real wealth of the world is in the children, who give promise of being better and of doing better than we have been and have done. Hayes observes that there is not a child in the Gospel of John, but that is not quite true, for Andrew tells Jesus of the lad with five barley loaves and two fishes (John 6:8 f.). Mark and Matthew both tell of the little children that were brought to Jesus, but Luke notes that they were "babes" (Luke 18:15). Luke alone gives the raising of the son of the widow of Nain (Luke 7), and Luke notes that the epileptic boy was the father's "only son" (9:38). Luke tells us most about the birth and childhood of Jesus, and gives us the only glimpse that we have of the boy Jesus, with a boy's hunger for knowledge and yearning for future service, this boy who already had the consciousness of peculiar relationship to God his Father, and yet who went back to Nazareth in obedience to Joseph and Mary to toil at the carpenter's bench for eighteen more years, till the voice of the Baptist should call him to the Jordan. No one who did not love and understand children could have so graphically pictured the boyhood of Jesus in this one short paragraph.

8. *Spiritual Insight.*—Luke's Gospel makes a point of prayer in the life of Jesus. He gives the example of Jesus and the instruction of Jesus on the subject. The Synoptic Gospels all tell of Christ's praying in Gethsemane. Luke[1] does not mention the praying of Jesus given in Mark 1:35 at Capernaum and in Matt. 19:23 (= Mark 6:46) after feeding the five thousand. But Luke alone notes that Jesus prayed at the baptism of Jesus (3:21), on his first clash with the Pharisees over forgiving the paralytic (5:16), before choosing the Twelve Apostles (6:12), before the first prediction of his death (9:18), at the transfiguration (9:18), before teaching the model prayer (11:1), on the cross (23:34, 46). Besides, as Plummer[2] further points out, Luke alone mentions Christ's special prayer for Peter (22:31 f.), the special command to the disciples to pray while in Gethsemane (22:32, 40). Luke alone gives the parables about persistence in prayer (11:5-13; 18:1-8) and the command to pray "at every season" (21:36). The parable of the Pharisee and the publican shows the difference between   real   and   perfunctory   (and   hypocritical)   prayer

[1] Plummer, *Comm.*, p. xlv.   [2] *Ibid.*

(18 : 11–13). Plummer's summary proves the point up to the hilt. Luke was himself a man of prayer, because of his interest in this aspect of Christ, who practised what he preached (11 : 9). "If the disciples of Jesus had learned to pray as their Master prayed, their victory would have been as sure and as continuous as his own." [1]

Luke's Gospel is not only the Gospel of Prayer, but also the Gospel of Praise. Plummer [2] notes that it begins and ends with worship in the temple (1 : 9; 24 : 53). Luke alone gives the Greeting of Elizabeth (1 : 42–45), the *Magnificat*, or Song of Mary the Mother of Jesus (1 : 46–55), the *Benedictus*, or Song of Zacharias (1 : 68–79), the *Gloria in Excelsis*, or Song of the Angels (2 : 14), the *Nunc Dimittis*, or Song of Simeon (2 : 29–32). Luke is fond of the expression "glorifying God" (2 : 20; 5 : 25 f.; 7 : 16; 13 : 13; 17 : 15; 18 : 43), "praising God" (2 : 13, 20; 19 : 37; 24 : 53?; Acts 2 : 47; 3 : 8 f.) and "blessing God" (1 : 64; 2 : 28; 24 : 53?).

So also it is the Gospel of Joy. Rejoicing is mentioned by verb or substantive twenty-two times in the Gospel and the Acts. All through the Gospel and the Acts there rings the note of praise and joy. The hymns in Luke's Gospel have thrilled the heart of the world. The *Magnificat* "is the highest specimen of the subtle influence of the song of purity, so exquisitely described by Browning. It is the 'Pippa Passes' among the liturgies of the world." [3]

Luke is fond of the ministry of angels. They are common in the Gospel and in the Acts, where they are mentioned twenty-two times. "Here and there throughout the Gospel we hear echoes of angel songs and catch glimpses of angel wings." [4] To be sure, some would term this trait superstition and lack of the scientific and the historical spirit. But that is a superficial attitude toward the deepest problem of humanity. The nineteenth century saw a recrudescence of materialism under the influence of the evolution hypothesis. But this very hypothesis now knocks at the door of the unseen and refuses to be satisfied with the negation of Mill and Huxley and Spencer and Haeckel. Wistfully scientists of the twentieth century are looking over the brim of eternity, if haply they

[1] Hayes, *op. cit.*, p. 259.　　　　　　　　[2] *Comm.*, p. xlvi.
[3] Alexander, *Leading Ideas of the Gospels*, p. 114.
[4] Hayes, *op. cit.*, p. 264.

may catch echoes from the other side. The wall seems thin at times to those who have loved ones who have passed over to be with Jesus.

Luke was a mystic, as every real Christian is. Scientist as he was, he had not lost his sense of wonder and awe in the presence of God and nature. He found in Christ the key to the mystery of life here and hereafter. Like McKenna (*The Adventure of Death*), another Christian physician of to-day who looked to Christ with a scientist's eyes from the trenches of France and Flanders, Luke saw in Christ the hope of the world. He gave himself with utter devotion to the task of recording the results of his years of research and of experience of Christ in his own life and in the lives of others. He wrote with whole-hearted consecration of his great gifts and with high standards before his eyes. He set his eyes upon Jesus, who alone makes life worth while. A man without spiritual insight has missed the meaning of his own life and the meaning of the world. Luke had the eyes of his mind opened (Luke 24 : 45) by the vision of Jesus which he saw. He saw Christ and he saw the world for which Christ died.

INDEX OF SUBJECTS

INDEX OF AUTHORS AND BOOKS
REFERRED TO

INDEX OF SCRIPTURE AND PAPYRI QUOTATIONS

A. NEW TESTAMENT

B. OLD TESTAMENT

C. PAPYRI